D1291857

AMERICAN EDUCATION

Its Men,

Ideas,

and

Institutions

Advisory Editor

Lawrence A. Cremin
Frederick A. P. Barnard Professor of Education
Teachers College, Columbia University

AMERICAN EDUCATION: *Its Men, Ideas, and Institutions* presents selected works of thought and scholarship that have long been out of print or otherwise unavailable. Inevitably, such works will include particular ideas and doctrines that have been outmoded or superseded by more recent research. Nevertheless, all retain their place in the literature, having influenced educational thought and practice in their own time and having provided the basis for subsequent scholarship.

WARTIME RELATIONS OF
THE FEDERAL GOVERNMENT AND
THE PUBLIC SCHOOLS
1917-1918

By Lewis Paul Todd, Ph.D.

ARNO PRESS & THE NEW YORK TIMES
*New York * 1971*

Reprint Edition 1971 by Arno Press Inc.

Copyright © 1945 by Lewis Paul Todd
Reprinted by permission of Lewis Paul Todd

Reprinted from a copy in
  The Newark Public Library

American Education:
  Its Men, Ideas, and Institutions - Series II
ISBN for complete set: 0-405-03600-0
See last pages of this volume for titles.

Manufactured in the United States of America

Library of Congress Cataloging in Publication Data

Todd, Lewis Paul, 1906-
    Wartime relations of the Federal Government
and the public schools, 1917-1918.
    (Teachers College, Columbia University.
Contributions to education, no. 907) (American
education: its men, ideas, and institutions.
Series II)
    Originally presented as the author's thesis,
Columbia, 1943.
    Includes bibliographical references.
    1. European War, 1914-1918--Education and the
war. 2. Education and state--U. S. I. Title.
II. Series: Columbia University. Teachers
College. Contributions to education, no. 907.
III. Series: American education: its men, ideas,
and institutions. Series II.
D639.E3T85 1971   379'.151'0973   76-165743
ISBN 0-405-03614-0

WARTIME RELATIONS OF THE FEDERAL GOVERNMENT AND THE PUBLIC SCHOOLS

1917-1918

By Lewis Paul Todd, Ph.D.

TEACHERS COLLEGE, COLUMBIA UNIVERSITY
CONTRIBUTIONS TO EDUCATION, NO. 907

BUREAU OF PUBLICATIONS
Teachers College, Columbia University
NEW YORK, 1945

TO

MY MOTHER AND FATHER

ACKNOWLEDGMENTS

IT IS difficult to express adequately my appreciation to those who assisted me in the preparation of this study. I am particularly grateful to the following individuals who, through correspondence, interviews, or both, shared with me their knowledge of some of the problems discussed in this volume: Dr. Guy Stanton Ford, formerly President of the University of Minnesota and now Editor of the *American Historical Review* and Executive Secretary of the American Historical Association; Dr. William H. Kilpatrick, Emeritus Professor of Education, Teachers College, Columbia University; Dr. Charles H. Judd, Emeritus Professor of Education, the University of Chicago; Dr. William C. Bagley, Editor of *School and Society;* Professor J. Montgomery Gambrill of The Johns Hopkins University; Dr. John C. Wright, Assistant Commissioner for Vocational Education, United States Office of Education; Dr. Philander P. Claxton, formerly United States Commissioner of Education; Mr. James F. Abel, formerly Chief Clerk in the United States Office of Education; Mr. Edwin C. Johnson, formerly Secretary of the Committee on Militarism in Education; and Dr. James R. Mock and Dr. Maxcy Dickson of the National Archives.

I wish to thank the following publishers for permission to quote from their publications: Association Press, D. Appleton-Century Company, George Banta Publishing Company, The University of Chicago Press, Harper and Brothers, Houghton Mifflin Company, The Macmillan Company, Princeton University Press, Charles Scribner's Sons, and Yale University Press.

I am also indebted to Professor Isaac L. Kandel of Teachers College, Columbia University, whose incisive criticisms helped me to define the study. Equally great is my debt to the following individuals, all of whom read the manuscript and made many valuable suggestions: Professors Harry James Carman and Robert S. Lynd of Columbia University; Professors John K. Norton, Benjamin Richard Andrews, R. Freeman Butts, and Alice W. Spieseke of Teachers College, Columbia University.

Finally, I reserve my deepest appreciation for Dr. Erling M. Hunt, Professor of History and Head of the Department of Teaching of Social Science at Teachers College, Columbia University, and for Dr. Merle Curti, formerly of Teachers College, now Professor of History at the University of Wisconsin. Both Professor Hunt and Professor Curti were generous in their criticisms, advice, suggestions, and encouragement. They gave unsparingly of their time and effort, sharing with me their invaluable fund of knowledge and experience. Where, in spite of this assistance, there are shortcomings in the study, I alone am responsible.

L. P. T.

Flushing, New York
May, 1943

CONTENTS

PART ONE

THE DRIVE FOR WARTIME UNITY

PART THREE

IN CONCLUSION

Wartime Relations of
the Federal Government and
the Public Schools
1917–1918

INTRODUCTION

1. Purpose and Scope of the Study

IN VIEW of the grave problems that confront statesmen and educators in the years that lie before us, it may be of some use to look back upon our experiences in 1917 and 1918. It was then that the shadow of total war fell upon the nation. To students of history, the wartime development of our economic and military machinery has long been a familiar story.[1] More recently, the place of propaganda in the mobilization of the American people has received considerable attention.[2] We know something of the attitude of churchmen in those troubled years,[3] and the effect of the war upon higher education has been in part revealed.[4] But curiously enough, in the light of its potential significance, we know little about the educational activities of the federal government among the 20,000,000 boys and girls then enrolled in the public schools.[5] What use was made of the school system? What was done by the federal authorities to prepare America's youth for the days of peace that lay ahead? Was our leadership in Washington primarily interested in the exigencies of the moment, or was it concerned with the broader implications of its educational activities? It is with questions of this kind that the present study proposes to deal.

Another reason directs interest in federal relations to public

[1] Bernard M. Baruch, *American Industry in the War. A Report of the War Industries Board* (New York: Prentice-Hall, Inc., 1941); Harold J. Tobin and Percy W. Bidwell, *Mobilizing Civilian America* (New York: Council on Foreign Relations, 1940).

[2] James R. Mock and Cedric Larson, *Words That Won the War. The Story of the Committee on Public Information* (Princeton: Princeton University Press, 1939).

[3] Ray H. Abrams, *Preachers Present Arms; A Study of the War-time Attitude and Activities of the Churches and the Clergy in the United States, 1914–1918* (Philadelphia: University of Pennsylvania Press, 1933).

[4] Charles F. Thwing, *The American Colleges and Universities in the Great War, 1914–1919* (New York: The Macmillan Company, 1920).

[5] The best single volume dealing with public education in the last war was written by Arthur D. Dean, *Our Schools in War Time and After* (New York: Ginn and Company, 1918). This was prepared in 1918, however, when the available information was far from adequate.

I

education during times of crisis. As we continue to move further into what Harold J. Laski chooses to call the era of the "positive state," the entire fabric of our educational system is destined to undergo great changes. This is to say that education is an integral part of a nation's life, and responds, as do all other institutions, to any alterations in the social, economic, and political structure. The federal government was strengthened to fight the First World War and again to combat the subsequent depression of the 1930's. It had to assume new powers to carry on the Second World War. Many of these powers will have to be retained, at least in part, if we are to combat successfully the disorganization that will inevitably follow the end of armed conflict. Our whole federal structure is being shaken and the individual states are losing, one by one, their former powers.[6] Not the least of these has been control of the educational system. It seems probable that the national authorities will to an ever greater extent undertake to influence· the education of American children. Upon educators falls the responsibility for seeing that in the uncertain days that lie before us our schools do not suffer from ill-advised and hasty action. Our experiences in the troubled years of 1917 and 1918 may be profitable to all those who are interested in charting the future course of our schools.

Certain limits have been set to the present study. It is concerned with the federal activities in the public elementary and secondary schools during the First World War. While these activities constituted an important part of our wartime educational program, it should be remembered that many other agencies sought to influence the schools and the nation at large in 1917 and 1918. No attempt has been made to deal, except incidentally, with the wartime work of professional educators and associations, with the influence of civic and patriotic organizations, or with the activities of the press. Nor has it been considered expedient to include a treatment of the role of higher education in the war, or of Americanization work among adults, in both of which the federal authorities were keenly interested. In brief, while the following discussion does undertake to indicate in a general way the effect

[6] Edward S. Corwin, *Constitutional Revolution, Ltd.* (Claremont, California: Published by Claremont Colleges, 1941), pp. 96–102.

of the war upon our educational institutions, its particular emphasis is upon the wartime relationship of the federal government to the public schools. For this reason, it is important to recall the educational situation which confronted our national leaders on the eve of 1917.

2. Public Education and the Federal Government on the Eve of 1917

During the years between 1865 and 1917 American society was shifting from an agrarian to an industrial base. Professional educators and other public officials were bewildered by the numerous social, economic, and political issues that were clamoring for attention. All institutions, including the schools, were struggling to adapt themselves to the new conditions. The migration from the farm to the city was throwing increased burdens upon school administrators. Problems of health, sanitation, child labor, and juvenile delinquency were being bred in the slums and industrial areas. For millions of Americans the home had lost much of its former meaning, with the result that heavier responsibilities were thrust upon public institutions. A vast influx of immigrants, many of them illiterate and almost totally ignorant of our democratic system, was presenting our national leaders with a problem of first magnitude. Faced with these changes in our socio-economic organization and with a rapidly growing school enrollment, educators were expanding the curriculum to include domestic science, vocational training, health, sanitation, and civic education. Nationalism, stimulated by the Spanish-American War and our subsequent colonial enterprises, was receiving a stronger emphasis in the school program.

Meanwhile, educational theory was transforming men's ideas about the learning process and the function of education. The evolutionary hypothesis had directed attention to the individual and the significance of environment. G. Stanley Hall's studies in psychology had furnished convincing evidence of the plasticity of child nature. John Dewey had pointed to the identity of life and the educative process. Edward L. Thorndike had provided the first tools and techniques for the measurement and evaluation of educational procedure. Commissions of prominent schoolmen had undertaken to adapt the educational institutions to the life about them. Both educational theory and social pressures were, therefore, forcing new subject matter, new methods, and a new philosophy upon our school system.

As school and society drew closer together, the federal authorities began to show an increased interest in public education. During our entire history the national government has sought to stimulate educational activities. Prior to the Civil War, however, federal participation was largely confined to grants of land for the endowment of education. But since the passage of the Morrill Act in 1862, the leaders in Washington have endeavored, both by land grants and by financial aid, to further specific types of education. Emphasis was at first upon the encouragement of agricultural education. By gifts of land in 1862, and by later financial appropriations, Congress induced the states to provide colleges for the study of agriculture and the mechanic arts. The Hatch Act of 1887 offered financial aid for the establishment of agricultural experiment stations. The Smith-Lever Act of 1914 went even further by providing support for home economics and agricultural extension agents who were charged with the duty of carrying on educational work among both adults and children in rural areas. A more sweeping innovation in federal relations to education took place when, in the Smith-Hughes Act of 1917, the government undertook to supply partial support for vocational education in the public schools.[7]

Because of the peculiar nature of our educational system, with legal control in the hands of the states, the national authorities could do no more than supply advisory services and financial aid. A Bureau of Education had been established as early as 1867,[8] but it was limited in personnel and operated with restricted appropriations; its principal function was to collect statistics and to supply

[7] The Advisory Committee on Education, *Report of the Committee* (Washington, D. C.: Government Printing Office, 1938), pp. 35–36. For an excellent summary of federal relations to education, see the *Encyclopedia of Educational Research*, Walter S. Monroe, ed. (New York: The Macmillan Company, 1941). A thorough study of the problem has been made by the National Advisory Committee on Education, *Federal Relations to Education: Report of the National Advisory Committee on Education* (Washington, D. C.: Government Printing Office, 1931).

[8] The Department of Education was created in 1867, but two years later it was reduced to the rank of a bureau in the Department of the Interior. Since 1933 it has been officially designated the Office of Education.

information. The Department of Agriculture, through its extension and home demonstration agents, conducted the program of education among farm children and adults. The Federal Board for Vocational Education, created in response to the demands of the new industrial age, was not established until 1917, and did not begin its educational activities until after we had entered the war. Neither the Bureau of Education nor the Department of Agriculture had the authority, the administrative machinery, the finances, or the staff to deal adequately with the complicated educational problems which faced our nation during the first two decades of the twentieth century. The character of education was undergoing radical changes. Leadership was badly needed to articulate the educational activities of the forty-eight states and to redefine federal relations to education, but this leadership was absent, both from Washington and from the ranks of professional educators.

3. Federal Relations to Public Education during 1917–1918

The effect of our entrance into the war was to focus attention upon those problems with which educators had been struggling for the last two or more decades. It was a matter of immediate national concern that American citizens should be united in spirit, sound in body, well fed, well clothed, well trained, and able to contribute effectively to the war program. Faced with the urgent need for action, a number of federal agencies called upon the public schools to aid them in the solution of the more pressing wartime problems.

Foremost among the educational campaigns was the drive to unite Americans behind the war effort. The Committee on Public Information was established to initiate and direct our propaganda activities. Although its early efforts were directed to the adult public, before long it became clear that the school system offered a ready-made approach to the minds and emotions of the millions of American parents. Propaganda began to pour into our educational institutions, and during the long months of the war the children carried home appealing messages from a score or more of federal organizations and a bewildering number of state and local patriotic societies. Indeed, the evidence indicates that many of the nation's leaders, and, it must be added, professional educators as well, looked upon the school children as little more than convenient messengers to reach the homes. It was adult action that was desired, and since the children could be used to precipitate this action, they too became important in the war program.

No less pressing was the need for soldiers. Although the War Department did not want immature boys for its fighting services, many Army officers felt that the secondary schools could furnish at least the rudiments of military training to the older pupils. With the approval of the War Department, and stimulated by the enthusiasm of numerous civilians, hundreds of schools organized cadet units and began to drill the boys on athletic fields and in vacant lots.

Because in total war the fullest contribution is expected from each individual, the problem of health assumed major significance. Aided by private organizations and individuals, the Children's Bureau conducted a vigorous campaign for the improvement of the health and welfare of the nation's youth. With the approval of the President, the year 1918 was designated as "Children's Year," and a widespread program of health education was energetically pursued. The United States Public Health Service, the quasi-public American Red Cross organization, the Bureau of Education, and the Food Administration actively supported the measures to improve the health and well-being of the boys and girls.

One of the most crucial of national problems was that of food. In an effort to increase production, the Bureau of Education organized the United States School Garden Army, and hundreds of thousands of home and community gardens were planted in backyards and vacant lots. To aid the farmers, the Department of Labor established the United States Boys' Working Reserve, organized it along the lines of an army, and recruited thousands of boys as farm hands; released from school in the spring and fall of 1917 and 1918, they did much to relieve the shortage of farm labor. By redoubling its prewar educational activities, the Department of Agriculture also sought to increase the production of foodstuffs. Meanwhile, the newly created Food Administration concentrated upon measures of conservation. An attempt was made to reach every home in the nation with a "Food Pledge Card," and during the school year of 1918–1919 Hoover's appeals to save food were carried home to millions of parents.

Both the Fuel Administration and the Treasury Department made similar use of the schools. The former organized a "Tag the Shovel" campaign and kept up a constant stream of exhortations to conserve coal, gas, and electricity. The latter sold millions of dollars worth of thrift stamps and war bonds through the public educational institutions.

Equally acute was the need for skilled workers. Both the Federal Board for Vocational Education and the War Department made use of the manual-training facilities of the nation's schools for the pre-induction training of soldiers. The woodworking shops, sewing rooms, and kitchens were also used by the pupils to prepare canned goods and handmade articles for hospitals, training camps, and the front line. These activities were sponsored by the Junior Red Cross, the Food Administration, the Department of Agriculture, and other federal organizations. In addition, both the Bureau of Education and the United States Employment Service established special placement agencies in an effort to relieve the critical shortage of teachers.

During the war years most of the public schools were veritable beehives of activity. Campaigns, sometimes several at a time, were going on almost constantly. The children made posters; spoke as "Junior Four Minute Men"; wrote letters to the soldiers; assembled scrapbooks, and collected magazines for the training camps; sewed on dresses, rolled bandages, and canned food; constructed furniture and packing boxes; adopted war orphans; rendered assistance of various kinds to official boards, such as filling out and filing cards, tabulating questionnaires, addressing envelopes, and preparing signs and posters; held patriotic celebrations, parades, and pageants; and salvaged peach pits, nutshells, and tinfoil.[9]

9 In this introduction, specific documentation of these activities has not been attempted. The reports of the state and city superintendents of education, the files of school journals and newspapers, and the records of the various governmental agencies are full of references to this work and summaries of the contributions made. In reply to a request by the Committee on Public Information, J. C. Wardlaw, Superintendent of the Atlanta Public Schools, sent a summary of the war

Through these activities, and through a heightened interest in the study of current events and recent history, the war was brought very close to the boys and girls in America's schools.

It is difficult to assess the value of this wartime education. There is little reason to doubt that, as carriers of propaganda, the children made an important contribution to the building of adult morale. Nor will many educators deny the value of bringing the problems of society into the classroom. Insofar as the conflict helped to vitalize methods and curriculum, and insofar as the pupils became more sensitive to the social advantages of cooperative effort, the effect of the war was to improve our educational system.

But the educator must think in terms of the future as well as of the immediate present, and it is on this point that one may question the wisdom of much of our wartime activity in the schools. Take, by way of example, the enormous amount of time that was consumed in the routine task of fashioning such articles as knitting needles and packing boxes. To say that these products were necessary and could have been provided in no other way, an assumption which is itself of questionable validity, is something entirely different from saying that the activities themselves had educational values. What skills did this work develop? How did it help to prepare the boys for future life? To take another illustration, was it better, in the long run, that the children learn to hate their enemies, or that they learn to appreciate the advantages of the democratic way of life? Questions of this sort are easy to ask, but hard, indeed, to answer. Yet if education is to have any meaning in terms of future conduct, similar questions must be raised constantly, even in wartime.

Two lessons emerge with particular clarity from our educational experiences in 1917–1918: First, as has been suggested, there was an amazing lack of understanding as to the function of education. Let some powerful federal agency claim that its work was important to the war effort, and, in many cases, the schools' doors were promptly opened wide. Second—and this problem is

work conducted in this one city system of Georgia during the winter of 1917–1918. Almost every one of the activities listed above was carried on in this single school system. Letter from J. C. Wardlaw to J. W. Searson, July 20, 1918. National Archives (CPI, 3-A1, C-131).

closely related to the first—federal relations to public education were poorly defined, the activities badly administered. Programs and campaigns followed each other in endless succession. Frequently, different national organizations were carrying on almost identical programs at the same time. The result was a needless duplication of effort, constant conflict, and an intolerable amount of confusion. Much of this was unnecessary. We had a Bureau of Education through which all national educational activities could readily have been cleared. Had this been done we might have secured a more intelligent decision when it came to choosing between packing boxes and education for a future democratic society.

It has been said that the Franco-Prussian War was won in the schools of Germany, the First World War on the playing fields of Eton. This is to say that, in the final analysis, a nation's strength rests upon more than armed might and productive capacity. Beneath all this there must be ideals and beliefs which are shared by the masses of people. It is at precisely this point that education is necessary, and by education we mean, of course, all those forces which influence society, such as the press, radio, motion picture, church, and school. The hope of a world made "safe for democracy," a hope for which millions died in 1917 and 1918, turned to ashes after the Armistice. Is it possible that the tragic history of the twenty-five years following the First World War was in part the result of an education which failed in wartime to prepare for the no less difficult problems of peace?

PART ONE

THE DRIVE FOR WARTIME UNITY

CHAPTER I

EDUCATION AND PROPAGANDA THROUGH
THE CREEL COMMITTEE

In war, the moral is to the physical as three to one.—*Napoleon*[1]

For war, completely seen, is no mere collision of physical forces: it is a collision of will against will. It is, after all, the mind and will of a nation—a thing intangible and invisible—that assembles the materials of war, the fighting forces, the ordnance, the whole physical array. It is this invisible thing that wages the war; it is this same invisible thing that on one side or the other must admit the finish and so end it. As things are now, it is the element of "morale" that controls the outcome. —*William E. Hocking, 1918*[2]

Morale is the quality of the spirit of the whole. It is the product of many elements, among them hope, determination, health, consciousness of strength, confidence—in the cause, the officers, the other men, the wisdom of the war program, the strategy, and the tactics—and belief in God. . . . It is confidence, not merely individual but collective. Morale is no more the sum of the feelings of the individuals than public opinion is the sum of individual opinions. It is the spirit of the whole.—*Luther H. Gulick, 1919*[3]

1. Purpose and Scope of Federal Propaganda, 1917–1918

With our entrance into the war in 1917, the federal government launched upon a vast program of education. Every conceivable device was used to unite 120,000,000 Americans behind the war effort. Starting with the general public, before many months had passed the government reached down into the public schools with a campaign designed to convince the children of the justice of our cause. How this propaganda campaign was started, what it sought to accomplish, and the machinery and methods through which it reached the school children are the subjects discussed in the following pages.

[1] William E. Hocking, *Morale and Its Enemies* (New Haven: Yale University Press, 1918), p. 5.
[2] *Ibid.*, p. 8.
[3] *Morals and Morale* (New York: Association Press, 1919), p. xi.

13

The director of our propaganda activities saw the problem clearly. As he later pointed out, "The war was not fought in France alone. Back of the firing-line, back of armies and navies, back of the great supply-depots, another struggle raged with the same intensity and with almost equal significance attaching to its victories and defeats. It was the fight for the *minds* of men, for the 'conquest of their convictions,' and the battle-line ran through every home in every country. . . . The trial of strength was not only between massed bodies of armed men, but between opposed ideals, and moral verdicts took on all the value of military decisions."[4] This need for a united public opinion was emphasized by President Wilson when he warned, shortly after our entry into the war, that "the whole nation must be a team in which each man shall play the part for which he is best fitted," that it is "our duty to give ourselves with thoughtful devotion to the common purpose of all."[5]

That a common purpose did not exist in the spring of 1917 Wilson knew only too well, and it was the President himself who was in part responsible for our divided feeling. It was only a few days after the outbreak of the European conflict that he warned the public to be "neutral in thought as well as in action"; constant emphasis upon this policy during the early months of the war convinced millions of Americans that they were merely spectators of another Old World quarrel. With this in mind, a large group of citizens registered their votes for Wilson in 1916 under the slogan, "He kept us out of war."

Our entrance into the conflict came as a shock to many Americans, and for several months large numbers remained apathetic to our participation. In August, 1917, the chairman of Oklahoma's State Council of National Defense claimed that "very few people yet understand the real nature of the enemy and the real danger to America."[6] Late in October, the leader of a teachers' institute in the Middle West called attention to much "indifference and even

4 George Creel, *How We Advertised America* (New York: Harper and Brothers, 1920), p. 3.
5 Proclamation of May 18, 1917. *President Wilson's State Papers and Addresses* (New York: George H. Doran Company, 1917), p. 398.
6 J. M. Aydelotte to Committee on Public Information, August 6, 1917. National Archives (CPI, 3-A7, L-1-272).

hostility to the war in country districts here."[7] Eight months after we had declared war upon Germany a trained historian warned that "we shall have to bring our people to support a long war in Europe . . . which many of them do not understand";[8] it was another historian who reminded a Congressional Committee that when we entered the war we were faced with the necessity of convincing many Americans that the United States was engaged in a "life and death" struggle.[9] But the hostility of those sympathetic to the Central Powers created a problem no less difficult; they were partisan since the opening days of the war, and our entry on the side of England only served to inflame their bitterness.

Responsible governmental leaders were troubled by the situation, and in the spring of 1917 much debate took place over the method of dealing with the problem. It was possible, of course, to erect rigid barriers of censorship behind which repressive measures could be instituted against all "un-American" expressions or activities. Although certain military leaders appear to have favored this course,[10] it was argued that such a procedure would not secure that common purpose so vital to a successful war effort. Indeed, in view of the traditional American belief in "free speech," the method might only serve to arouse greater dissention. This feeling was shared by Josephus Daniels, Secretary of the Navy. Writing a number of years after the war had ended, he recalled:

When we entered the World War, the President, Mr. Baker and I particularly—all the members of the Cabinet also agreeing—were very anxious that we should not fall into the stupid censorship which had marked the action of some countries in dealing with war news. Immediately upon our entrance into the war I called in all the newspapermen of Washington, and particularly the representatives of the press associations, and told them that we would have no censorship, but that the President and his Cabinet wished them and all newspapermen in

[7] S. B. Hepburn to S. B. Harding, October 20, 1917. National Archives (CPI, 3-A1, L-1-458).

[8] W. E. Dodd to G. S. Ford, December 9, 1917. National Archives (CPI, 3-A7, L-1-91).

[9] Guy Stanton Ford. His testimony is contained in *Sundry Civil Bill, 1919,* "Committee on Public Information." *Hearing before Subcommittee of House Committee on Appropriations.* Part III, 61, Cong., 2 sess. (Washington: Government Printing Office, 1918), p. 95. Hereafter cited as "CPI, *Hearing, 1918.*"

[10] Creel, *How We Advertised America,* pp. 19–20; Mark Sullivan, *Over Here, 1914–1918* (Vol. V of *Our Times, 1900–1925.* New York: Charles Scribner's Sons, 1933), p. 424.

America to impose self-censorship; that we would give them freely the information that would let them know what was going on and request them from time to time to publish nothing which might fall into the hands of the enemy or embarrass war operations. Ninety-nine per cent of them patriotically accepted this suggestion but we soon found that now and then the zeal for scoops outran patriotism. Determined to have no censorship and to give the public all information possible, we decided to establish the Committee on Public Information. . . .[11]

This decision had evidently been reached after considerable discussion, for one week after our declaration of war upon Germany the Secretaries of State, War, and Navy in a written memorandum to Wilson urged him to implement the proposal by the creation of a "committee on public information." The three cabinet officers felt that "America's great present needs are confidence, enthusiasm, and service, and these needs will not be met completely unless every citizen is given the feeling of partnership that comes with full, frank statements concerning the conduct of the public business."[12] In full accord with the views of his associates, and prompted by their letter, the President immediately issued an Executive Order creating the Committee on Public Information.[13] Headed by a civilian appointed by the President, the committee was also to include the Secretaries of State, War, and Navy.

George Creel's was the only name proposed to direct the organization[14] and, from the moment he assumed office, it became, in fact as well as in popular terminology, "Creel's Committee."[15] A journalist who for many years had wielded a trenchant pen in behalf of liberalism, a man of intense enthusiasms with a brilliant mind that leaped restlessly from idea to idea, an ardent advocate of the principles of the "New Freedom," and a devoted friend of the President himself, none could have been found better qualified for the job. Such, at least, was the estimate of Creel's friends.[16]

[11] Mock and Larson, *Words That Won the War,* pp. 49–50.
[12] *Ibid.,* p. 50.
[13] In this study the Committee is cited as the "CPI."
[14] Mock and Larson, *Words That Won the War,* pp. 49–50.
[15] Newton D. Baker, Secretary of War and himself a member of the Committee, gave this as his testimony. The whole group met only once, he said, and from that early meeting until the Committee was disbanded at the end of the war, Creel was responsible for everything that was done by the CPI. For Baker's remarks see Creel, *How We Advertised America,* p. xi.
[16] Sullivan, *Over Here,* pp. 424–426; 436–440.

Before accepting the position, Creel demanded from the President assurances that his job was not to exercise merely negative censorship. Convinced in his own mind that, in spite of the title given to the organization, the prevailing idea was to establish a committee whose primary purpose was to suppress information, Creel submitted to Wilson a written statement of his views, and only after the President had given unqualified approval to the plans did Creel assume the chairmanship. "I accepted the position," he later said, "because I felt that this work was going to be a great deal wider than mere censorship; that it was a war of 110,000,000 people rather than a war of the administration, and so the committee began to broaden its work in the sense of making it a great publicity bureau—a publicity bureau not only for the expression of what was being done in Washington but to bring home the truths of this great war to every man, woman, and child in the United States, so that they might understand that it was a just war, a holy war, and a war in self-defense."[17]

Creel's primary objective was to mobilize the American people by means of an extensive educational program;[18] as the work developed he expanded his activities to the rest of the world.[19] The problem, as he visualized it, was threefold: First, to make "America's own purposes and ideals clear both to ourselves and to the world"; second, to give "a thorough presentation of the aims, methods, and ideals of the dynastic and feudal government of Germany"; and third, to give "information which would help in a constructive way in the daily tasks of a nation at war."[20]

The press viewed the establishment of the Committee on Public Information with suspicious eyes. "Expression, not suppression,"[21] was a happy term; "self-censorship" sounded well on paper; but what, exactly, did all this mean? As the weeks passed, these suspicions were lulled. Then, in May, Congress established the Cen-

---

[17] CPI, *Hearing, 1918,* p. 4.
[18] The term "mobilize" was used by Newton D. Baker in an informal address given at a dinner in honor of Creel, Washington, November 29, 1918. Creel thoroughly approved. See Creel, *How We Advertised America,* pp. xiii, 5.
[19] *Complete Record of the Chairman of the Committee on Public Information. 1917: 1918: 1919.* (Washington: Government Printing Office, 1920), p. 2. Hereafter cited as *RCPI.*
[20] Creel, *How We Advertised America,* pp. 104–108.
[21] The phrase was Creel's. *RCPI,* p. 1.

sorship Board, and Creel was appointed a member. The newspapers immediately broke into a torrent of denunciation. Now they saw clearly. The CPI was a smokescreen behind which the Board of Censorship was to exercise real power, voluntary censorship was a mockery, and the whole procedure was a clever trick to drive the papers into line and to destroy the freedom of the press.[22] Although the storm did subside as a large portion of the press was eventually convinced of Creel's sincerity, a number of newspapers continued to hammer away at the Committee on Public Information until it disbanded in 1919.

How much censorship did Creel actually exert? He directed the release of all war news, carefully suppressing that information judged to be of military value to the enemy. Here his powers as chairman of the propaganda committee definitely ended. But Creel had other connections with the federal government. Behind him stood the extraordinary force of the Espionage Act, the Trading-with-the-Enemy Act, and the Sedition Act; he was a member of the Censorship Board; he worked in close collaboration with the Military and Naval Intelligence; the Department of Justice was at hand to make his word as good as law;[23] and the President aided him with close cooperation.[24] The glove did indeed conceal a mailed fist. Yet the fact remains that greater freedom for the press existed in this country than was found in any of the belligerent nations of Europe, and for this Creel deserves the "largest share of credit."[25] Had he chosen to secure an ironclad grip upon the American press, he could, by rubbing his Aladdin's lamp, have called to his side any one of several forces fully adequate to achieve his purpose. There is no reason to doubt that under such circumstances the public, particularly during the

[22] Interview with G. S. Ford, New York, December 28, 1940. The April, May, and June, 1917, files of almost any newspaper will furnish convincing proof that the press was suspicious.

[23] Mock and Larson, *Words That Won the War*, p. 46.

[24] CPI, *Hearing, 1918*, p. 160.

[25] Mock and Larson, *Words That Won the War*, p. 46. Creel insisted that he did not hold these powers (*How We Advertised America*, p. 27). As Chairman of the CPI, he did not. Had he chosen to use them, however, they were available, and the mere fact of their existence undoubtedly exerted some indirect influence on the press. Bernard Baruch used his power over industry with extreme reserve, yet the industrialists knew that the power was implicit in all of Baruch's requests and responded accordingly. The cases are somewhat analogous.

latter months of the war, would have patriotically rallied to his support. That Creel did not choose to exercise the influence that was his in such large measure is the clearest indication of his sincerity in advocating "unparalleled openness."[26] On the whole, press censorship during the war was largely self-administered. The Committee on Public Information did little more than to establish certain general principles, leaving the newspapers free to make their own decisions as to what should be printed.[27]

The propaganda committee had many enemies. Many Americans favored rigid censorship along European lines, and vented their anger upon Creel when these demands were not met.[28] A number of Congressmen were ignorant of the true nature of the work being done by the committee;[29] others chose to use Creel as a "whipping boy" in their efforts to strike at the President.[30] Creel himself, caustic in expression, impetuous in action, did little to correct the misunderstanding and allay the ill-feeling, perhaps causing more dissension than was necessary with other branches of the government.[31] "The heavens may fall, the earth be consumed," he remarked bitterly some months after the war had ended, "but the right of a Congressman to lie and defame remains inviolate."[32]

Having decided that his job was to be "a vast enterprise in salesmanship," Creel wasted no time in starting what he called "the world's greatest adventure in advertising."[33] Within a few months he had created an educational organization that touched every part of the war machine, that utilized every medium of appeal—the written and spoken word: the telegraph, cable, and wireless; the motion picture, poster, and signboard; the college,

[26] The expression is quoted by Sullivan, *Over Here*, p. 425.

[27] Mock and Larson, *Words That Won the War*, pp. 46–47. Chapter II of Mock's study contains an interesting analysis of the entire problem. Ford firmly supports Creel in the latter's contention that no censorship was exercised by the Committee on Public Information, and insists that even Mock and Larson have not given Creel his full measure of credit. Interview with G. S. Ford, New York, December 28, 1940.

[28] Creel, *How We Advertised America*, pp. 16, 27.

[29] CPI, *Hearing, 1918*. This lack of understanding is revealed on almost every page of the testimony.

[30] Interview with G. S. Ford, New York, December 28, 1940.

[31] Sullivan, *Over Here*, pp. 425–426; 436–438; Mock and Larson, *Words That Won the War*, p. 46.

[32] Creel, *How We Advertised America*, p. 52.

[33] *Ibid.*, p. 4.

public school, and kindergarten. News was the life blood of the Committee on Public Information.[34] It came from every conceivable source: from mining camp and front-line trench, from ships at sea, from office, factory, farm, and home. More than fifty federal bureaus and departments daily released as many as eighty columns of publicity. In an unending torrent it poured through the offices of the News Division where relays of trained men working twenty-four hours a day read, interpreted, and released the "most important" information to thousands of papers throughout the United States. Much of it was translated and went into the foreign press.[35] At Wilson's insistence, the Committee issued an official newspaper[36] which, to Creel's surprise and delight, reached a circulation of over 100,000 copies daily and served every department of the government.[37]

To the "Four Minute Men" went forty-six different bulletins prepared by the propaganda bureau. Data, illustrations, and sample addresses from these pamphlets furnished the raw material for an army of 75,000 speakers who, it was estimated, delivered over 1,000,000 speeches before some 400,000,000 people gathered in lodges, theaters, churches, synagogues, labor unions, and on Indian Reservations.[38] Even the school children were organized in a "Junior Four Minute Men" program. Meanwhile, hundreds of more experienced speakers carried messages of greater length to audiences presumably more thoughtful.[39]

Films showing the various phases of the war effort were released by the Committee and shown in the nation's theaters; slides were prepared and over 200,000 distributed;[40] 750 cartoonists were supplied each week with "inspiration" from a bulletin containing suggestions for their work;[41] and artists of the stature of James Montgomery Flagg, rallying under the leadership of Charles Dana Gibson, produced scores of effective posters. As Wallace Irwin so picturesquely phrased it, "art put on khaki and went into action."[42]

[34] Mock and Larson, *Words That Won the War*, p. 77.
[35] CPI, *Hearing, 1918*, p. 47.
[36] *The Official Bulletin.*
[37] CPI, *Hearing, 1918*, p. 11.
[38] Creel, *How We Advertised America*, pp. 86–94.
[39] *Ibid.*, p. 148.
[40] *Ibid.*, pp. 121–124.
[41] *Ibid.*, p. 226.
[42] *Ibid.*, pp. 133–141.

Creel's work started in a pattern of public relations rather than of education. Advertising men from all sections of the country volunteered their services and were formed into a special division of the Committee.[43] A women's division sent out weekly releases to the press and magazines in an attempt to reveal the part women were playing in the war effort.[44] War expositions toured the country, bringing to the people the weapons used by the men at the fighting fronts. The citizens of Chicago were invited to share vicariously the thrills of war by witnessing a sham battle; Creel was particularly pleased with the effectiveness of the demonstrations. As he later wrote, "This daily spectacle of men going over the top to the rattle of rifles and machine-guns, and the roar of the navy ordnance, aroused the assembled thousands to the highest pitch of enthusiasm."[45]

A Service Bureau was opened in Washington to facilitate inter-departmental communication and to make it easier for visitors to locate a particular bureau or official.[46] The Committee organized and directed twenty-three societies and leagues designed to appeal to certain classes of people, especially the foreign language groups; each of these organizations carried the government's messages to a selected portion of the population.[47] Even the traveling men were called into service by means of a pamphlet prepared by the Creel Committee and addressed to "The Commercial Travellers of America." Copies of this bulletin were placed in the hands of salesmen who were urged to "swat the lie" that the Kaiser's "paid agents and unpaid sympathizers are spreading by word of mouth."[48]

As has been indicated, the Committee's activities did not stop at America's frontiers. Every capital of the world, with the exception, naturally, of those of the Central Powers, was served daily by cable and mail with important news releases; in several countries reading rooms were opened and stocked with American books, periodicals, newspapers, and literature of a selected nature; while speakers chosen from the foreign born in this country toured the continent lecturing to labor unions, university circles, and busi-

43 *Ibid.,* p. 158.
44 *Ibid.,* p. 212.
45 Creel, *How We Advertised America,* p. 146.
46 *Ibid.,* pp. 222–223.
47 *RCPI,* p. 3.
48 CPI, *The Kaiserite in America. One Hundred and One German Lies,* p. 8.

nessmen, carrying Creel's messages to the peoples of Europe.[49] Not even the enemy's lines were a barrier; American propaganda crossed the trenches by "balloons, mortars, and aeroplanes."[50]

No summary can possibly make clear the extent of Creel's work. Through it all ran an enthusiasm which can never be recaptured in cold type. It has been estimated that over 150,000 of the nation's most talented artists, writers, business leaders, and professional men contributed freely of their time and experience.[51] It was an amazing exhibition, and novel in the world's history. Not until the days of Stalin and Goebbels were men to realize how effectively Creel had used the new weapon of propaganda in a different, and total, type of war. Nor should it be forgotten that Creel was without benefit of those instruments which have made the work of later propagandists so much easier—the sound effect of the improved motion picture and the radio.[52]

2. Printed Propaganda

The Division of Civic and Educational Cooperation[53] was of fundamental importance in the success of Creel's work. Before the war had ended this organization was responsible for the preparation and publication of more than one hundred separate bulletins and pamphlets,[54] ranging from liberally documented books of some 300 pages down to tiny leaflets written in the simplest terms. More than 75,000,000 copies of these bulletins were distributed throughout the United States, a number of them in fourteen dif-

---

[49] Creel, *How We Advertised America*, p. 50.

[50] *RCPI*, p. 5.

[51] Sullivan, *Over Here*, p. 427.

[52] The standard account of the Committee on Public Information is the admirable study by Mock and Larson, *Words That Won the War*. General readers will find in this volume a colorful treatment of the activities of the Creel Committee; the student will value it as an extremely careful piece of research based on the voluminous records of the CPI now located in the National Archives. Mock and Larson were the first to make extensive use of these records. Creel's book, *How We Advertised America*, was written a few months after the end of the war "as a matter of duty and as a partial discharge of my debt of gratitude to the men and women who worked with me," the author explained (p. ix). It is Creel's own interpretation and should, of course, be read with care. The so-called *Complete Record of the Chairman of the Committee on Public Information, 1917: 1918: 1919* throws little additional light on Creel's work.

[53] The name was changed on March 11, 1918, to "Division of Civic and Educational Publications." National Archives (CPI, 3-A1, L-1-482).

[54] Mock and Larson, *Words That Won the War*, p. 162.

ferent languages. This total does not include the millions of additional copies which were reprinted and distributed by private agencies and individuals at their own expense, nor does it include the publications which were translated from the English and circulated in foreign countries.[55] Here was one of the greatest publishing ventures in history, and it is of particular interest to this study because it was through the Division of Civic and Educational Cooperation that much of the federal propaganda was carried into the public schools.

Creel, wishing to make the justice of America's cause "a matter of definite intellectual conviction" to the American people, started at first to prepare state papers and documents for publication. He soon decided that "long, tedious state papers" would be of little value, and discarded this plan in favor of "popular pamphleteering."[56] In the course of his search for a "writer skilled in investigation," a historian "who knew Europe and America equally well," he chanced upon a pamphlet written by Guy Stanton Ford, Head of the Department of History and Dean of the Graduate School of the University of Minnesota.[57]

This incident catapulted Dean Ford into the very center of our war effort. Little did he realize as he sat before his desk in those spring days of 1917 the far-reaching consequences that were to result from the paper he was preparing. Years later he told the history of this little pamphlet:

Early in the spring of 1917 I wrote an open letter to school principals about the possibility of using the coming high school commencements for patriotic purposes. I wrote it for the signature of the Commissioner of Education, but he modestly declined to sign it and sent it out, however, over my name. A copy of that fell into George Creel's hands. I think it must have reached him through some member of the National Board for Historical Service, already partly formed in Washington, possibly through Professor Shotwell. Something about it made him think that I would be valuable as a writer. Presumably his earlier idea was that the Committee on Public Information would largely serve as writers, supplementing the utterances of the President and other leaders, and in doing what its name implied.[58]

55 *RCPI*, pp. 2, 18.
56 Creel, *How We Advertised America*, p. 101.
57 *Ibid.*, p. 101.
58 Mock and Larson, *Words That Won the War*, pp. 158–159.

It was characteristic of Creel that immediately upon reading this pamphlet he drafted a telegram to Dean Ford: "Committee Public Information desires your service. Need imperative. Work continue during war. Salary satisfactory. Wire reply time of departure."[59] This telegram reached Ford on May 8, and he promptly wired Professor James T. Shotwell of Columbia University for advice. Shotwell, already active in Washington as chairman of the National Board for Historical Service, "strongly" advised acceptance,[60] and Ford notified Creel that he was leaving for Washington without delay.[61]

While other choices might have been made, it is difficult to believe that any could have been more fortunate. Even as Creel was to surprise everyone, including perhaps himself, with the extent of his activities, so Ford was to conduct the greatest campaign in popular education that the country had ever witnessed. Creel never regretted his choice. He and Ford became firm friends, each with the utmost confidence in the integrity and ability of the other. As a result of this mutual respect, Ford was given an entirely free hand by the chairman of the Committee on Public Information, and the whole responsibility for the educational publications and the bulletins issued for the use of the "Four Minute Men" rested upon Ford's shoulders.[62] When the propaganda committee, seeking an appropriation in June, 1918, was compelled by a Congressional committee to defend its activities, Ford was asked how decisions were reached as to what should be published. He replied: "The initiation of every publication has come from me as a suggestion to Mr. Creel. Mr. Creel has never said to me in reference to any of these pamphlets, 'This is what I want to put in that pamphlet.' "[63]

In addition to his personal qualities, which combined tact,

[59] National Archives (CPI, 3-A1, L-1-3).

[60] *Ibid.*

[61] *Ibid.*

[62] Interview with G. S. Ford, New York, December 28, 1940. James R. Mock, who with painstaking care has gone through the voluminous records of the CPI in the National Archives, corroborated this statement. Mr. Mock was impressed with the extent to which Creel relied upon Ford. Repeatedly, Mock pointed out, Creel would ask his colleague for advice, and the records reveal that it was always followed in its entirety. (Interview with James R. Mock, Washington, December 10, 1940.)

[63] CPI, *Hearing, 1918*, p. 106.

patience, and an unassuming manner with a sincerity of purpose and a firm devotion to principles,[64] Ford came well equipped for his task. He had studied at Wisconsin, Berlin, and Columbia. At the latter university he did a doctoral study on a subject dealing with Hanover and Prussia, receiving his degree in 1903. His career in the educational field had been widely varied, starting in the public schools, first with classroom teaching, later as superintendent. Subsequently he had served successively at Yale, Illinois, and Minnesota in both professorial and administrative capacities.[65]

The Committee's first publication was the President's War Message of April 2, 1917, annotated by Professor W. S. Davis and a group of historians from the University of Minnesota.[66] After a study of the newspaper directories, it was estimated that about 20,000 copies would cover the requirements of the press.[67] "That," Ford later remarked, "was our idea of our job." It was a bad miscalculation. The newspapers pounced upon the bulletin, and the CPI was overwhelmed with the consequent publicity. Letters demanding further copies poured into Ford's office. The day after the bulletin appeared in print, he received a peach basket full of mail; the next day, two bushels; "and then," Ford stated, "the flood just opened on us."[68] Requests came from all ranks and kinds of people—from fathers and mothers, from boys on their way to camp, from superintendents of schools, from State Councils of Defense and local patriotic societies—and by the time the war had ended more than 2,500,000 copies had been distributed.[69]

From that time on, new bulletins rolled from the press in constantly increasing variety and volume. There were two major series—the Red, White, and Blue Series of ten bulletins, and the War Information Series of twenty-one bulletins.[70] These were published according to a definite plan. As Ford stated:

[64] The record is revealed in his own correspondence on file in the National Archives.

[65] Who's Who in America, vol. XXII, 1942–1943. (Chicago: The A. N. Marquis Company, 1942.)

[66] CPI, The War Message and Facts Behind It. Annotated Text of President Wilson's Message, April 2, 1917.

[67] Creel, How We Advertised America, p. 102.

[68] CPI, Hearing, 1918, p. 96.

[69] RCPI, p. 16.

[70] Nothing will reveal more clearly than these bulletins the nature of our propaganda activities. They should be read in their entirety. Short summaries will be found in the general literature covering the subject. See supra, p. 22.

We have not done it haphazard. We have concentrated, first, on the thing that was most evident, which was to make our own purposes and our own ideals clear. If you follow the order of the publications, you will notice that that is primarily what we did first, and then we turned to stripping the mask off this thing that is called the Prussian military machine, showing how it works. We have gone at that point by point, e.g., in the way they treated subject populations in Belgium and Holland, in the way they stripped conquered territory of even the door knobs and name plates, in the way they taught their officers in their military code to do, to feel justified in doing, exactly the things that they have done and might be expected to do . . .[71]

3. Methods of Preparation and Distribution

Trained scholars prepared each of the bulletins issued by the Committee on Public Information. Topics were suggested by state and local Councils of Defense, by patriotic societies, and by individuals; from this list Ford chose those topics which appeared to be most promising. Creel's approval was then secured, and a scholar was selected to prepare the bulletin. If a trip to Washington were required for purposes of consultation, the author received from thirty-five to fifty dollars for each week he spent in the capital; with this exception, no compensation was available for any of the writers. The finished manuscript was given a general examination by the Committee, was checked by the various bureaus and departments of the government concerned with the problem—in the case of a study dealing with foreign affairs, it was read by the Secretary of War, the Secretary of State, or perhaps the Attorney General—and, after final approval by the President, was released for publication.[72] Ford claimed that although he selected the topic and broadly outlined the study he wished prepared, his only instructions to the writer were to do the job "so carefully" that "you will be willing to stand for it twenty years from now." He affirmed that, had any attempt been made to bind the scholars to predetermined conclusions, "I know that none of those men would have touched it with a ten-foot pole."[73]

This explanation of how the pamphlets were prepared appears to have satisfied the Congressmen, whose primary concern was for

[71] CPI, *Hearing, 1918*, p. 99.
[72] CPI, *Hearing, 1918*, p. 107.
[73] *Ibid.*, pp. 99, 107.

the political power latent in Creel's control of the machinery of persuasion. They were content to know that Creel was trying only to advance the war effort, not to further Wilson's political ambitions. But there was another problem about which the legislators showed little, if any, concern. That was the problem of scholarship.

Were the historians who prepared these bulletins as objective as Ford's remarks would seem to indicate? One who reads their pamphlets now can answer only in the negative. These men faced a dilemma common to all scholars in wartime. The academician is pledged to the search for truth, but he is also a citizen of a nation battling for its very existence and he has civic responsibilities which cannot be evaded. In the First World War, as in all other conflicts in which the United States has been engaged, many scholars left their caps and gowns to devote their efforts to the struggle for victory. Not all had Ford's integrity. "If," as one able student recently observed, "in the ardor of patriotism some forgot altogether the cannons of scholarship, they no doubt took satisfaction in thinking that the pen might be as mighty as the sword."[74] How far the publications of the Creel Committee departed from the standards of scholarship the reader may judge for himself; how far the Committee might have gone is revealed by the pamphlets it refused to publish. The files of the CPI are full of these unpublished documents, sent in by ardent "patriots" from all sections of the country. Many of them are brutal and degrading perversions of the truth.

To understand why the Creel pamphlets were so effective, it is necessary to remember that the propagandist may avoid the outright falsehood and still achieve his purposes. The selection of subject matter is in itself the finest art of propaganda. One needs only to run through the titles of the bulletins issued by the Division on Civic and Educational Cooperation to see how the thing was done: *The Government of Germany; A War of Self-Defense; German Plots and Intrigues in the United States During the Period of Our Neutrality; American Loyalty; The German War Code Contrasted with the War Manuals of the United States,*

[74] Merle Curti, "The American Scholar in Three Wars," *Journal of the History of Ideas*, vol. III (June, 1942), pp. 250–252.

*Great Britain, and France; The Prussian System; American Inter-
est in Popular Government Abroad; German Militarism and Its
German Critics; The War for Peace;* and so forth. Each publication was an argument for the justice of the American cause or an
indictment of the German Imperial Government. Many of them,
as an examination of the titles will indicate, can be paired one
against the other. There were only two sides: the right and the
wrong, the white and the black; shaded areas in between were
not explored. Topics not susceptible to this one-sided treatment
were discreetly laid aside. This point is illuminated by the correspondence which Ford carried on with one historian in regard
to a contemplated bulletin.

Shortly after he had assumed the chairmanship of the Division
of Civic and Educational Cooperation, Ford was struck with the
idea of preparing a pamphlet on the German War Code, and
selected Professor J. W. Garner of the University of Illinois to
do the job. Further thought led him to doubt the wisdom of such
a publication, and he expressed his uncertainty in a letter to
Garner. "War codes," he wrote, "even in humane nations, are
likely to contain things which when taken out of their texts and
apart from the spirit in which they are executed sound quite as
barbaric as similar passages in the Prussian War Code."[75] Additional reading and thought confirmed Ford's fears, and he sent a
second letter to the University of Illinois: "The more I look over
our own field regulations with the citations from Moltke and other
German writers and their utter confusion of necessity and right,
the more doubtful I am about the effectiveness of the subject I
suggested to you." He then proposed that they substitute for the
war code pamphlet a study which "might be called 'Neutral Europe and the U-boat.' I think," Ford said, "there would be great
value in the northwest in presenting the disastrous consequences
of the submarine campaign, particularly in the Scandinavian
countries but not omitting Holland, Spain, etc."[76]

Another illustration of how material was selected for its propaganda value is revealed in a letter from Ford to one of his colleagues in the University of Minnesota. "I have been looking,"

[75] G. S. Ford to J. W. Garner, June 7, 1917, National Archives (CPI, 3-A1, L-1-34).
[76] *Ibid.*, June 11, 1917.

he stated, "for something which would do as a text upon which we could hang a collection of excerpts from German publicists and newspapers regarding the pan-German idea. The Flag Day speech has made that possible."[77] Three months later a thirty-page pamphlet was issued by the Creel Committee. The propagandists had outdone themselves. Ford had asked for something upon which to "hang" a collection of excerpts, but it is difficult to tell from the bulletin which is hanging—the excerpts from the German publicists or the President's "Flag Day Address." Frequently only two or three lines of the President's remarks appear at the top of a page; the remainder of the space, and in several instances the next two or three pages, are filled with "annotations."[78]

The task of the propagandist does not, of course, end with the judicious selection of a topic; he must also know what to include in the pamphlet and what it is better to leave unsaid. This technique was employed with considerable skill in the preparation of a study of the German war code. Evidently Ford's earlier doubts were resolved, for the bulletin was eventually written by Professors J. W. Garner of the University of Illinois and G. W. Scott of Columbia.[79] The pamphlet was prefaced with a note of explanation:

Many good loyal Americans have hesitated to believe the charges of wholesale brutality and ruthlessness made against the German authorities. . . .
The facts here set forth are not new. They have been known for years to those whose business it is to be informed on such matters. They are, however, unknown to the general public. We ask you to read them and then consider whether the brutality, ruthlessness, terrorism, and violence of the German forces have not been cold-bloodedly programmed for years by the German authorities.[80]

The facts that the reader was asked to examine were taken from the *German Army-Law Manual (Kriegsbrauch im Landkriege).* This manual contained the rules by which German soldiers were to conduct themselves in the field, outlining in detail such prob-

[77] G. S. Ford to W. Notestein, National Archives (CPI, 3-A1, L-1-19).
[78] CPI, *The President's Flag Day Address. With Evidences of Germany's Plans.*
[79] CPI, *The German War Code Contrasted with the War Manuals of the United States, Great Britain, and France.*
[80] *Ibid.*, p. 2.

lems as the procedure to be followed by the army in conquered
territory and the treatment to be rendered prisoners of war. The
facts presented by the authors of the Creel pamphlet were exact
quotations from the German manual, and did appear to prove that
the Germans "nullify in more or less express language nearly
every important rule of warfare." Nearly half of the propaganda
leaflet was devoted to these excerpts from the German code. Then,
turning to the manuals in use by the United States, Great Britain,
and France, the authors noted a "refreshing contrast." As evidence of this contrast, two pages of quotations were offered from
the manual in use by the United States; one page from that manual
followed by the English armies; while France, with a code "striking" in its contrast, was given one half page of quotations.

It is obvious that the reader who sought in a few short pages of
excerpts to compare the war manuals of the principal belligerents
was completely dependent upon the integrity of the editors. As
Ford had warned in reference to the American war code, quotations torn from their context may be devoid even of the spirit in
which they were written.[81]

The history of the German manual serves to cast even further
doubt upon the accuracy of the conclusions reached by the editors
of Creel's leaflet. The first code of this sort ever used was prepared for the United States Union Army during our Civil War.
Francis Lieber, international lawyer and Professor of Political
Science at Columbia University, who undertook this task at the
request of Lincoln, was well pleased with the result of his efforts.
"I think," he said, "the No. 100 will do honour to our country.
It will be adopted as a basis for similar works by the English,
French and Germans. It is a contribution by the United States to
the stock of common civilization." His prophecy was realized, for
the code he had drawn up did become the basis for future works
on this phase of international law.[82] The articles were adopted by
the German Government for the conduct of its armies in the war
of 1870 with France.[83] From it were derived those laws of war

---

[81] See *supra*, p. 28.

[82] Brainerd Dyer, "Francis Lieber and the American Civil War," *Huntington
Library Quarterly*, vol. II (July, 1939), pp. 456–457.

[83] Elihu Root, "Francis Lieber," *The American Journal of International Law*,
vol. VII (1913), p. 456.

which were adopted by the Conference of Brussels in 1874; which were re-enacted a second and third time by the Hague Conferences of 1899 and 1907; and which were in force when the World War broke out in 1914.[84] With the war codes of the belligerents all based upon the same source, it is difficult to accept the conclusion that there was a "refreshing contrast" between the codes of Germany and the Associated Powers.

This is not to say that the actual conduct of the German armies in the field was exemplary; whether or not they were less humane than their opponents is another problem. The point here emphasized is that the propagandist may quote exactly, yet still vitiate the truth by a careful process of selection. Much of the material prepared for the Committee on Public Information was the product of such a technique. This discovery in the postwar years may have been a contributing factor in the disillusionment of the next generation.

As publications of this sort flowed from the press, they were widely advertised through newspapers and magazines, through educational circles, through more than 1,500,000 self-addressed postcards distributed by the Creel Committee, and through the numerous national, state, and local patriotic organizations that were active during the war. With two exceptions, all material was mailed only on request. *The President's Flag Day Address* was delivered by the Boy Scouts with instructions to secure from the recipient his promise first to read the pamphlet and then to pass it on to his friends. The bulletins translated into foreign languages were sent into those areas where Ford felt that the need for propaganda among the foreign-born groups was most vital.[85] Most of the pamphlets were free; a few were sold at cost.

4. Criticisms of the War Bulletins

Hardly had the work been started before criticisms began to reach the offices of the Division of Civic and Educational Cooperation. Many people agreed with the energetic chairman of the Illinois State Council of Defense, Harold L. Ickes, who claimed

---

[84] Ernest Nys, "Francis Lieber—His Life and Work," *The American Journal of International Law*, vol. V, part I (1911), p. 86.

[85] CPI, *Hearing, 1918*, p. 103.

that the material was too scholarly, that nothing had been published to "appeal to the farmers, to the laboring men, or to the
average run of citizens who do not do profound reading."[86] It was
clear that millions of Americans were not being reached.

Ford's reply to objections of this nature was the publication of
a new series known as the "Loyalty Leaflets." There were seven
of these tiny pamphlets, and more than 1,500,000 of each were distributed.[87] They were simply written, aimed obviously at the least
literate of America's population; but the criticisms continued to
pour in. Although it was admitted that the new leaflets did help
to reach a "distinct class" not previously circularized, Ford was
urged to prepare "special material for farmers."[88]

Other critics were not so much interested in the preparation of
new pamphlets as in the adequate distribution of those already
printed. A letter from the Illinois Council of Defense, written
early in 1918, referred to the embarrassment of the Committee
when asked by the University of Chicago for the *War Cyclopedia*.
"We had to confess," the letter complained, "that we had not even
heard of it."[89] Some months later a member of the Union League
Club of Chicago wrote to an official of the Department of the Interior pleading with the latter to get him 80,000 copies of seven
different pamphlets. The supply is "so far below the demand,"
he said, "that apparently the only person who gets the documents
is the person who sits on the doorstep and grabs them from the
wagon. . . . If in your department you have an able-bodied and
persuasive genius who can extract the above documents from the
Committee on Public Information, I promise you that every one
of them will be put where it will do great good."[90] An Assistant
Professor of History at Teachers College, Columbia University,
found it difficult to get materials for use in summer school. In
fact, he wrote, "I find it almost impossible to get satisfactory an-

[86] H. L. Ickes to G. S. Ford, October 24, 1917, and February 2, 1918. National
Archives (CPI, 3-A7, L-1-329).

[87] *RCPI*, p. 16. Leaflet No. 5, written by Elihu Root, had a circulation of only
112,492.

[88] A. M. Simons to G. S. Ford, April 19, 1918. National Archives (CPI, 3-A7,
L-1-283).

[89] V. G. Chandler to G. S. Ford, February 8, 1918. National Archives (CPI, 3-A7,
L-1-558).

[90] A. O. Pond to S. T. Mather, April 13, 1918. National Archives (CPI, 3-A7,
L-1-558).

swers to inquiries and requests, and it often takes several weeks to hear anything."[91]

These criticisms were fully merited, but the fault was not entirely that of the propaganda committee. Ford's 75,000,000 bulletins were prepared, printed, and circulated at a total cost of $568,306.08.[92] The first year the Committee had operated under a special grant from the President's Emergency War Fund; after June, 1918, operations were continued under an appropriation from Congress, but the amount was insufficient and the supply of pamphlets was always hopelessly below the demand. Nor was the situation helped by the policy of distributing materials only upon request. The customary procedure was for various organizations to secure quantities of the different bulletins and circulate them throughout a limited area. Where the organizations were active, the spread of propaganda was heavy; where vigorous local groups did not operate, Creel's publications were given only a limited circulation.[93]

A third group of critics was concerned because the public schools were not being asked to play a more active role in the war effort. Their letters usually contained either requests for assistance or suggestions as to ways by which the propaganda committee could more effectively extend its influence into the educational system. One book publisher recommended the preparation of a "brief and cogent statement of why we are at war, which could be read in all the secondary schools of the country at the opening exercises at stated intervals."[94] The Educational Director of the National Security League claimed that he had received 20,000 requests in a single week for one of the League's publications, a manual designed to help teachers to "instill into the minds of their pupils patriotic ideals."[95] Typical was the letter from a Michigan teacher who asked for "any publications bearing on the present

[91] J. M. Gambrill to S. B. Harding, August 14, 1918. National Archives (CPI, 3-A1, L-1-604).

[92] RCPI, p. 9.

[93] CPI, Hearing, 1918, pp. 103–104; G. S. Ford to S. H. Clark, April 1, 1918. National Archives (CPI, 3-A1, L-1-478).

[94] F. Greenslet, Houghton Mifflin Company, to W. B. Pitkin. National Archives (CPI, 3-A1, L-1-142).

[95] R. R. McElroy to G. S. Ford, December 3 and 15, 1917. National Archives (CPI, 3-A1, L-1-161).

war" for use by "the Patriotic Committee organized in our public schools."[96]

Ford's procedure in such cases was to send at once all free publications. These had not been prepared for boys and girls of school age, however, and as requests and suggestions continued to reach the Committee from those connected with the schools and those interested in using the schools, it became increasingly apparent that the propaganda committee had a new problem to tackle.

5. Carrying Propaganda Activities to the Public Schools

That the public schools could be of use to the war effort was not a new idea to Ford. From the beginning of his work with the Creel Committee he had tried to enlist the aid of educators. The National Board for Historical Service was practically an affiliate of the Committee on Public Information, and Ford repeatedly urged the political scientists to form a similar organization for war work, but his efforts in this direction were fruitless.[97] With the National Education Association he had greater success, and he was delighted when he heard that the program for the annual convention of 1917 was to be built around the theme of "Preparedness, Nationalism, and Patriotism."[98]

Ford believed that the public schools were in great need of guidance in "making readjustments that the war will reveal as necessary." It was his conviction that "in no field will new problems or old problems in new light be more frequent than in that part of the high schools covered by the social sciences. All questions touching citizenship and civic service will take on a new meaning." Meanwhile, leadership was needed, and Ford proposed the immediate formation of an organization of secondary school social studies teachers similar to that of the National Board for Historical Service. He suggested that this association maintain permanent representatives in Washington where, in close touch with

[96] H. Beach to J. T. Shotwell, February 2, 1918. National Archives (CPI, 3-A1, L-1-163).

[97] Correspondence between G. S. Ford and C. L. Jones, June, 1917. National Archives (CPI, 3-A1, L-1-43).

[98] G. S. Ford to D. W. Springer, May 28, 1917; Memorandum of the N.E.A., May 19, 1917. National Archives (CPI, 3-A7, L-1-32).

the work of the government, they would be in a position to furnish leadership to the public school teachers of America. Printed material especially valuable for school use could be secured through the Bureau of Education and the Creel Committee, speakers could be sent out to teachers' meetings and educational conferences, and "other avenues of publicity would open up."[99] The teachers of New York City were urged to take the initiative in the organization of such a project. A conference was actually held in the spring of 1917, but action was postponed until the fall.[100] By that time, other groups, such as the National Security League, had begun to function, and propaganda was being prepared and injected into the public school system in constantly increasing volume.

The idea was sound, and had it been developed much of the confusion that was later to trouble public school administrators might have been avoided. That the Creel Committee did not press the proposal was the result, at least in part, of the pressure of more important work. By September, 1917, the Division of Civic and Educational Cooperation had printed and was in the process of distributing twelve bulletins. Although these had not been designed for school children, it was felt that they might have some value if placed in the hands of teachers.

At this point the Committee ran into difficulties. How could these bulletins be brought to the attention of the teachers? A number of suggestions were made, including one proposal to use the Boy Scouts as distributing agents, but all were rejected.[101] The plan which was finally adopted with only slight modifications originated with Professor David S. Snedden of Teachers College, Columbia University. He proposed that the Bureau of Education prepare a single sheet leaflet containing a prospectus of each pamphlet and a concluding statement urging teachers who were interested to send for a copy. This procedure had the added merit, as he saw it, of advertising the federal bureau and thus enhancing its prestige.[102] Here a second difficulty was encountered. Nothing indicates more clearly how completely our educational system was

99 G. S. Ford to T. J. Jones, June 2, 1917. National Archives (CPI, 3-A1, L-1-40).
100 E. Dawson to G. S. Ford, June 13, 1917. National Archives (CPI, 3-A1, L-1-41).
101 J. T. Shotwell to G. S. Ford, July 12 and 13, 1917. National Archives (CPI, 3-A1, L-1-163).
102 *Ibid.*

decentralized than the fact that in August, 1917, Ford was unable to secure from the Bureau of Education a list of the officers and teachers employed in the nation's schools.[103] In October he was still trying to get the names and addresses of the state superintendents, and as late as the fall of 1918 the Bureau of Education had been unable to compile a complete directory of the schoolhouses of the United States.[104] It was obvious that if the propaganda committee relied upon direct circularization of the teachers, its campaign could expect only limited success. Additional publicity was necessary.

Ford then approached the McKinley Publishing Company, publishers of *The History Teacher's Magazine*, with the proposal that they advertise the Committee's bulletins in their educational journal. Foreseeing the possibility of an increased circulation, the publishers gave enthusiastic support to the project. Their judgment was correct. By the end of September, 1917, they were able to report "a great many new subscriptions," and Ford, in turn, was gratified by "definite practical results."[105] Teachers in growing numbers were requesting the bulletins which they had read about in *The History Teacher's Magazine*.

It is impossible to estimate how many of the 75,000,000 pamphlets ever reached the public schools. The records reveal that fewer than 350,000 copies were distributed directly to the schools themselves. Hundreds of local groups, from Kiwanis Clubs to churches, disposed of the remainder; many of these undoubtedly ended in the hands of educators.[106] Of the bulletins issued for the general reader, there were three which the Creel Committee believed might be of particular value to school children. *The President's Flag Day Address* reached a peak of nearly 7,000,000 pamphlets,[107] but almost all of these were distributed by the Boy Scouts,[108] evidently to parents.[109] About 2,500,000 copies of *The*

---

[103] G. S. Ford to the Bureau of Education, August 1 and October 9, 1917. National Archives (CPI, 3-A7, L-1-30).

[104] *School and Society*, vol. VIII (August 17, 1918), p. 199.

[105] Correspondence between Ford and the McKinley Publishing Company, October 2–4, 1917. National Archives (CPI, 3-A1, L-1-311).

[106] CPI, *Hearing, 1918*, p. 104.

[107] *RCPI*, p. 15.

[108] CPI, *Hearing, 1918*, p. 103.

[109] Creel, *How We Advertised America*, p. 110.

War Message and Facts Behind It were printed;[110] there is no way of telling how many of these were made available to the children. *The Battle Line of Democracy*, a collection of prose, poetry, and songs, sold for fifteen cents; not 100,000 copies were purchased.[111]

Two other bulletins were prepared specifically for use in the schools. One of these was Samuel B. Harding's syllabus,[112] prepared for high school students, of which approximately 700,000 copies were issued by the Creel Committee.[113] The second was a semi-monthly magazine called *National School Service;* an effort was made to place it before every teacher. In addition, the Committee on Public Information sponsored an outline for the elementary grades.[114] It is also important to remember that practically all of this material was reprinted in large quantities by newspapers and private organizations.[115] Yet when one recalls that in 1918 the public school system enrolled about 20,000,000 boys and girls and employed about 650,000 teachers,[116] it is evident that the educational institutions were not flooded with propaganda from the Creel organization. Some schools got more than their share, more than they wished; others never saw more than a handful of pamphlets.

As has been indicated, there were substantial reasons why the work was not done more thoroughly in the public schools. Money was limited; distributing facilities were inadequate; the actual field work for the Committee had to be handled by local groups, stimulated whenever possible by Creel's Committee in Washington; and, finally, Ford was never persuaded that the public schools were his primary responsibility.[117] The Committee first tried to get copies into the hands of all community leaders; it made a less vigorous attempt to reach the school administrators;[118] and its

110 *RCPI*, p. 16.

111 *Ibid.*, p. 15.

112 *The Study of the Great War. A Topical Outline, with Extensive Quotations and Reading References.* See *infra*, pp. 54 *et seq.*

113 *RCPI*, p. 15.

114 Charles A. Coulomb, Armand J. Gerson, and Albert E. McKinley. *Outline of an Emergency Course of Instruction on the War* (Bureau of Education, Teachers' Leaflet No. 4, 1918). See *infra*, pp. 58 *et seq.*

115 *RCPI*, pp. 2, 18.

116 *Biennial Survey*, 1916–1918 (Bureau of Education Bulletin, 1919, No. 90), vol. III, p. 54.

117 Interview with G. S. Ford, New York, December 28, 1940.

118 Memorandum (no date). National Archives (CPI, 3-A7, L-1-495).

efforts to influence the teachers and pupils were always subordinated to other activities. Here and there throughout the country, local societies were particularly energetic. The Wisconsin Loyalty Legion, for example, attempted to make a complete coverage of the schools, but it was continually thwarted by its inability to secure sufficient materials from Washington.[119] Whatever the reasons, the activities of the Committee on Public Information were far from satisfactory to many individuals interested in the public schools, and by the end of 1917 the volume of criticism was swelling rapidly.

The nature and extent of this criticism may be illustrated by the activities of Professor S. H. Clark of the University of Chicago. For months he peppered Ford and Creel with inquiries, suggestions, requests, and even demands. During these same months, he traveled extensively from New York to California, talking to and corresponding with schoolmen from the rank of teacher to that of normal school and university president. By March, 1918, he was filled with "despair over the educational system," and had practically abandoned hope of getting much done by the Committee on Public Information. He wrote to Creel:

This is my third and last attempt to urge a campaign having for its objective training in patriotism of every public school and high school teacher besides teachers in parochial and private schools; students in normal schools and high schools and, in some way, even pupils in our grammar schools. So far as I can learn the public school system has gone to sleep on its job. The direction from Washington has been slipshod and haphazard, and there has been comparatively little initiative on the part of individual superintendents and schools. In refutation of my argument you may hear from various parts of the country that I am mistaken: that the pamphlets issued by your committee have been used in this and that school, that there have been a great many lecturers talking to teachers and students on the war. Granted; but if you will look into the matter carefully you will find that where the pamphlets are used in any quantity at all it is in connection with a history class in the fourth year of high school or something like that. My contention is that 90% of our teachers could not pass a fair examination on the background of the war, the legal as well as the moral justification of our entering it, and (except in a very general way) why we must fight it through.

[119] Correspondence between A. M. Simons and G. S. Ford, winter of 1917–1918. National Archives (CPI, 3-A7, L-1-283).

Clark was convinced that the teachers were potentially "the greatest single factor . . . in extending war propaganda," but he insisted that they must be given adequate materials, including lesson plans for every grade from the kindergarten to the university. But Clark was fighting for more than the distribution of materials; he wanted "a national system of education." Until the federal government established state and local committees with power to enforce the study of its propaganda materials, it was his opinion that the work would continue to be neglected or, at best, would be done haphazardly.

In reply to criticisms of this sort, Ford pointed out that the Committee on Public Information was an emergency organization, operating under considerable difficulties, and that neither it nor any other federal agency had the power to make demands upon the public educational system. He did, however, admit discouragement and impatience, and promised to do something about the public school situation.[120] These promises bore fruit, as has been indicated, in the sponsorship of two courses of study and a semi-monthly magazine. Since the lessons in patriotism embodied in this material were used by millions of school children, it is instructive to examine them in some detail.

[120] Correspondence between S. H. Clark and G. S. Ford, March 1918, National Archives (CPI, 3-A1, L-1-478).

CHAPTER II

STIMULATING PATRIOTISM IN THE SCHOOLS

Patriotism is the last refuge of a scoundrel.
                                        —*Samuel Johnson*

We want no teachers who say there are two sides to
every question including even our system of government;
who care more for their academic freedom of speech and
opinion (so-called) than for their country.
                                        —*President of the D.A.R., 1923*[1]

This royal throne of kings, this sceptered isle,
This earth of majesty, this seat of Mars,
This other Eden, demi-paradise,
This fortress built by Nature for herself
Against infection and the hand of war,
This happy breed of men, this little world,
This precious stone set in the silver sea,
Which serves it in the office of a wall,
Or as a moat defensive to a house,
Against the envy of less happier lands,
This blessed plot, this earth, this realm, this England.
                                        —*Shakespeare, King Richard II*

1. Interpretations of Patriotism

Patriotism is an awkward term to define. Those who sing, "I
love thy rocks and rills, thy woods and templed hills," are echoing
a sentiment which has its roots deep in the past. Men have always
shared what one scholar has called a "natural local patriotism,"
or devotion to their native land. In the past, it was a relatively
small social group and a limited area for which men professed this
devotion; as transportation and communication have developed
and the state has become larger and more complex, the simple
patriotism of this earlier period has expanded into the "nationalism" or "imperial patriotism" of the nineteenth and twentieth

[1] Bessie L. Pierce, *Citizens' Organizations and the Civic Training of Youth* (New
York: Charles Scribner's Sons, 1933), p. 21.

40

centuries.[2] These new, or modified, sentiments have created their own problems. On the world stage, nationalism has been for centuries the breeding ground of war. Equally disturbing for the internal security of the state have been the contentions frequently advanced by specific groups that their particular ideals represent the true interests of the nation; it follows that those who do not identify themselves with these ideals are unpatriotic.

Patriotism is not, to borrow a happy phrasing, "a single, integrated sentiment the same at all times and places and among all groups."[3] Chameleon-like, it is ever adapting itself to changing situations, and its protective coloration is often utilized by different groups to win adherents to their particular points of view. In this chapter we shall examine the type of patriotism fostered by the lessons prepared during the last war for use in the schools.

It may be of interest first to point out the interpretation that was officially accepted by the educational authorities of Wales. England had been at war for more than a year when the Welsh Board of Education issued what in the light of later American experience was an unusual document. It contained suggestions for the educators of Wales to aid them in the teaching of patriotism:

Patriotism is very like loyalty to our side in a school game. We do not feel proud of, and ought not to support, our side if it cheats or fouls the other side, or loses its temper and does not play a fair game. Wrongful actions by one's own country (and our country has not always done right) [are] just as despicable as foul play in a school game. 'Our country, right or wrong,' [is] a bad motto. Our duty [is] to do to others as we would they should do to us. Any other standard of patriotic conduct [is] really unpatriotic because it does harm, not good, to our country, and injures its good name. . . . The Germans' 'Hymn of Hate' is unworthy of any great nation. No nation is really

2 Carleton J. H. Hayes, *Essays on Nationalism* (New York: The Macmillan Company, 1926), pp. 23–24.
3 Merle Curti, "Wanted: A History of American Patriotism," *Proceedings of the Middle States Association of History and Social Science Teachers*, vol. XXXVI (1938), p. 24. A number of interesting studies have been published on the subject of patriotism and pressure groups. See Norman Hapgood, ed. *Professional Patriots* (New York: Albert & Charles Boni, 1927); B. L. Pierce, *op. cit.*, and *Public Opinion and The Teaching of History in the United States* (New York: Alfred A. Knopf, 1926); Earle L. Hunter, *A Sociological Analysis of Certain Types of Patriotism. A Study of Certain Patriotic Attitudes, Particularly as These Appear in Peace-Time Controversies in the United States* (New York: Columbia University Press, 1932).

great whose Patriotism takes the form of hating other nations. . . .
The future peace of the world must be built upon the broad basis
of mutual esteem and understanding, not of jealousy, ambition, and
hate.[4]

These views of the Welsh educators differed radically from the
sentiments promoted in a number of the propaganda bulletins
sponsored by responsible federal officials for use in American
schools. Presumably, patriots of 1914 were those who best obeyed
Wilson's injunction to be "neutral in fact as well as in name,"
but by 1918 all this had changed, and the depth of an individual's
devotion to his country was measured by his efforts to "win the
war." Each citizen was expected to subordinate his will and to
direct his intelligence to the war effort. The superiority of the
American nation was proclaimed from every angle; the brutality
and degradation of the German Empire admitted of no argument.
Most of the propaganda emanating from the federal government,
not excluding the courses of study prepared for school children,
had its beginning and end in the one thought of military conquest. Barely considered was that larger view suggested by the
Welsh Board of Education, which looked beyond the immediate
conflict to the fundamental problem of reconstructing a world
along more rational lines.[5]

That instruction in patriotism was, to the American propagandists, primarily a method of implementing the military activities may be demonstrated by an example drawn from a course
of study issued to the schools in the summer of 1918. Prepared by
three public school administrators, sponsored by a group of emi-
nent historians, published under the name of the Bureau of Education, and distributed with the approval of the Committee on
Public Information, the document expressed a point of view close
to what might be called official.[6] Teachers were asked to develop

[4] *Patriotism. Suggestions to Local Educational Authorities and Teachers in Wales
Regarding the Teaching of Patriotism* (Issued by the Welsh Board of Education,
1916), pp. 15–17.

[5] This is not to imply that all English educators subscribed to the views expressed
by the Welsh authorities. There, as in America, opinions varied. See John Langdon-
Davies, *Militarism in Education. A Contribution to Educational Reconstruction*
(London: The Swarthmore Press, Ltd., no date), pp. 45–46.

[6] Coulomb, Gerson, and McKinley, *Outline of An Emergency Course of Instruction on the War*. Interestingly enough, the title itself suggests the haste with
which we approached the problem of instruction in patriotism.

the three ideas of "patriotism, heroism, and sacrifice." Children
in the first two grades were told that their fathers and brothers
were fighting for two reasons: "(1) To protect the people of France
and Belgium from the Germans, who were burning the homes and
killing the people, even women and children; (2) to keep the
German soldiers from coming to our country and treating us in
the same way."[7] A clear distinction between the evil that was in
Germany and the good that was in America (we generously included our associates) was drawn through all the lessons. This was
one way to teach patriotism; the Welsh educators had suggested
another.

It would be extremely misleading, however, to conclude that
throughout the war our school children were taught only to be
self-righteous and to hate their enemies. There were many in the
nation's capital—among them President Wilson, Commissioner of
Education Claxton, and Ford himself—who consistently urged the
maintenance of educational standards on the grounds that the
problems of reconstruction in the postwar world were of para-
mount importance. There were many others who raised indignant
voices against chauvinistic propaganda from whatever source; and
there were still others who had clear ideas as to what should be
taught in the public schools.

Not the least influential of this latter group was Professor
William H. Kilpatrick of Teachers College, Columbia University.
In vigorous words he called upon Ford to liberalize the educational materials issued by the federal government. "The conception of democracy as an attempt to place society upon an ethical
basis," he wrote in the summer of 1918, "is the foundation stone
upon which, in my thinking at least, I try to erect my whole social
structure." This introduced the question of a citizen's relationship to his country, a matter upon which Kilpatrick had strong
views. "There is," he said to Ford, "a parochial patriotism which
belongs, I hope, to *ante-bellum* affairs. I recognize the difficulty
of presenting or even discussing this point, but unless we are going
to attempt the impossible task of maintaining the *status quo ante
bellum,* there will need to be a broader, more intelligent patriotism." He believed that the schools should develop in the chil-

7 *Ibid.,* p. 6.

dren a "flexibility of attitude with reference to impending social changes." As to the methods by which this might be accomplished, the war offered an unusual opportunity to introduce that "purposeful activity" which would vitalize education.[8]

Meanwhile, Kilpatrick put some of his ideas into practice at Teachers College. The student societies, organized as study groups, met regularly to discuss problems of postwar reconstruction. Of larger significance was his proposal to establish a new educational journal to serve as a forum for the interchange of ideas on the part education should play in both war and peace. Growing out of a conference called by Dean James E. Russell early in 1918 to consider a thorough reorganization of the educational system, Kilpatrick's plan secured strong support within the university, but the war ended before this plan could be completed.[9]

John Dewey, after reminding his readers that they were fighting to protect their democratic institutions, suggested that it might be well for the country "to take a survey of its own educational resources and see what our system is adapted to, and how it will prepare its future generations for a purely democratic society."[10]

Similar views were expressed by the President of the University of Montana in an address before a large group of educators. The National Education Association had just passed a resolution proclaiming a new aim—"World-Citizenship." President Sisson saw in this "an omen of brightest promise. . . . We need," he announced, "not less, but more and wiser patriotism; but we need also more and wiser and broader humanity." Sisson did not hold the Germans solely responsible for the war; it was their misfortune to play "the terrible role of frightfulness in becoming the last champion of war as the final arbiter of human affairs," but other nations, and educators everywhere, must also accept their share of responsibility for the disaster. In his concluding remarks he made a strong plea for a new kind of education:

The schools have had a large share in fostering this false idea of national superiority and of the inferiority of other peoples. In every

8 W. H. Kilpatrick to G. S. Ford, May 16, 1918. National Archives (CPI, 3-A7, B-52).

9 Interview with W. H. Kilpatrick, New York, April 9, 1941.

10 *Education for Democracy*, Address delivered at Detroit, Michigan, February 3, 1918 (Pamphlet, Teachers College Library, Columbia University, New York), p. 7.

controversy we are right and our opponents wrong; all the honesty and fair-mindedness are on our side, all the meanness and treachery with our opponents. In every war all the heroism and splendor are attributed to our troops, and all the flight and defeat to the enemy. We are always outnumbered and win by incredible valor and prowess; the troops of the enemy are overwhelmed in spite of all their advantage. All this is so unutterably false and silly that one would never believe it could exist except that it does exist and is common to all people. It is the pernicious remnant in civilization of the grotesque war-dance of the barbarian, in which he brags and boasts of his achievements and derides his antagonists. One of the healthy signs today is the protest against the falsehoods and evasions of our American school histories, and the demand that the plain truth be told as to our diplomacy and our wars, even when it is not entirely to our national credit. Let the good work go on: we shall know the truth and the truth shall make us more and more free.[11]

A short time before this Albert J. Beveridge had appealed to the educators to color every program of instruction with a "policy of nationalism."[12] The contrast was striking.

At this same conference another college president reminded his associates that it was their duty "to reconcile *outside* your borders the people you have reconciled *within* your borders." Listing as our objective a "brotherhood of men," he warned: "War—which elsewhere breeds brutality, bigotry, cupidity, race-hatred, intolerance—must in our schools and colleges be interpreted to develop catholicity of spirit, human sympathy, sacrificial devotion to convictions, and passion for truth and justice. . . . For what shall it profit us if we gain the whole world for democracy and thereby lose the soul of democracy?"[13] Other speakers, including the President of the National Education Association, called upon the schoolmen to teach internationalism.[14] Indeed, Wilson's ideals had many advocates at the N.E.A. conventions of 1917 and 1918.

These views were not, however, shared by some of those individuals most actively engaged in propaganda activities, as Professor J. Montgomery Gambrill was disappointed to discover. Early in the war, he decided that victory would not be facilitated by arous-

[11] N.E.A., *Proceedings*, 1917, pp. 124–127.
[12] *Ibid.*, pp. 678–679.
[13] *Ibid.*, pp. 30–31. The speaker was William T. Foster, President of Reed College, Portland, Oregon.
[14] *Ibid.*, pp. 54, 136.

ing the passions of school children. Fearing that only harm would result from such a course, he prepared a syllabus designed to bring before both teachers and pupils some conception of the problems involved in making the world safe for democracy. Gambrill believed that if there was to be any hope of realizing our professed war aims it was necessary to develop an awareness of world issues, and that any but the most perfunctory treatment would inevitably reveal the difficulties created by certain types of nationalism and imperialism. Working along these lines he completed the syllabus, only to have it rejected by the National Board for Historical Service.[15] The representatives of the Board made it clear that they did not believe the teachers were prepared to deal with such ideas.[16]

Many individuals, including educators, although eager to work for a new world built upon the foundation of Wilsonian ideals, felt that, as a matter of expediency, the task of reconstruction and education should wait upon the end of the war. This view was expressed repeatedly at a conference called by the Commissioner of Education to devise plans for better teaching of international relations.[17]

The student of American history will not be surprised at this situation. Our reluctance to accept a broader interpretation of patriotism was rooted deeply in America's past. Those who agreed with Kilpatrick, Sisson, and the others, were advocating a viewpoint that ran counter to these strongly held traditions. Most powerful of the social forces inclining us toward certain patterns of action were adherence to a policy of isolationism, the doctrine of our mission to democratize the world,[18] and the tide of nation-

15 The National Board for Historical Service was a semi-official organization formed early in the war as the result of a conference called by the department of historical research of the Carnegie Institute. Representing over 3,000 historians of the United States, it had as its object the dissemination of trustworthy information to the public and assistance to the government "through direct personal service." Ford told a group of Congressmen that this was the most important of the agencies collaborating with the Committee on Public Information. CPI, *Hearing, 1918,* p. 100; Mock and Larson. *Words That Won the War,* p. 183.

16 E. B. Greene to J. M. Gambrill, May 29, 1918. Gambrill MSS. in J. M. Gambrill's possession. Interview with J. M. Gambrill, New York, April 8, 1941.

17 "Minutes of an Educational Conference at Atlantic City," February 25, 1918. Gambrill MSS. in J. M. Gambrill's possession.

18 Ralph H. Gabriel. *The Course of American Democratic Thought. An Intellectual History Since 1815* (New York: The Ronald Press Company, 1940), pp. 339–340.

alism which had risen during the nineteenth century. This latter force was not, of course, confined to the American continent.[19]

Since the founding of the Republic, most Americans had been isolationists, scorning to look at the larger horizon of world affairs. Although the Spanish-American War had opened our eyes to imperial vistas, it had at the same time stimulated the sentiment of nationalism. This was reflected in our educational system. It took the form of growing pressure from patriotic societies, courses of study and manuals in patriotism, and laws requiring patriotic observances. An examination of the available manuals in patriotism indicates that the authors thought in terms of emotionalized responses to the stimulus of symbols, rather than along the lines of a critical study of the bases of American life. As one writer put it, not the textbooks, but the exercises, "appealing . . . to the imaginations and emotions will captivate the pupil."[20] Another manual, prepared under the direction of New York State's Superintendent of Public Instruction, contained forty programs designed to encourage patriotic sentiments in the schools; here, too, the emphasis was upon flag, song, and poetry.[21] This wave of patriotism swept into the legislative halls. Two-fifths of all the educational laws enacted during the period from 1903 to 1923 attempted "to foster local, provincial, and national pride."[22] Our entrance into the war gave additional vigor to this attitude of self-glorification. It is easy to understand, therefore, why any attempts to liberalize the commonly accepted interpretations of patriotism were doomed to failure.

There was, it is true, an inherent contradiction between our traditions of isolationism and our mission to democratize the world. Under the stress of war, however, the isolationist viewpoint readily yielded to the greater vitality of our crusade to make the

[19] Hayes, *Essays on Nationalism.*

[20] Geo. T. Balch, *Methods of Teaching Patriotism in the Public Schools* (New York: D. Van Nostrand Company, 1890), p. 109.

[21] Charles R. Skinner, ed., *Manual of Patriotism. For Use in the Public Schools of the State of New York* (Authorized by Act of the Legislature, 1900); see also John W. Davis, ed., *Young America's Manual. The Child's Guide to Patriotism* (Rev. ed., New York: Educational Publishing Company, 1908); Kate Upson Clarke, *Teaching the Child Patriotism* (Boston: The Page Company, 1918).

[22] Jesse K. Flanders, *Legislative Control of the Elementary Curriculum* (New York: Bureau of Publications, Teachers College, Columbia University, 1925), pp. 61, 174–175.

world "safe for democracy." It was not difficult to defend our war with the German autocracy, for all autocracies were bad and the German particularly so, but our association with other European powers, obviously a marriage of convenience, was at times highly embarrassing. The Tsar was awkward to explain; the virtues of the English, for over a century hidden behind a cloud, now shone forth clearly, or so we argued to ourselves. Official propagandists labored diligently to strengthen the ties with our new associates, but these associates remained at best merely companions in a crusade of which the Americans were the self-appointed leaders.

By a judicious emphasis upon our "mission" to make the world safe for democracy, with a clear recognition of the responsibilities that this threw upon us, the American propagandists might have helped to divert our thinking from the narrow channels of isolationism and self-glorification. Kilpatrick is of the opinion that never before or since had American leadership been faced with such stirring possibilities.[23] Gambrill, writing shortly after the war had ended, was "convinced that a widespread campaign of education [for a realistic study of the problems of "democracy" and "enduring peace"] could have been carried on had Washington so willed."[24] On the whole, Washington did not so will. We were taught to feel only aversion for the German Empire; this inevitably carried over to the individual German, the "Hun." The crusade "to make the world safe for democracy" was used all too frequently to emphasize the superiority of American institutions. Our disillusionment after the war and our return to the traditional paths of isolationism is a familiar story. As has been indicated, it is open to conjecture whether a vigorous educational campaign to liberalize American nationalism might have helped to prevent this development. Certainly our wartime encouragement of a provincial type of patriotism did not, in the postwar years, help us to think in terms of world problems.

2. Lessons for the High School

The first pamphlet prepared by a federal agency to stimulate patriotism in the schools was Samuel B. Harding's *Study of the*

---

23 Interview with W. H. Kilpatrick, New York, April 9, 1941.
24 J. M. Gambrill to S. Duggan, January 9, 1919. Gambrill MSS.

Great War.[25] This was originally intended for use in the training camps.[26] A number of people felt that the boys inducted into service did not sufficiently understand the reasons why they had to fight. It was reported that speakers from the National Security League who went from camp to camp found "young men of the nation eager and anxious to undertake the task to which the government had called them, but quite unable, without special instruction, to understand what it was all about."[27] Harding, a professor of history at the University of Indiana, was asked to enlighten them through the medium of a short, topical outline.

With the "active cooperation" of the National Board for Historical Service and the Committee on Public Information, Harding began work in the fall of 1917.[28] It was at about this time that the clamor arose for materials which could be used in the public schools. The "Outline" obviously had value for this purpose. It was completed as a manual for both high school teachers and pupils.[29]

The "Outline" was first published in *The History Teacher's Magazine* for January, 1918,[30] appearing as a separate pamphlet in April. Teachers welcomed this aid to instruction in patriotism, and requests for copies began to multiply. By the end of the war nearly 700,000 bulletins had been sold at five cents per copy by the Committee on Public Information.[31] In addition, approximately 5,000 copies of *The History Teacher's Magazine* were circulated, and over 40,000 additional copies were sold at twenty cents each by the McKinley Publishing Company.[32]

[25] *Supra*, p. 37.

[26] Interview with G. S. Ford, New York, December 28, 1941.

[27] Ernest Carroll Moore, *What the War Teaches About Education. And Other Papers and Addresses* (New York: The Macmillan Company, 1919), p. 238.

[28] *The History Teacher's Magazine*, vol. IX (January, 1918), p. 30.

[29] G. S. Ford to R. M. McElroy, November 30, 1917. National Archives (CPI, 3-A1, L-1-161).

[30] Founded in 1909, this magazine maintained close connection with the American Historical Association, which had appointed an advisory committee to work with the managing-editor, Albert E. McKinley. During the war it became one of the mouthpieces of the National Board for Historical Service and gave extensive publicity to the publications of the Committee on Public Information. With the January, 1918, issue, the magazine started to publish a "War Supplement," Harding's syllabus being the first pamphlet to appear in this manner. Starting with the October, 1918, issue, the name was changed to *The Historical Outlook*.

[31] *RCPI*, p. 15.

[32] McKinley Publishing Company to the author, April 8, 1941.

In any attempt to estimate the possible influence of Harding's course in patriotism, it should be borne in mind that these 800,000 or so copies were more than sufficient to reach the hands of every high school senior in the country. This is not to suggest that they did reach all seniors; poor distributing facilities would in themselves have prevented that. But that so many were eager to secure the "Outline" at a cost of twenty cents (the CPI sold its copies for only five cents), is evidence that the lessons did have wide use among teachers and students. The Creel Committee was so gratified with the favorable reports received that in the spring of 1918 it made plans to utilize the course systematically in the high schools during the following year. Also under consideration was a companion bulletin to be composed of excerpts from the other propaganda publications of the Committee;[33] lack of funds and the signing of the Armistice cut short these plans.

George Creel once referred to the publications of the Committee on Publication Information, taken collectively, as the most damning indictment of a sovereign nation ever penned. One who reads the pamphlets is inclined to agree with him. Harding's "Outline" concentrated this material in a logical, polished, and devastating argument. Since both the Division of Civic and Educational Cooperation and the National Board for Historical Service accepted this syllabus as that view of the war which it was desirable to inculcate in the minds of the public school pupils, listing it first when replying to requests for material to use in the classroom,[34] it is enlightening to examine the contents of this course of study.

Each important statement was documented. This documentation appeared to clinch every argument, gave the bulletin a semblance of scholarship, and made it difficult for any but the trained historian to dispute the contents. Bearing the name of a professor of history from one of the country's largest universities, and appearing under the authorization of the government of the United States, the syllabus was in some respects an impressive publication. As propaganda, and that was its purpose, the "Outline" had real merit, but to the historian looking at it from the

[33] Correspondence between S. B. Harding and M. Hill, Spring, 1918. National Archives (CPI, 3-A7, L-1-509).
[34] *Ibid.*

perspective of over twenty years, the flaws are all too evident. Although Harding told the truth, he did not always tell the whole truth, and, in a few instances, he failed to confine his statements to what might be accepted as reasonable evidence in any court of law. In this respect he followed the method employed by so many other historians during the war years. It is not our task to pass judgment upon the sincerity of these men; that many were over-zealous is indubitably true. Perhaps it is sufficient to observe that the drawing of an indictment and the preparation of a well-balanced historical explanation are totally different problems, both in method and intent; the one is for the pleader and the propagandist, the other for the historian. We are dealing here with the historian turned propagandist.

The documentation, on the surface impressive, did not measure up to historical standards. Approximately 500 references were made to more than one hundred different sources. Fully one third of the citations sent the reader to Creel's other propaganda leaflets! This is curious documentation. The method was, nevertheless, effective, giving the pamphlet the semblance of authority while at the same time directing the student to further reading of the Creel materials. As propaganda it had great value; as history, it left much to be desired.

A second source from which Harding drew about one third of his references was the published diplomatic correspondence of the various warring countries—the *Red Books, Blue Books, Orange Books,* and so forth. Issued at the beginning of the war by each of the belligerents in an effort to justify its cause and to thrust the onus of guilt upon the enemy, these documents were the rawest of propaganda. To Harding, however, they offered a rich storehouse from which to draw materials to support his arguments. The critical reader will discover that in over ninety per cent of cases he is referred to the arguments of the Allied Powers, while less than one tenth of the references direct him to the case presented by Germany and her allies. It is perhaps unnecessary to repeat that this method gave an appearance of respectability to the "Outline," but that taken as a whole the document was damning to the German case and indefensible as history.

The remaining citations refer the student to a wide variety of sources, yet one cannot read the "Outline" carefully without reaching the conclusion that the author first stated his opinion, then sought and found suitable documentation to prove and clinch it. The highly scattered nature of the materials cited is in itself a clue that leads one to suspect that Harding sometimes found it necessary to go far afield to "prove" his point. Quotations from German sources go back to Bismarck, and most frequently appear over the names of William II, Treitschke, and Bernhardi. One could hardly argue that the most violent statements by this quartet offered a balanced picture of the aspirations of the German people. But this matter of documentation need not be labored; the shortest cut to understanding is the reading of the pamphlet itself.

Throughout the "Outline" the assertions are sweeping and conclusive. There is only one side to the case. Germany is charged with every brutality and crime; the Allies are long suffering and kind. In Chapter III, headed "Indications that Germany and Austria Planned an Aggressive Stroke before June 28, 1914," a quotation is taken from Elihu Root's speech in Chicago, delivered on September 14, 1917:

> **It now appears beyond the possibility of doubt that this war was made by Germany pursuing a long and settled purpose.** For many years she had been preparing to do exactly what she has done, with a thoroughness, a perfection of plans, and a vastness of provision in men, munitions and supplies never before equaled or approached in human history. **She brought the war on when she chose, because she chose, in the belief that she could conquer the earth nation by nation.**[35]

This is part of the summary with which each topic ends, and is one of the more temperate expressions in the chapter. Many of the statements are much more extreme and violent.

Chapter VII is titled, "The War Spreads: Character of the War." Here the German ruthlessness, brutality, and violation of all international law and the basic principles of humanity are revealed in page after page of quotations. Professor A. S. Hershey, writing in the *Indiana University Alumni Quarterly* for October, 1917, is authority for the statement that

[35] Harding, *The Study of the Great War*, p. 26. Bold type appears in the original.

Germany does not really wage war. She assassinates, massacres, poisons, tortures, intrigues; she commits every crime in the calendar, such as arson, pillage, murder, and rape; she is guilty of almost every possible violation of international law and of humanity—and she calls it war.[36]

Eyewitness accounts recovered from the diaries of captured German soldiers (it is curious how many diaries are conveniently found on the battlefield) form the basis for the most damaging charges of brutality. The following illustrates the extremes to which the pamphlet went:

By leaps and bounds we got across the clearing. They were here, there, and everywhere hidden in the thicket. Now it is down with the enemy! And we will give them no quarter. . . . We knock them down or bayonet the wounded, for we know that those scoundrels fire at our backs when we have gone by. There was a Frenchman there stretched out, full length, face down, pretending to be dead. A kick from a strong fusilier soon taught him that we were there. Turning round he asked for quarter, but we answered: "Is that the way your tools work, you ————," and he was nailed to the ground. Close to me I heard odd cracking sounds. They were blows from a gun on the bald head of a Frenchman which a private of the 154th was dealing out vigorously; he was wisely using a French gun so as not to break his own. Tenderhearted souls are so kind to the French wounded that they finish them with a bullet, but others give them as many thrusts and blows as they can.[37]

In the last chapter of the "Outline," various "proposals for peace" were discussed. The German propositions of December 12, 1916, were termed "empty and insincere";[38] the Kaiser's reply to the Pope's appeal was "filled with the vaguest generalities" and "in part it consisted of hypocritical and lying protestations."[39] America's peace proposals were summarized in Wilson's "Fourteen Points," and it was made quite clear that the President's views had the full approval of the Allied nations.[40] The question was asked: "Will this be the last great war?" Harding answered with a qualified affirmative: "The triumph of the United States and

36 *Ibid.*, p. 55.
37 *Ibid.*, pp. 60–61.
38 *Ibid.*, p. 84.
39 *Ibid.*, pp. 86–87.
40 *Ibid.*, pp. 87–90.

the Entente Allies over militarist and despotic Germany gives the best assurance of the establishment of a League of Peace and the practical ending of war."[41]

It is worthy of note that this section, devoted to the problem of peace, continues to portray the German Government as perfidious and rapacious, raising in sharp contrast the idealism of America and her associates. Even in a discussion of the vital question of postwar settlements, the authors felt it incumbent to emphasize national antagonisms.

Ford referred to the bulletin as "an exceptionally effective thing,"[42] and recommended it "for the schools and clubs desiring to study the war."[43] In this praise he was joined by the National Board for Historical Service, when, at the head of "A Short Reading List" which they prepared for teachers, this pamphlet was cited as the "best introduction to a course of reading; [with] extensive and interesting quotations."[44] Another member of Creel's organization was of the opinion that "Dr. Samuel B. Harding has contributed the most scholarly outlined history of the war yet produced."[45] One educator told Creel that the "Outline" was a "magnificent job . . . among the greatest contributions your department has made," adding, however, that it was written for "advanced students" and should be simplified for use in the lower grades.[46] This pamphlet was widely advertised in the pages of *The History Teacher's Magazine*. Teachers and professors of education were eager to secure it. Encouraged by the response, Creel's Committee made plans to introduce it systematically into the classrooms of America during the school year of 1918–1919. These plans were abruptly terminated by the Armistice.

3. Lessons for the Elementary School

The first lessons in patriotism for the elementary grades issued by a federal agency were not published until August, 1918. Nearly

41 *Ibid.*, pp. 93–94.

42 G. S. Ford to R. M. McElroy, November 30, 1917. National Archives (CPI, 3-A1, L-1-161).

43 G. S. Ford to I. T. Jones, September 21, 1917. National Archives (CPI, 3-A1, L-1-378).

44 Memorandum (no date). National Archives (CPI, 3-A1, L-1-295).

45 J. W. Searson to W. L. Bryan, May 11, 1918. National Archives (CPI, 3-A7, B-55).

46 S. H. Clark to G. Creel, March 2, 1918. National Archives (CPI, 3-A7, L-1-478).

a year earlier, the National Board for Historical Service had asked Professor J. Montgomery Gambrill of the History Department of Teachers College, Columbia University, to prepare a thirty-two page syllabus for use by grammar school teachers and pupils. As Gambrill reflected upon his task, it loomed "bigger and more difficult" in his mind.[47] He unburdened himself in a letter to his sponsors:

The problems of the time are so tremendous, so complex, and of such fundamental importance, that it is indeed a staggering question as to just how one should best go at them for the education of our people . . . The more I have actually wrestled with the problem, however, the more convinced I have become that mere suggestions about teaching this or that set of facts is of relatively small importance. I think in whatever I work out, the primary purpose must be to inform the teachers themselves, as an influential body of citizens, about the nature of these crises as they appear to those who have seriously studied them. Such a presentation is not of exclusive interest to elementary teachers.[48]

As his ideas matured during the winter months, Gambrill kept in constant communication with the historians of the National Board, and through conversation and correspondence they were at all times fully informed of the direction of his thoughts. In addition, he lectured before many groups of teachers, from the Atlantic Coast to Omaha, discussing the problems which must be solved before we could realize our war aims. He also consulted numerous school officials and officers of teachers' associations in different sections of the country. He was accorded everywhere a sympathetic reception of his views.[49] As the weeks passed, his conviction became stronger that what he was writing should be for the education of teachers. By this means he hoped to reach both pupils and parents. To him, intellectual preparedness for victory seemed immensely more important than trying to make children of six to twelve years of age hate and fear the enemy. He assumed that the members of the Board for Historical Service were in substantial agreement with these views.

It was, therefore, a shock to Gambrill when the finished manu-

47 J. M. Gambrill to W. G. Leland, November 28, 1917. Gambrill MSS.
48 J. M. Gambrill to E. B. Greene, January 26, 1918. Gambrill MSS.
49 Interview with J. M. Gambrill, New York, April 8, 1941.

script was abruptly rejected in May, 1918, by the Board for Historical Service. The nature of the pamphlet prepared by Gambrill, the reasons given for its rejection, and the syllabus that was subsequently published in its place, furnish a revealing commentary on the type of patriotism fostered in the public schools by the federal propaganda agencies.

Like many others, Gambrill did not believe that victory alone could "end war." He expressed this thought in his outline:

Defeat of autocratic and militarized Germany there must be, but even that great result, if the free nations fighting her keep faith, will be only the first necessary step toward the goal of a better world order. Too many people entertain the delusion that a decisive defeat of Germany would *ipso facto* bring permanent peace. There could be no greater mistake. The problem of abolishing or even greatly reducing war is complex and difficult. Its solution will require a careful analysis of the sources of international strife, the collection of a great mass of information about existing conditions in all parts of the world, a coolness of temper difficult to command immediately after a long and bitter war, and a capacity to deal with all questions from the broadest viewpoint of international welfare.[50]

It appeared to Gambrill that the bitter struggles through which the national state had emerged from the ruins of feudalism and the city state were, in a sense, being repeated on a larger scale, with the national state of the twentieth century beating against the concept of an international order.[51] In the light of this world-wide upheaval, "fine words and ringing resolutions about the brotherhood of man and the beauties of peace will accomplish nothing," he wrote in his syllabus. Although conceding that "the legitimate demands of nationality [must be] everywhere satisfied," he insisted that "there would remain the larger problem of reconciling nationalism with internationalism; of providing military and economic security, equality of opportunity in the world's markets and in the development of backward and undeveloped countries." The narrow viewpoint of nationalism and imperialism must be replaced by the larger concept of a world order."[52] These ideas he developed at considerable

50 J. M. Gambrill, Unpublished MSS., p. 56. Gambrill MSS.
51 Interview with J. M. Gambrill, New York, April 23, 1941.
52 J. M. Gambrill, Unpublished MSS., p. 58. Gambrill MSS.

length in a historical treatment of the origins and growth of imperialism and nationalism and their relationship to the First World War.

The National Board for Historical Service was frank in explaining why it could not publish the manuscript. "It is not suited to the specific purpose for which it was designed, namely, that of offering practical suggestions to teachers especially in elementary schools," the spokesman for the Board wrote. This, obviously, was sufficient reason for the rejection of the pamphlet. But why the Board delayed its basic criticism until such a late hour is more difficult to understand, for the original purpose of the bulletin had been changed with the full knowledge of the historians as early as January, to embrace the viewpoint which was finally incorporated in the text.

At this late date, criticism was also made of the treatment of nationalism and imperialism. "The comparatively untrained teacher is sure to underestimate the liberalism of Western Europe," E. B. Greene pointed out. "The positive values of nationalism seem also to deserve more attention. Similarly, the discussion of imperialism seems to take into account exclusively the predatory type, as distinguished from that exemplified in the present relation of the self-governing colonies to the British Empire." A further objection was raised in regard to the pamphlet's discussion of Pan-Germanism. This, it was noted, "is not adequately presented in its relation to the origins of the European war . . ."[53]

Which of the objections weighed most heavily, in the minds of those responsible for rejecting the syllabus, it is impossible to say, but one fact is clear: The historians were afraid that "the comparatively untrained teacher" would fail to see the war as a clash between autocracy and liberal democracy; they were concerned that he might see instead only the disastrous effects of the unbridled nationalism and imperialism in which all the belligerents had been engaged. Inasmuch as the Committee on Public Information had been vigorously developing the thesis of Germany's exclusive war guilt, it is evident that frank discussion such as Gambrill advocated would have seemed to discredit much of the

[53] Correspondence between E. B. Greene, Chairman of the National Board for Historical Service, and J. M. Gambrill, May 21, to June 8, 1918. Gambrill MSS.

previous propaganda, and it is not surprising that the syllabus was finally rejected. The episode furnishes an interesting commentary on the "climate of opinion" in 1918.

The leaflet that was hurriedly prepared and published as a substitute for the original project was of a somewhat different nature.[54] In its opening pages the teachers were reminded that "The general topic of the war and America's part in it should form an integral part of the course of study in every grade of our public schools." The authors admitted that "incidental instruction on this subject can and should be provided through the opportunities offered by such subjects as American history, European geography . . . English composition and literature . . . the floating of Liberty Loans and the sale of thrift stamps." At the same time, they warned that "if definite results are to be obtained . . . , our schools must go further and provide for systematic instruction." in patriotism. Two fifteen-minute periods a week, it was suggested, should be provided for this work in the first two grades; two periods of twenty minutes each were recommended for grades three and four; while for the last four years of elementary school, at least two thirty-minute sessions each week should be devoted to the study of patriotism.

Since the materials offered for instruction in the upper grades of the high school have been described with some detail, it might be interesting at this point to contrast the course of study recommended for children six and seven years old. As a suggestion for teachers, the following outline was published in the pamphlet:

COURSE FOR GRADES ONE AND TWO

Instruction on the war in the first two grades should take the form of:

I. Stories of War Incidents.
II. Celebrations of Special Holidays.
III. Talks on the War and the Children's Relation to It.

I. Stories of War Incidents.

True incidents of the war, illustrating the three ideas of *patriotism, heroism,* and *sacrifice,* should be selected and told the children. So far as possible, incidents centering about the actions of children in France, Belgium, and other invaded countries should be selected.

[54] Coulomb, Gerson, and McKinley, *Outline of An Emergency Course of Instruction on the War.*

The stories should by no means be limited to those about children, however, as children take a very real interest in the actions of grown-ups—brave soldiers, self-sacrificing mothers, and the like. Besides inculcating an admiration for the virtues of patriotism, heroism, and sacrifice, these stories should incidentally give the children some notion of life "over there."

The treatment throughout should be informal. Pupils should not be held for "facts." Informal conversations should be encouraged, but the children should not be required to retail stories nor to answer questions about them.

II. Celebrations of Special Holidays.

Columbus Day. Thanksgiving Day. Lincoln's Birthday. Washington's Birthday. Liberty Day (anniversary of April 6, 1917). Memorial Day. Flag Day. Fourth of July. Bastille Day.

These celebrations should be treated from a national and international rather than from a personal point of view. For example, on Columbus Day emphasize the relations of the Old World with the New, and of our country with the countries of Latin America; in connection with Lincoln emphasize the preservation of our country and the freeing of the slaves rather than the personal characteristics of Lincoln; on Flag Day discuss the meaning of the flag rather than the story of Betsy Ross. Dramatics should form a part of most holiday celebrations in lower grades.

The celebration of each of these holidays should center about its relation to the present war. Washington founded this Nation and Lincoln saved it; so that today we may do our part toward establishing liberty and democracy for the world. Flag Day should serve as an occasion for reference to the flags of our associates in the war.

III. Talks on the War and the Children's Relation to It.

A. Reasons why father, brother, uncle, cousin, had to go to war: (1) To protect the people of France and Belgium from the Germans, who were burning their homes and killing the people, even women and children; (2) to keep the German soldiers from coming to our country and treating us the same way.

B. How little children can help:

1. Save pennies for thrift stamps.
2. Eat less of things the soldiers and the people of the allied countries need.
3. Eat less candy and sweet cakes.
4. Do not waste food. (The "clean plate" idea.) Remind brothers and sisters not to waste.
5. Do not waste water. Faucets left running mean wasted coal at the pumping station.
6. Be careful of health. Doctors and nurses are needed just now

for more important work than curing children's ailments that are the result of carelessness.

7. Be careful of shoes and clothes. We need all the cloth and leather we can spare for the soldiers. [The teacher is here referred to a "suggestive" lesson on the "Care of Shoes" printed in the appendix of the pamphlet.]

8. Save labor by not giving other people extra work. Avoid—
   a. Throwing paper about the streets.
   b. Breaking windows or otherwise destroying or defacing property.
   c. Carelessness with school books and other public property.

9. Try to be better boys and girls, so that older folks will not be troubled or worried about you and so can work harder.[55]

The topics suggested for the first two grades were retained in the three other courses of study for the upper grades. The teacher is reminded that the material must "be adapted to the older pupils,"[56] and that "while in Grades Five and Six the stories of war incidents and the celebration of special holidays are not such a vital part of the course as they are in the lower grades, they can, nevertheless, help much in securing that emotional response which is so essential to successful teaching of the war."[57] The authors again and again stress the value of arousing the emotions. At one point they make certain suggestions as to methods, and warn that:

1. In teaching the war to young pupils the appeal should be directed primarily to the imagination and to the emotions. It is not enough that our pupils shall be informed of the events of the war, their causes and their results; their imaginations must be awakened and their feelings aroused to an appreciation of the significance of the great happenings of the time. To secure this result it is suggested that the teacher supplement her instruction throughout with appropriate stories and poems. Her manner also should be interesting and dramatic. Above all, the teacher should in her whole personality express an enthusiastic and patriotic interest in her topic; the contagion of her spirit will be of more value than the facts she is trying to impart.

2. While the horrors inseparable from war and peculiarly characteristic of the present struggle must necessarily be referred to, the wise teacher will not dwell unduly on this phase of the subject. Permanent injury may result to young children through emphasis on the terrible and the repulsive.[58]

[55] Coulomb, Gerson, and McKinley, *Outline of An Emergency Course of Instruction on the War*, pp. 5–7.

[56] *Ibid.*, p. 7.   [57] *Ibid.*, p. 9.

[58] *Ibid.*, p. 23.

It is evident that this course of study presents war as a glamorous adventure filled with deeds of "patriotism, heroism, and sacrifice." Although there is much of value in the lessons, one may well question the authenticity of the picture the children received of life "over there." There is also reason to feel concern over the emotional reactions of six-year-old children to whom the Germans were portrayed as brutes who killed, burned, and plundered in Europe, and who threatened to invade America and treat "us the same way." Nor is it easy to understand how in the last two grades the teachers could hope to discuss, as the authors recommended, "the idea of a League of Nations." With this emotionalized treatment as a prelude, one can only wonder how the "foundations" were "laid for a broad attitude of mind toward the possibility of 'world-citizenship' in the days to come."[59]

The basic pattern for grades one and two was expanded for the older pupils by the addition of other study topics. These included comparisons of the German life and government with our own (the material covered in this section suggests that the word "contrast" would be more accurate); discussions of the American soldiers and sailors; further ways in which the children could help to win the war; and "war biographies." The latter are of particular interest.

Seven of these "brief biographies" are presented in the outline. Joan of Arc, Lafayette, and Joseph Joffre represent the traditions of France; William Pitt, Lord Kitchener, and David Lloyd George speak for England, Ireland, and Wales respectively; while Italy is upheld by the picturesque Giuseppe Garibaldi.

Certain characteristics are common to these biographical sketches. Each of the characters played a prominent part in military adventures; all but William Pitt and Lloyd George were soldiers. The "patriotism, heroism, and sacrifice" of each life was emphasized: "Joan gave up her life for France, but France was saved"; "we should honor Lafayette for the sacrifices he made on behalf of a weak nation struggling for independence"; Garibaldi "was noted for his simplicity of manner and his matchless bravery. Always and everywhere he was a devoted patriot."[60]

[59] *Ibid.*, p. 13.
[60] *Ibid.*, pp. 27–29.

Joan of Arc must have given the authors considerable difficulty. The sketch opens with the statement, "France overrun with enemies." Yet, in spite of the fact that Joan was in the end "treacherously captured by the enemies of France,"[61] at no time are they identified. It is amusing to think of the awkward comments that must have arisen in many classrooms when some ten-year-old child naïvely asked: "Who were the enemies of France?"

This course of instruction was not prepared for high school use. A few pages are, nevertheless, set apart for suggestions to high school teachers. The program followed at the William Penn High School of Philadelphia is recommended as worthy of note. Two full periods a week were here spent on a study of the war. These periods occurred simultaneously in all classes, the pupils receiving their instruction on the war under the teacher whose room they happened to be in at the hour assigned for such study.[62] Educators interested in following a similar program were referred to Harding's "Topical Outline" for reading material. Those who wished to secure "an insight into the racial, political, and economic life of the great nations" were referred to the *Community and National Life Leaflets* of the Bureau of Education.[63]

These lessons in patriotism, prepared by private authors, supported by the National Board for Historical Service, and published by the Bureau of Education, were welcomed with enthusiasm by the Committee on Public Information. When the authors proposed to publish a companion textbook for use with the outline,[64] the Committee's chief concern was for a low sales price in order to insure a larger circulation.[65] Moreover, when the Committee on

[61] *Ibid.*, p. 27.

[62] *Ibid.*, pp. 19–20.

[63] These leaflets were edited by Charles H. Judd and Leon C. Marshall, both of the University of Chicago. They were issued jointly by the Bureau of Education and the United States Food Administration. Appearing monthly from October 1, 1917, to May 1, 1918, the lessons were not directly concerned with the building of a war spirit, and for that reason they are not included in this chapter.

[64] This project created some difficulty for the Bureau of Education, which, having published the syllabus, was now in the awkward position of tacitly sponsoring a purely commercial textbook, an arrangement which was likely to net the publishers and the authors a handsome profit. In spite of these difficulties, the text was published, appearing, however, a month after the war had ended. See Albert E. McKinley, Charles A. Coulomb, and Armand J. Gerson, *The World War. A School History of the Great War* (New York: American Book Company, 1918).

[65] G. S. Ford to E. B. Greene, August 30, 1918. National Archives (CPI, 3-A1, L-1-141).

Public Information began the publication of the *National School Service* in September, 1918, one of the authors of the elementary school leaflet became an active member of the staff, adapting much of the material in the leaflet for further circulation.

4. Coordinated Program for All Grades
(National School Service)

The *National School Service,* issued by the Creel Committee, was a sixteen-page semi-monthly bulletin for the public school teachers of America. Although George Creel claimed that the paper was "an early and cherished plan,"[66] it was not published until the fall of 1918. It was one answer to those educators who for months had been demanding greater coordination in the educational activities of the federal government. Each agency in Washington interested in using the public schools was awarded a definite allotment of space; if a campaign were contemplated, the time was set well in advance. By this means the school men were freed from the inevitable confusion that resulted from the attempt to conduct several campaigns simultaneously.[67] The activities of these other federal agencies will be discussed later. It should be noted, however, that the campaigns conducted by such organizations as the Treasury Department and the Food Administration had more than incidental value in stimulating patriotism.

But the periodical contained a great deal of material that was inserted with the sole design of arousing the nationalistic ardor of the readers. The value of poetry for this purpose was not overlooked, and every issue contained a sprinkling of verse. Lieutenant-Colonel John McCrea's "In Flanders' Fields" was printed, and a rather bloody poem of the same title, written by C. B. Galbreath.[68] Typical of this poetry is the following verse, taken from the "Wings of War" by Minna Irving:

> Some day a flier from afar
>   Will pass the city gate,
> Upon its wings the sable cross,
>   Of unrelenting hate,

---

[66] *National School Service,* vol. I (September 1, 1918), p. 8.

[67] The reasons for the organization of the *National School Service* are discussed more fully in the next chapter. See *infra,* pp. 85 *et seq.*

[68] *National School Service,* vol. I (September 15, 1918), p. 4.

And bombs will fall, and flames arise,
And precious blood will run—
Leave not the azure fields above
Unguarded to the Hun![69]

Pupils were told, among other things, that "If we had not fought Germany after her false and brutal conduct, we should have been despised by all the world, even by the Germans."[70] They read that "Germany not only makes war in the most savage and merciless way. She thinks war in itself a good thing, and desires it."[71] They were taught about the "bad faith of the German Government," and they learned that the German schools were "nurseries of autocracy" where the people were "not trained to do independent thinking." It is unnecessary to question the accuracy of these assertions; the point is that here was material selected with the one thought of winning approval for the war effort, "to mobilize," as Creel put it, "the minds of the American people." That to secure this mobilization of minds we were resorting to methods dangerously similar to those used in the "nurseries of autocracy," apparently did not occur to the editors.

The bulk of each issue consisted of lessons carefully prepared for both rural and city school systems, and graded for primary, intermediate, upper, and high school classes. These lessons were much the same as those published earlier in the special bulletins. This was to be expected, for Samuel B. Harding, author of the "Topical Outline" used in the high schools, was in charge of the "Historical Section"; while Charles A. Coulomb, co-author of the *Outline of an Emergency Course of Instruction on the War* for the elementary grades, was responsible for the preparation of all lessons printed in the periodical.[72] Even the sand table was drawn into the service of war. The following suggestion was made for the instruction of pupils in the primary grades:

Natural War Interests of Children

One of the agencies most prone to promote the war spirit is the sand table. Children are no longer satisfied to build peaceful ditches, pleasant farms, or high mountains, as they used to do. Now trenches

[69] *Ibid.* (October 1, 1918), p. 2.
[70] *Ibid.* (September 15, 1918), p. 4.
[71] *Ibid.*, p. 5.
[72] *Ibid.* (September 1, 1918), p. 8.

appear fortified by whatever accessible material may serve as cannon. Sometimes the sand dashes its waves over the edge of the table itself in a great storm created by small hands to sink an enemy ship. No form of occupation material can claim exemption from war service. Drawings of ponies and friendly cows are supplanted by galloping cavalry horses. Crayoned ships sail the ocean bringing supplies to our soldiers, while bits of folded paper floating through the air become miniature air ships. Clay cannon, bullets, and soldiers are a common sight on the modeling table. Soldier games and marching songs are called for. 'Over There' seems to be known to all and is more popular than the most tuneful childish melody.

The primary teacher who is awake to her opportunities will allow this natural war interest of the children to run its course. More than that, she will follow the lead thus given her by the children themselves and will provide the mediums for its full play.[73]

There was much excellent material in the *National School Service,* including discussions of current events, articles on food production and conservation, lessons in thrift and health, and general information of interest to children. In the later issues, the League of Nations was given a generous amount of space. But there was also a large percentage of material intended to arouse the emotions of the pupils. This periodical, like practically all of the propaganda issued by the federal government for use in our public schools, stressed what William H. Kilpatrick called "a parochial patriotism." There was one outstanding exception; the leaflets edited by Charles H. Judd and Leon C. Marshall were lessons in citizenship, rather than instruction in patriotism.[74]

5. Lessons in Citizenship

Early in August, 1917, a conference was held by representatives of the Bureau of Education and the Food Administration. Although the original subject for discussion was an educational campaign designed to conserve food, it was agreed at the outset that "if such a campaign was to be effective and to justify itself as a school enterprise it must be carried out along broad lines dealing with every phase of community life and not confine itself merely

---

[73] *Ibid.* (September 15, 1918), p. 12.

[74] *Lessons in Community and National Life.* (Prepared by the Bureau of Education in cooperation with the United States Food Administration. Washington: Government Printing Office, 1918.) These sold for from five cents a copy to as low as $9.50 per thousand.

to the matter of immediate food administration."[75] Within a few weeks formal arrangements had been completed between the two federal agencies, work and expenses had been allocated, the editors had begun the preparation of the first lessons, and nation-wide publicity was under way. The first leaflets were printed and ready for distribution by October 1, 1917.

The purpose of these lessons was explained by President Wilson in a letter addressed to the educational authorities;[76] his remarks were amplified by Professor Judd in his introduction to the series. "The Lessons in Community and National Life," he wrote, "are intended first of all to lay the foundations for an intelligent enthusiasm for the United States. Our schools have lacked that emphasis on nationalism which has been characteristic of European schools." But what Judd had in mind by "nationalism" was something entirely different from the type of patriotism that was even then being fostered by the federal propaganda agencies. He believed that national unity could best be secured through an understanding of our way of life, and that this understanding could be most effectually achieved through "concrete descriptions of American institutions."

A second purpose of the lessons was "to bring industry into the schools in a way which will appeal to the intelligence of the pupils and will intellectualize all later contact with practical affairs." Judd insisted that there would be no educational gain if the schools did nothing more than provide skilled workmen; industry itself was in a position to do that much. But, he added, if "by appropriate recognition of industry as the expression of human genius and human cooperation we can give pupils ideas as well as skills to guide them in later practical life, then the schools will have made a genuine and positive contribution to industrial training."

Finally, the lessons were "intended to create a sense of personal responsibility, which can result only when the pupil is shown how his life is interdependent with the life of other members of society." Children, as Judd pointed out, learn first to consume; it is the job of society to teach them how to produce. As for food

[75] P. P. Claxton to F. K. Lane, Secretary of the Interior, October 26, 1917. National Archives (Bureau of Education, 106–18).

[76] *Lessons in Community and National Life* (Series A. 1918–1919). pp. 5–7.

conservation, "American children are not to be ordered to deprive themselves of familiar luxuries; they are to be told how urgent the need is. The lesson of civic responsibility, if learned in this rational way, will effect the saving that the Nation needs."[77] These views of an outstanding educator offer an interesting contrast to those expressed in the literature of our propaganda agencies.

Hardly had the lessons appeared in print before letters of congratulation began to pour across the desk of the Commissioner of Education. By the end of October more than 300,000 copies of the entire series had been ordered;[78] a month later the city of Cleveland asked for 70,000 for its own use;[79] by June, 1918, nearly 3,500,-000 copies had been sold.[80]

There were also criticisms. Most serious was the disapproval of Herbert Hoover. As head of the Food Administration, he did not feel that the lessons were vigorous enough in their attack on the war situation and particularly on the problem of food conservation.[81] For a time it appeared as though the entire undertaking might be abandoned, and at one point the Food Administration actually ruled against any further support, but appeals were made to Hoover by the Secretary of the Interior[82] and by the President himself.[83] As a consequence, an understanding was reached whereby Judd agreed to publish a special food number at the earliest possible date,[84] and Hoover generously paid the entire cost of printing the series out of his own personal funds.[85]

This misunderstanding as to the nature of the leaflets was aggravated by differing conceptions of the place of the schools in the war effort. The Food Administration, interested primarily in the problem of conservation, wished to use the schools to reach the parents, and early in the fall of 1917 began preparations for a food pledge campaign to be conducted through the school children.

77 *Ibid.,* pp. 7–8.
78 P. P. Claxton to F. K. Lane, October 26, 1917. National Archives (Bureau of Education, 106–18).
79 P. P. Claxton to C. H. Judd, November 15, 1917. National Archives, *op. cit.*
80 P. P. Claxton, Open letter to schoolmen throughout the country. National Archives, *op. cit.*
81 C. H. Judd to P. P. Claxton, October 30, 1917. National Archives, *op. cit.*
82 P. P. Claxton to F. K. Lane, October 26, 1917. National Archives, *op. cit.*
83 C. H. Judd to P. P. Claxton, October 30, 1917. National Archives, *op. cit.*
84 F. C. Walcott to C. H. Judd, November 14, 1917. National Archives, *op. cit.*
85 P. P. Claxton to the author, May 15, 1941.

Judd protested vigorously. "The plan to use the schools to distribute pledges for mothers is in my judgment doubtful from the point of view of that enterprise itself," he wrote. "It will certainly furnish dangerous, if not disastrous, competition for the Lessons which we are editing. Finally, such a use of the schools is fundamentally wrong in principle. . . . No program is right in principle which distracts the schools and uses them as a mere means to an end. The only way to use the schools is to use them for purposes which are educative. Children should be taught in schools something which they can absorb; they ought never to be used in a public institution to which they are brought by compulsory education laws as messengers to their parents."[86] Many people believed that Judd's views on wartime education were sound, but in this particular battle he went down to overwhelming defeat, not only at the hands of the Food Administration, but before the onslaught of scores of propaganda agencies' and campaigns.

There was an unbridgeable gap between the educational viewpoint of Judd and many of his critics. Typical were the remarks of the leader of one patriotic society who charged that "these community leaflets are grotesque when compared with the serious need and the wonderful opportunity." The "need," as he visualized it, was to compel all children to master a "list of essential facts" before they could graduate from school.[87] What he really wanted, of course, was to have the schools present in an uncritical way certain lessons designed to stimulate patriotic ardor. He should have been well pleased with many of the educational programs sponsored during the war.

Criticism of this sort was echoed in a somewhat different form by the National Industrial Conference Board, publicity bureau for the associated manufacturers of the country. In a thirteen page pamphlet, this organization condemned the leaflets for their radicalism:

Through the whole fabric is woven a thread of propaganda in favor of the eight-hour day, old age pensions, social insurance, trade-unionism, the minimum wage, and similar issues. Likewise there is an

[86] C. H. Judd to P. P. Claxton, September 24, 1917. National Archives (Bureau of Education, 106–18).
[87] W. H. Allen, Director of the Institute for Public Service, to F. K. Lane, March 13, 1918. National Archives, *op. cit.*

obvious effort to place before the scholar's mind a highly prejudiced picture of the hardships and hazards of factory life, injustices of present wage systems, and the attitude of employers in general toward their workers. This partisanship is well illustrated in the footnote questions which accompany each lesson. Here insidious suggestion in favor of certain theories is so subtly done that it cannot easily be challenged in specific cases.[88]

The reader who approaches these leaflets from the "climate of ideas" prevailing in the 1940's will find it difficult to understand this criticism by the manufacturers' association. Judd himself was not content to let the matter rest, and secured a hearing before the Board. He evidently convinced the Educational Committee that the published charges had been inaccurate, and that his own educational views were sound. "I think," Judd later commented, "the Committee was on the point of helping to continue the issuance of such material when at the annual meeting of the Board the Educational Committee was abolished.[89]

It is clear that these leaflets were in no sense lessons in patriotism as that word was understood by those interested in stimulating a lively nationalism in the school children. Carefully graded on three different levels to meet the requirements of the lower, intermediate, and upper grades of the public schools, the materials were designed, as Judd expressed it, to develop "an intelligent enthusiasm for the United States."

But, although Judd may have been dismayed at the "violent opposition" he encountered from certain sources, he had some reason to feel gratified with his work. The lessons were received more generously by educators than any of the propaganda materials issued during the war, as the sale of 3,500,000 copies indicates. Moreover, their influence persisted; more than a decade after the war had ended, one of Judd's former critics in the manufacturers' association took steps to revive the lessons.[90]

[88] *A Case of Federal Propaganda in Our Public Schools* (Boston, Massachusetts: National Industrial Conference Board, 1919), p. 4.

[89] C. H. Judd to the author, May 14, 1941.

[90] *Ibid.* The critic was Magnus Alexander. In response to his call, a conference was held to discuss the publication of a similar series of lessons. Judd was present, together with Ex-President Coolidge, Secretary of the Interior Wilbur, and Henry Suzzalo. Alexander indicated that the National Industrial Conference Board might be willing to aid in financing the project. He died before these plans could be carried out.

This is not to deny the influence of the other courses in patriotism prepared by literally scores of patriotic societies and educational organizations. As a result of the war, many people realized for the first time that our educational system was a powerful instrument of social control, and in the postwar period a growing number of pressure groups sought to inject their own special doctrines into the public school curriculum. This led to confusion, for educators were frequently bewildered in the face of these conflicting demands. Uncertain as to the course they should follow, particularly during the war years, they sometimes lashed out blindly at those who, by word or action, questioned their decisions. The activities of these pressure groups contributed in no small degree to our failure to build an effective wartime educational organization.

CHAPTER III

EFFORTS TO STEM HYSTERIA AND TO COORDINATE EDUCATIONAL ACTIVITIES

Every powerful passion brings with it an impulse to an attendant system of false beliefs. . . . Most men meet few foreigners, especially in time of war, and beliefs inspired by passion can be communicated to others without fear of an unsympathetic response. The supposed facts intensify the passion which they embody, and are magnified still further by those to whom they are told. Individual passions, except in lunatics, produce only the germs of myths, perpetually neutralized by the indifference of others; but collective passions escape this corrective, and generate in time what appears like overwhelming evidence for wholly false beliefs.

—*Bertrand Russell*[1]

If you have any new insight, any original ideas, if you present men and affairs under an unwonted aspect, you will surprise the reader. And the reader does not want to be surprised. He seeks in history only the stupidities with which he is already familiar.

—*Anatole France*[2]

1. The Schools and War Hysteria

Although many of the wartime activities carried on in the public schools were initiated by federal agencies, a large proportion originated with private or semi-public patriotic societies, organized along national, state, or purely local lines.[3] The federal government had little control over these groups; indeed, in a number of cases, it cooperated with them, using their facilities for the distribution of its own publications. Among the more prominent of the nationally organized societies, for both the scope and the vigor of their work, were the National Security League and the Council for National Defense. The latter, through its state,

[1] *Justice in War-Time* (Chicago: The Open Court Publishing Co., 1916), pp. 4–5.
[2] Quoted by Bessie L. Pierce, *Civic Attitudes in American School Textbooks* (Chicago: The University of Chicago Press, 1930), p. 255.
[3] Pierce in several studies has discussed the educational activities of the more prominent of these organizations.

county, and local committees covered the entire country with a fine web. There were scores of others, not the least active of which were the National Chamber of Commerce, the National Board for Historical Service, and International Rotary.

Excessive zeal on the part of certain of these organizations not infrequently aroused popular feeling in some localities to a point bordering on hysteria. The schools, traditional symbols of democracy, became the object of solicitude and suspicion. As emotions rose closer to the surface and nerves wore thin, the pressures upon the schools increased.

City after city abolished the teaching of German in the public schools, and a number of states took similar action. The Washington State Board of Education, convinced by the summer of 1918 that the "sentiment of our citizens is now such that this may be done without arousing resentment in any part of the state," ordered the teaching of German to be stopped. It is significant that this was done at the "request" of the State Council for National Defense.[4] South Dakota followed the same procedure when its State Council for National Defense "ordered that all teaching of the German language during the period of the war be discontinued in all the schools and educational institutions of the state."[5] A proposal was made at the Portland convention of the National Education Association to place that organization on record as favoring the abolition of the German language and literature from the public schools of the entire country; this was defeated.[6] The principal of a Michigan high school commented tersely: "The less we have of German the better."[7] A fellow educator from the same state was more explicit: "The previous efforts of German teachers," he flatly stated, "have been more of an effort to advance German Kultur than to teach literature. It has been propaganda to overthrow English, pure and simple. It has been a purely selfish means of implanting German Imperial Government ideals among our people rather than a pure desire to teach them literature.

[4] *Twenty-Fourth Biennial Report of the Superintendent of Public Instruction for the Biennium Ending June 30, 1918* (Olympia, Washington: Frank M. Lamborn, Public Printer, 1919), p. 52.
[5] *Fourteenth Biennial Report of the Superintendent of Public Instruction of the State of South Dakota. July 1, 1916 to June 30, 1918* (South Dakota, 1919), p. 16.
[6] N.E.A., *Proceedings,* 1917, p. 381.
[7] *School and Society,* vol. VII (June 22, 1918), p. 750.

Everything with the tag 'Made in Germany' must go. We resent any German influence. It is dishonest."[8] Senator Young of Iowa held identical views. "Ninety per cent of all the men and women who teach the German language are traitors and out of sympathy with the Government," he angrily charged before a group of prominent educators and government officials.[9] The California State Board of Education, in banning the teaching of German from the schools of the state, referred to it as "a language that disseminates the ideals of autocracy, brutality and hatred."[10] But it remained for Governor Alexander of Idaho to best sum up the attitude of many of the super-patriotic individuals and societies. "Law or no law . . . ," he announced, "German is not taught in the State of Idaho, probably will never be, even after the war is over. . . . You can count on Idaho. Whatever is wanted we will furnish, no matter what it is."[11]

With such an emotionally charged atmosphere, the persecution of teachers was inevitable. From all sections of the nation came reports of punishments meted out to those instructors who dared to resist the general unreason and popular hysteria. Loyalty oaths and dismissals for "pro-German" activities were noted with increasing frequency. Even the National Education Association joined in the hue and cry by canceling all honorary memberships of persons residing in Germany.[12]

The contagion spread. Some individuals felt that the time had come for educators to reinterpret the facts of history. "There should be an honest attempt," one patriot wrote, "to overcome the prejudice, amounting at times to hatred of England, which has been instilled into the American youth through our common school histories."[13] The Bureau of Education lent its name to this

8 *Ibid.*

9 *Americanization as a War Measure* (Bureau of Education Bulletin, 1918, No. 18), p. 35.

10 *Third Biennial Report of the State Board of Education, State of California, 1916–1918* (Sacramento, California: State Printing Office, 1918), p. 14.

11 *Americanization as a War Measure, op. cit.,* p. 55.

12 H. K. Beale, *Are American Teachers Free? An Analysis of Restraints Upon the Freedom of Teaching in American Schools* (New York: Charles Scribner's Sons, 1936), pp. 22 *et seq.* Beale is convinced that "any presentation of obtainable and publishable facts is an inevitable understatement of the truth (p. xvi)." See *infra,* pp. 217 ff.

13 H. B. Snell to J. W. Searson, May 16, 1917. National Archives (CPI, 3-A7, B-143).

recommendation.[14] Textbooks of long-standing respectability
were attacked. One prominent educator called attention to "the
careful elimination in various cities . . . of all material in high
school textbooks that seemed directly or indirectly to support
autocratic government."[15]

An awkward situation developed in California. In 1915 the
state educational authorities had adopted a music book for use in
the schools, only to discover three years later that "the psycho-
logical effect on the children of the appearance in their music
books of several songs designated as 'German Folk Songs,' or songs
'From the German,' was not considered good." Although the
books had not yet been distributed, the State Board of Education
was faced with a painful question. The problem was handed to
the State Council for National Defense which, after "full discussion," decided to issue the books with the un-American songs and
passages eliminated. The authorities were forced to confess that
"the process has necessarily eliminated some unobjectionable songs
appearing on opposite sides of pages cut out, and has left an occasional line or two of music on pages immediately following those
removed, which it will not be possible to utilize in study," but a
new edition was promised "at as early a date as possible." The
investigating committee also discovered an "astonishing amount
of German material" and "particularly vicious propaganda" in the
supplementary school books. "Fortunately," the committee observed, "the German influence in the state series books was confined to a few selections in some of the readers and to a number
of songs from the German . . ."[16]

Textbook problems were not confined to the Pacific coast. New
York State's well-known "Lusk laws" of 1918 prohibited the use
of any textbook which was found to contain statements "seditious
in character, disloyal to the United States, or favorable to the
cause of any foreign country with which the United States is now
at war." To a commission created by the law, any person might
present written complaints against any textbook in "civics, eco-

[14] *Opportunities for History Teachers. The Lessons of the Great War in the
Classroom* (Bureau of Education, Teachers' Leaflet No. 1, 1917), p. 5.

[15] Thomas H. Briggs, "Secondary Education," *Biennial Survey, 1916–1918* (Bureau
of Education Bulletin, 1919, No. 88), p. 217.

[16] California, *Third Biennial Report of the State Board of Education* (1918),
pp. 31–33.

nomics, English, history, language, and literature."[17] Montana barred from her public schools Willis Mason West's textbook on modern history because it was "pro-German." George Creel claimed that a principal reason for this charge was the statement that " 'Christianity advanced from the Rhine to the Elbe' "; presumably, West's critics believed that any identification of Christianity with the Germans was un-American.[18] In Michigan vicious attacks were made on a textbook by James Harvey Robinson for its allegedly insidious German propaganda. These attacks were made, according to one historian, "mainly or wholly because of an unfortunate cut of the Kaiser's family."[19] Carried on the winds by salesmen and publishers hungry for profits, charges of this sort— and the inevitable counter-charges—swept the country, and investigations were the order of the day. Even the War Department took a hand in the game. A memorandum from the Department of Military Censorship, dated September 30, 1918, listed seventy-seven books which were to be withdrawn from circulation in the military camps.[20]

All over the country people lived in an atmosphere of suspicion and recrimination. One federal judge enjoined the production of a film portraying the Wyoming Massacre and Paul Revere's ride because it tended " 'to make us a little bit slack in our loyalty to Great Britain in this great emergency.' "[21] Because two mothers refused to sign a Junior Red Cross pledge carried from school by their children, a local committee of patriots in a small Oregon town decided to "investigate fully to see if there can be any pro-Germanism."[22] In view of such incidents, it is not surprising to find the German language, teachers, and textbooks under assault

[17] Pierce, *Civic Attitudes in American School Textbooks*, pp. 232–233. The so-called "Lusk Report" makes valuable reading for those who wish to understand the war hysteria. See Clayton R. Lusk, *Revolutionary Radicalism: Its History, Purpose and Tactics. With an Exposition and Discussion of the Steps Being Taken and Required to Curb It* (Albany: J. B. Lyon Company, Printers, 1920).

[18] Creel to F. K. Lane, June, 1918. National Archives (CPI, 3-A7, L-1-71).

[19] W. M. West to G. S. Ford, August 23, 1918. National Archives (CPI, 3-A1, L-1-632).

[20] Memorandum. National Archives (CPI, 3-A1, L-1-196). For an extended discussion of the textbook problem, see H. K. Beale, *Are American Teachers Free?* chap. xi.

[21] Pierce, *Public Opinion and the Teaching of History in the United States*, p. 245.

[22] *Twenty-third Biennial Report of the Superintendent of Public Instruction in Oregon* (Salem, Oregon: State Printing Department, 1919), p. 8.

by patriotic organizations. Nor is it surprising that these same patriotic groups, not content with the suppression of what, to them, were dissident elements, should prepare lessons embodying their own interpretations of American history for use in the public schools.

2. Attempts to Prevent Hysteria

It has been claimed that the federal propaganda agencies were responsible for creating this state of feeling in the country.[23] To a certain extent, this is true. No organization which deliberately undertakes to arouse and direct the emotions of school children and of the larger public can avoid a share of responsibility for the excesses that may follow. But to say that the federal authorities acted with complete disregard for the consequences is to ignore an important aspect of their activities.

Not only did the director of the Division of Civic and Educational Cooperation advise the historians who prepared his bulletins to write so that they would feel no shame in twenty years,[24] but he himself read every pamphlet and took a rigid stand against the inclusion of even the word "hun," a term then in frequent use by the press and by public speakers.[25] When this opprobrious word did appear in the *War Cyclopedia*,[26] one of Ford's publications, it was mildly defined as "a term of reproach leveled at the Germans by their enemies since the war began," and a speech of the Kaiser, delivered in 1900 at the time of the Boxer Rebellion, was quoted to indicate how the word came to be associated with the German soldiers.[27] The files of the Committee on Public Information are full of unpublished manuscripts, many of which are brutal and degrading in nature. Although some scholars may in

---

[23] According to one critic, the Creel Committee was responsible for everything under the sun, from "causing cyclones in Kansas to starting revolutions in Mexico, originating Spanish influenza, or starting forest fires in Minnesota, firing ammunition dumps, or giving the baby the measles." August Schinderhans, *The Truth in the World War. An Exposé for Better Americanism* (Dallas, Texas: 1920), p. 16. This was a cheap, sensational, viciously inaccurate pamphlet. Few people could have taken it seriously, but it did represent the extreme point of view.

[24] CPI, *Hearing*, 1918, p. 99.

[25] Interview with G. S. Ford, New York, December 28, 1940. W. C. Bagley confirmed this in an interview with the author, New York, April 9, 1941.

[26] Frederick L. Paxson, Edward S. Corwin, and Samuel B. Harding, editors. *War Cyclopedia. A Handbook for Ready Reference on the Great War.*

[27] *Ibid.*, p. 132.

peacetime deplore the injudicious use of historical materials by the Creel Committee, they must recognize the fact that only authority in high places kept the propaganda from even greater immoderation.

As has been indicated, neither Ford nor Creel felt that the public schools were a primary responsibility of the Committee on Public Information; consequently, they spent a relatively small part of their time in efforts to influence the school children. They were, on the other hand, much disturbed over the hysteria aroused by the private patriotic organizations, and they expended considerable effort in an attempt to subdue and control these groups.[28] Writing shortly after the war ended, Creel expressed his indignation at the persecution of the foreign-born in America, and described the measures he had taken to subdue what he called the "savagery" of " 'leagues' and 'societies' operating in the name of 'patriotism.' "[29]

Other federal agencies were more concerned with the public schools than was the Creel Committee. The Children's Bureau was interested in maintaining and improving health standards; the Department of Labor and the Food Administration in the task of increasing and conserving foodstuffs; the Treasury Department in disposing of war bonds; the Department of Labor in supplying skilled workmen for the war-machine and in maintaining prewar standards of labor. The activities of these and other agencies, such as the Junior Red Cross, inevitably took time from regular school work. They certainly stimulated war feeling when, through posters, poems, "Junior Four-Minute Men" speeches, and campaigns of every sort, they called upon the pupils to sacrifice to win the war; yet their appeals were never based on or near the level of the atrocity stories so frequently used by the independent patriotic groups.

During the entire war the Bureau of Education waged an unceasing campaign against the misuse of the schools for merely war purposes. To the Commissioner of Education, P. P. Claxton, all war was abhorrent; he felt that the last place it should secure a foothold was in the public school system. In a constant stream of

---

[28] Interview with G. S. Ford, New York, December 28, 1940.
[29] Creel, *How We Advertised America*, pp. 443 *et seq.*

speeches and written statements, he pled with the school men of the country to maintain educational standards. *School Life*,[30] official organ of the Bureau of Education, from the date of its first publication on August 1, 1918 devoted almost its entire space to the improvement of the normal educational program. In spite of constant pressure, Claxton refused to join in the attack against Germany; it was with extreme reluctance, and then only to a limited extent, that he consented to cooperate with the National Board for Historical Service and the Creel Committee in their propaganda activities.[31] While it is true that several of the bulletins prepared by the National Board were published under the imprint of the Bureau of Education, the most notable being the elementary school syllabus, Claxton gave these publications only the most perfunctory advertising in the pages of his journal, *School Life*. This position was maintained against a storm of criticism from his enemies and the impatience of his friends. The Commissioner remained undisturbed, often repeating to his friend, James F. Abel, that "the Bureau of Education can't cooperate; it can only invite cooperation."[32]

The federal authorities took a firm position against the barring of German from the schools. Claxton, in particular, made vigorous efforts to bring educators to a more reasonable point of view. Emphasizing that our war was "with the Imperial Government of Germany and not with the German language or literature," he urged that "for our own and for the sake of the future of the world, let us hope that we may finish this task for the establishment of freedom and the safety of democracy without learning to chant any hymn of hate . . . For practical, industrial and commercial purposes we shall need a knowledge of the German lan-

---

[30] This was a semi-monthly publication. Since it was designed primarily for administrators, it was not discussed in the chapter dealing with lessons in patriotism.

[31] James F. Abel claimed that, as he recalled the situation, the Secretary of the Interior insisted that Claxton take an active part in the propaganda work of the federal government (Interview, Washington, April 15, 1941). Claxton denied that any pressure was ever exerted by his superiors (P. P. Claxton to the author, May 15, 1941).

[32] Interview with J. F. Abel, Washington, April 15, 1941. During the World War, Abel was chief clerk of the Bureau of Education and a close friend of the Commissioner. His statements are confirmed by the addresses and printed statements of Claxton, by the files of *School Life*, and by the correspondence of the Bureau of Education now in the National Archives.

guage more than we have needed it in the past . . . The fewer hatreds and antagonisms that get themselves embodied in institutions and policies the better it will be for us when the days of peace return." These views, the Commissioner reminded school men, were fully "in harmony with those of the administration at Washington."[33] His reward for this temperate statement was a violent outburst of criticism and abuse from all parts of the country.[34]

By using similar methods, the director of the Division of Civic and Educational Cooperation threw all the prestige of his position into the effort to stop this hysterical reaction against the German language. Speaking to groups throughout the nation, Ford reminded them of the President's declaration that our quarrel was with the Imperial Government, not with the German people.[35] In the fall of 1917 he sent a circular letter[36] to the forty-eight state superintendents of education recommending for their use the German translation of President Wilson's "War Message."[37] Schools which followed Ford's suggestion would thus retain the study of German and at the same time would become inoculated with the "official" view of Germany's war guilt and the justice of the American cause. These were indirect methods, but they were the only ones available to the federal authorities. While there is no evidence to indicate that the efforts of these men had any effect, it is clear that it was not the federal authorities who were responsible for the expulsion of the German language from the public schools.

The textbook problem was unusually difficult. It caused Ford some of his most unpleasant moments. With other reasonable people, he could view the situation only in dismay. He had, moreover, personal reasons for his discomfiture. Through his activities in the field of history, his membership in and close relationship

[33] P. P. Claxton to R. L. Slagle, March 12, 1918. Published in *School and Society*, vol. VII (March 30, 1918), p. 374.

[34] Interview with J. F. Abel, Washington, April 15, 1941. According to Abel, this criticism greatly disturbed the Commissioner. It was not inspired, but was obviously the spontaneous reaction of a large number of individuals.

[35] Interview with G. S. Ford, New York, December 28, 1940.

[36] G. S. Ford to Dr. John Finley, State Commissioner of Education, New York, October 25, 1917. National Archives (CPI, 3-A1, L-1-427).

[37] CPI, *The War Message and Facts Behind It. Annotated Text of President Wilson's Message, April 2, 1917.*

with the National Board for Historical Service, and his work on the Creel Committee, he had been brought into close touch with many of the men who were accused of spreading German propaganda in their textbooks. He knew how preposterous the charges were, for most of these men were his friends and colleagues; as a consequence, he exerted all his influence—which, since he was head of an important division of Creel's Committee, was considerable—to bring the emotionally aroused public to a more rational point of view. Here, again, he was forced to the use of indirect methods.

For example, in the spring of 1918, Professor Willis Mason West found it necessary to visit Montana to defend himself and his textbook against the accusation of spreading German propaganda. By sheer chance he met Ford in a hotel lobby. West unburdened himself of the entire story of his difficulties with the textbook. That afternoon Ford addressed a large gathering. In the middle of his speech he paused, expressed his delight at seeing in the audience his "good friend," Professor Willis Mason West, and proceeded to voice his appreciation for the valuable aid West had rendered the Committee of Public Information and the nation in the present crisis. It is distressing to add that Ford's comments on this particular occasion were of no avail, for that evening the State Council for National Defense met and barred West's book from the Montana schools.[38]

The effort to aid his friend and to calm public hysteria did not end with this speech. In June, from his offices in Washington, Ford replied to a letter from Allyn and Bacon, publishers of the West text. Ostensibly addressed to the publishing house, Ford's letter was in reality a veiled defense of West's text. "Professor [Willis Mason] West's *Modern History*," he wrote, "published in 1903, was certainly the first textbook that pushed aside the German mask and showed behind it the features we now know so well as Prussian militarism with its immoral statecraft and worship of force. To have done this fifteen years ago is proof of Professor West's penetration and prevision."[39]

On another occasion Ford answered a letter from the Macmil-

---

[38] Interview with G. S. Ford, New York, December 28, 1940.
[39] Mock and Larson, *Words That Won the War*, p. 177.

lan publishing house. Pointing out that his position with the
federal government made it impossible for him to endorse a textbook openly, he went on to praise Charles A. Beard for his splendid scholarship and unimpeachable patriotism, concluding with
a glowing reference to Beard's services in behalf of the Committee
on Public Information. The Macmillan officials printed this
letter and distributed it to their salesmen in the field, where,
presumably, it was used with telling effect in many an argument
over Beard's pro-Germanism.[40]

Slight as the result of Ford's efforts appeared to be in the light
of the hysteria that was sweeping the country, they must have
been of some value. The files of the Committee on Public Information contain a number of letters from publishing houses and
from individuals asking for approval of their textbooks or maps.
Denoyer and Geppert offered to sell their maps to the Committee.[41] Albert Bushnell Hart prepared a series of war maps which
he felt would be helpful to "teachers in the grade and high
schools," and asked Ford to publish them.[42] Another company
inquired if it "would not be possible . . . to publish one or more
books that would be commercially feasible and, at the same time,
carry a certain amount of propaganda with them."[43] The editor
of *Current History Magazine* felt that his periodical would be
invaluable as "collateral" reading in the schools, and suggested
that Ford or the agencies that he controlled might utilize it for
this purpose.[44] These letters are typical of many that passed across
Ford's desk during the war years. To those requests which sought
merely to use government channels for additional publicity, or to
those which sought to carry on their own particular propaganda
through federal agencies, Ford returned a courteous but firm re-
fusal. But to those companies whose books were under attack by
the super-patriots, as in the cases mentioned, he replied with letters which were in reality endorsements.

Ford's methods did not, of course, begin to solve the textbook

40 Interview with G. S. Ford, New York, December 28, 1940.
41 Letter to G. S. Ford, November 2, 1918. National Archives (CPI, 3-A7, L-1-504).
42 Letter to G. S. Ford, January 8, 1918. National Archives (CPI, 3-A1, L-1-250).
43 D. Appleton and Company to G. S. Ford, February 26, 1918. National Archives
(CPI, 3-A1, L-1-140).
44 G. W. Ochs Oakes to G. S. Ford, September 6, 1918. National Archives (CPI,
3-A1, L-1-186).

problem. A number of other individuals had their own ideas as to how to reach a satisfactory solution. The advertising manager of the Wells-Fargo Company, E. Hungerford, who was also a member of the Publicity Committee of the American Defense Society, had a suggestion to offer. Although he deplored the "praise of the Kaiser" and the "criticism of our British allies" in "many of the textbooks used across the land," Hungerford admitted that "it would be difficult if not practically impossible to change all these textbooks now." He then went on to ask "if it would not be a big stunt to prepare a patriotic poster on Government paper, telling what the war really means in simple, concise language, such as any child might understand? After heading it with the official seal of the United States, send it out to boards of education all across the land, with instructions to have children paste it in the fly-leaves of their histories or other textbooks. You might go further and have an attached receipt—worded as a sort of covenant of national faith, which each child could sign and send to the President, at Washington. As you can see," he concluded, "this is still a crude idea, but I do think it has merit." Creel, to whom the letter was addressed, evidently did not share the author's faith in the idea. After notifying Hungerford that the Committee on Public Information was "buried out of sight" with other projects, he added that the problem of textbooks was receiving some "consideration."[45]

This incident is mentioned only as an illustration of a strong desire on the part of many individuals to have the federal propaganda agencies take a more vigorous role in controlling the thoughts of the school children. It is clear, in retrospect, that this plan and those of similar nature would have served to fan the flames of the misguided nationalism that raged throughout the country. Such a procedure would only have accentuated the problems which had emerged, in large part, because of the interference of private interests in the work of the schools.

More feasible was the solution proposed by the National Board for Historical Service. Feeling that the Bureau of Education and the Committee on Public Information could exert a stabilizing

[45] Correspondence between E. Hungerford, Advertising Manager of the Wells-Fargo Company, and G. Creel, October, 1917. National Archives (CPI, 3-A1, L-1-435).

influence by endorsing a "list of books, designed for the use especially of teachers and libraries," the Board actually had such a list prepared by several of the nation's leading historians. This plan was abandoned when the Board was advised that the Department of the Interior forbade "any expressions of opinion about the relative merits of articles offered for sale, even books."[46]

Meanwhile, Creel himself was devoting a considerable amount of thought to the problem. In characteristically robust terms, he expressed his opinion of the whole situation in a letter to the Secretary of the Interior:

> Your interest as much as my own in the schools leads me to call your attention to certain phases of the textbook question, especially in the field of history that is now precipitated by rival publishers and patriots suffering from civic shell shock. Within the past two weeks we have been appealed to by publishers and authors in three separate cases to get a reasonable hearing and treatment of school books in history, which were being thrown out of cities or whole states, for reasons essentially trivial—a picture of the present German Emperor, of Frederick the Great, that the author's son (in fact only eleven years old) had been disloyal and the father equally so, or that the text said, 'Christianity advanced from the Rhine to the Elbe,' therefore the author was trying to show that Christianity originated in Germany.
>
> In some cases state defense councils have been the agency appealed to, in others the Department of Justice.
>
> Whatever the reason, and some objections are more vapid than the above, I suspect a rival book company (in a glass house) has a stone missing from its garden walk. We can hardly expect that the Department of Justice will discriminate or defend.[47]

Ford shared Creel's distrust of the book companies, and there is evidence to indicate that this distrust was not misplaced. In one letter to Professor West, the Allyn and Bacon Company denied that their salesmen had made any attacks upon the books of rival publishing houses. "Of course," the letter admitted, "as soon as our men find that Robinson is scheduled to be dropped, they try their best to have our book introduced in its place, and very naturally they invite comparison."[48]

[46] C. H. Hull to G. S. Ford, August 27, 1917. National Archives (CPI, 3-A1, L-1-295).

[47] G. Creel to F. K. Lane, June, 1918. National Archives (CPI, 3-A7, L-1-71).

[48] This letter is now on file in the National Archives (CPI, 3-A1, L-1-632). Other evidence of a similar import is also available in these records.

The solution to the problem, as Ford saw it, was to establish a neutral commission to judge all such charges of pro-Germanism in textbooks.[49] He agreed with the Chairman of the National Board for Historical Service, J. T. Shotwell, who stated that the "historians have got to bring pressure on both publishers and the public, not to mention Departments, in order to secure a sane handling of the teaching of history. My guess," Shotwell concluded, "is to have the Department of Justice refer all these matters to you."[50]

A similar proposal was advanced by the War Department a few weeks later. Their "Index Expurgatorius," a list of seventy-seven books banned from all military camps, was exciting adverse comment. "Would it be fair to ask your office," a spokesman for the War Department wrote to Ford, "to let me know informally the books which it might be profitable to have someone read with a view to their restoration to respectability?"[51] Ford, replying promptly, agreed that the War Department's list was "a curious one," and added that he had "wondered about its origin." Ford did not, however, feel that he should be the one to pass judgment upon the questionable books. It would be much better, he thought, to set up a neutral commission. This idea, he pointed out, had been discussed with the Secretary of the Interior and the Commissioner of Education; both had joined him in the belief that such a commission should be created. An organization of this sort "might well undertake," as one of its first jobs, "to examine the War Department's Index Expurgatorius."[52]

Perhaps this exchange of views spurred Ford to action; at any rate, within two weeks he wrote again to the War Department. He was pleased, he said, to notify the Department that a "committee of five, representing the Bureau of Education, Committee on Public Information, Historical Section of the War College, the American Historical Association, and the National Education Association" was being formed under the direction of the Com-

---

[49] G. S. Ford to W. M. West, August 27, 1918. National Archives (CPI, 3-A1, L-1-632).

[50] J. T. Shotwell to G. S. Ford, August 22, 1918. National Archives (CPI, 3-A1, L-1-163).

[51] F. P. Keppel, Third Assistant Secretary of War, to G. S. Ford, October 3, 1918. National Archives (CPI, 3-A1, L-1-196).

[52] G. S. Ford to F. P. Keppel, October 5, 1918, *op. cit.*

missioner of Education. Ford then suggested that the group start its activities by a review of the War Department's list of doubtful books.[53]

Since the Armistice intervened before this Commission really began to function, it is impossible to do more than conjecture upon the value it might have had as a stabilizing force in the text-book field. It is interesting to bear in mind that, although the proposal came too late, it was the only really constructive attempt made to deal with the problem of textbooks, and that the plan was worked out by the very men who were accused of inciting war hysteria.

3. Measures to Coordinate Wartime Activities in the Schools

As has been indicated, the schools were among the first to be affected when the watchdogs of patriotism were turned loose during the early days of the war. Federal agencies, scores of patriotic societies, and many school systems proceeded to formulate courses in patriotism and to initiate war activities. Whatever the merits of these varied programs, it is certain that in many schools a conspicuous by-product was confusion.

Under the decentralized system of education in the United States, this was perhaps inevitable. The Bureau of Education was the only federal organization with any interest in the public school system as a whole, and it operated merely as a fact-finding and advisory body. Not even the state departments of public instruction were in a position to exert much control over the activities of the local districts. The Creel Committee, created for the express purpose of mobilizing the thoughts and feelings of the American people, had neither the authority nor the machinery to control the public schools.

As the months passed and the patriotic groups warmed up to their tasks, the situation became increasingly difficult. The Bureau of Education, noting "considerable confusion . . . regarding the origin and purpose of the various agencies at work," took a feeble step to clarify the situation in the spring of 1918. At this

[53] G. S. Ford to F. P. Keppel, October 16, 1918. National Archives (CPI, 3-A1, L-1-196).

time, in collaboration with the National Board for Historical
Service, it issued a small pamphlet giving "a synopsis" of the
activities and publications of a few of the national agencies interested in the public schools.[54] Although this manual undoubtedly
helped teachers to secure additional propaganda materials, it is
hard to see how it could have helped to dispel confusion. What
educators needed was not more activities, but a coordinated program.

This need for a more systematic procedure in the war activities
of our public school system was revealed in the reports of city and
state superintendents of education. Few forthright condemnations
of the situation were made publicly. It is an interesting commentary on the times that many educational leaders dared not
protest for fear of being "considered lacking in patriotism."[55]
There were many veiled protests, however, and demands and suggestions for a coordinated program became increasingly insistent.

From the start of the war, the Committee on Public Information had been held up as the logical agency behind which to con-
solidate the wartime activities of our educational system. Some,
at least, of the National Board for Historical Service shared this
view with Ford and others. The chief obstacles to such a plan
were the unpopularity of Creel's organization and the lack of
adequate finances.[56] It was also proposed that the Council for
National Defense should head the war activities of the nation's
schools. This organization had the merit of being a quasi-public
enterprise, thus escaping the charges of political partisanship
which were so frequently directed at Creel and his Committee.
To offset this obvious advantage was the varying effectiveness of
the State Councils; in some sections of the country these were
strong organizations, in many states they were ineffectual.[57]

Perhaps most insistent of all were the proponents of the Bureau of Education,[58] many of whom saw in the troubled war

[54] *Education in Patriotism, A Synopsis of the Agencies at Work* (Bureau of Education, Teachers' Leaflet No. 2, April, 1918).

[55] U. S. Conn, President of the State Normal School, Wayne, Nebraska, to J. W.
Searson, May 14, 1918. National Archives (CPI, 3-A7, B-66).

[56] W. B. Pitkin to G. S. Ford, August 21, 1917. National Archives (CPI, 3-A1,
L-1-237).

[57] *Ibid.*

[58] Parke R. Kolbe, "War Work of the United States Bureau of Education," *School
and Society*, vol. VII (May 25, 1918), p. 606.

years an opportunity to elevate that body into the status of a full department of the federal government.[59] A statistician for the Bureau of Education put the case with considerable clarity when he pointed out that the educational activities of the federal government were "scattered among half a hundred different agencies in twenty-three distinct departments, bureaus, or commissions. It is estimated," he remarked, "that the work done by at least thirty-five of these agencies, representing an expenditure of close to thirty millions of dollars, could profitably be brought together into a single adequately equipped department of education, and that, given such a department, the remaining educational agencies would either come into the department or at any rate find it valuable to cooperate very definitely with it in educational work." The writer then presented a plan for his proposed organization.[60] This was obviously too sweeping a proposal to hope for success during the war years; moreover, it offered no solution for the confusion created by the patriotic societies operating throughout the country.

The National Education Association brought the situation to a head when, on April 12, 1918, the Commission on the National Emergency on Education and Necessary Readjustment during and after the war unanimously adopted a resolution. In this resolution, the Commission called upon "the National Council of Defense, the various federal departments, divisions, bureaus, commissions and committees [to] provide at once a clearing house and coordinating agency for those propagandas and activities that they wish the schools to present." It was further proposed that this material should be prepared in suitable form for use in the schools, arranged in order of importance, and distributed through the educational authorities of each state.[61] In compliance with this request[62] and the rising volume of demands from other sources, the Creel Committee immediately took steps to establish such a coordinating agency.

[59] John H. MacCracken, "The Bill for a National Department of Education," *School and Society,* vol. VIII (September 14, 1918), p. 329.

[60] Carson Ryan, Jr., "The Federal Government and Education," *School and Society,* vol. VIII (July 13, 1918), pp. 54–57; Parke L. Kolbe, "War Work of the United States Bureau of Education," *op. cit.*

[61] *School and Society,* vol. VII (May 4, 1918), pp. 529–530.

[62] Memorandum, June 1, 1918. National Archives (CPI, 3-A7, A-1).

After some discussion, it was decided to publish a bulletin. Professor J. W. Searson was chosen to direct the enterprise. With Ford's approval, he drew up a tentative program; this was sent to the leading educators of the country, with requests for comments and suggestions.[63] At the same time, a second letter was forwarded to all summer schools, asking for data as to dates of opening, length of terms, and number of students.[64] Searson proposed to issue two bulletins in the summer of 1918, one to appear in June for use by the teachers in the summer schools, the other to be sent in August to the Community Institutes. Starting in the fall, the bulletin was to be mailed semi-monthly.[65] The purpose was explained in Searson's letter to the educators: First, to appeal to the ideals of patriotism; second, to set forth the causes of the war and the problems growing out of the conflict; third, to determine the priority of the various campaigns and propagandas; fourth, to serve as a clearing house for the interchange of ideas; and fifth, to call attention to important articles in current publications.[66]

Letters from school men indicated general approval. Most educators were delighted that at last some measures were being taken to put an end to the confusion in the schools. Searson had mentioned five reasons for publishing the bulletin. On three of these points there was some disagreement as to the value of the bulletin, but over two thirds of those who replied were enthusiastic over the proposal to use the magazine as a clearing house for propaganda. The reply of one superintendent was typical: "I think," he remarked, "the plan of having a Clearing House for School Activities is certainly a wise one. Up to the present time we have been very much like the crowd at a fire in a country town. Everybody has been trying to tell everybody else what to do and how to do it and the result has been that everybody has been in everybody else's way."[67]

[63] Form letter, copy to P. Monroe, May 8, 1918. National Archives (CPI, 3-A7, B-1).

[64] Form letter, copy to A. A. Goodyear, May 3, 1918. National Archives (CPI, 3-A7, D-6).

[65] Form letter "To the Teachers of America." National Archives (CPI, 3-A1, L-1-234).

[66] L. D. Coffman to J. W. Searson, May 10, 1918. National Archives (CPI, 3-A7, A-2).

[67] L. H. Minkel to J. W. Searson, May 21, 1918. National Archives (CPI, 3-A7, B-98).

An Advisory Editorial Board was set up; this group was assisted by a consulting editorial board established in each of the forty-eight states. These state boards were to serve two major functions: (1) To give to the regular editorial staff such help, advice, and suggestions as was needed to make the bulletin vital for the teachers; and (2) to constitute a standing advisory committee which could be consulted as to the best means for adapting the war service material to school needs and for promoting the harmony of local, state, and national programs of war education. Each of the state boards was composed of five members, four appointed by the State Superintendent of Education, and the Superintendent himself serving as the fifth member and chairman.[68] This organization insured greater coordination of the country's educational forces, and the schools were at last to have a voice in the determination of both the policy and the administration of the war program.

Delays in completing the administrative details and in securing the necessary appropriation from Congress prevented the publication of the summer bulletins.[69] Meanwhile, the name of the bulletin was changed to National School Service. With Professor W. C. Bagley, of Teachers College, Columbia University, acting as editor-in-chief, the various governmental agencies swung into line, and the first issue of the periodical appeared on September 1, 1918.

As we have seen, each of the major departments of the federal government interested in conducting educational campaigns in the public schools was given an allotment of space; all lessons were graded for rural and city schools and for the different age levels. Generous portions of the courses of study previously prepared by Harding, Coulomb, and others, were rewritten and republished in the pages of National School Service. Messages from the President, from Hoover, and from other national leaders were delivered to the school children through the pages of the periodical. Current events were summarized, and the extra space was filled with stirring quotations, slogans, poetry, and pictures.

[68] Form letter to State Superintendents of Education, May 22, 1918. National Archives (CPI, 3-A7, A-1-31).

[69] J. W. Searson to G. M. Wilson, July 19, 1918. National Archives (CPI, 3-A1, C-142).

An effort was made to place the publication in the hands of every teacher in the country. This in itself was a difficult task, for, as has been indicated, when the war began no such list was available, and as late as the summer of 1918 the Committee on Public Information and the Bureau of Education had not been able to complete a mailing list of even the school houses.

So it was, in the closing months of the war, that a means was devised to reduce the confusion and inefficiency of the educational activities of the federal agencies. Although this service did not directly reduce the interference of the many private patriotic societies, it did serve to focus attention upon those materials and programs that the directors of *National School Service* considered most valuable. In this way the periodical speedily demonstrated its usefulness. When the war ended, the demand for its continuance was so insistent that the service was carried on until the summer of 1919.

PART TWO

USING THE SCHOOLS TO ADVANCE THE WAR EFFORT

CHAPTER IV

SCHOOLBOYS IN UNIFORM

We who desire peace must write it in the hearts of children.[1]

An instructor's success will be measured by his ability to instil into his men the will and desire to use the bayonet. This spirit is infinitely more than the physical efforts displayed on our athletic fields . . . it is an intense eagerness to fight and kill hand to hand. . . . Bayonet fighting is possible only because red-blooded man naturally possesses the killing instinct. This inherent desire to fight and kill must be carefully watched for and encouraged by the instructor.[2]

Like other agues that shake the body politic, militarism is intermittent.[3]

In modern times both military leaders and educators must face the problem of the age at which military training is most desirable for youth. Some individuals have insisted that the best time to start this education is while boys are still in school; others have vigorously opposed such action on the grounds that military training for schoolboys cannot hope to produce good soldiers, and that it is actually harmful to children.

Military training in the public schools was initiated during the heat of conflict in the years from 1861 to 1865;[4] since that date interest in the problem, as well as the number of schoolboys in uniform, has risen and fallen with the beginning and end of every war. As a result of the Spanish-American War, for example, by

[1] Motto over the door of a memorial building erected in northern France by the Red Cross after the First World War. *War Work in the Public Schools of the City of New York.* Compiled by the Teachers' Council, Committee on School Records and Statistics (New York: F. Hubner and Company, Inc., 1933), p. 122.

[2] Colonel Jas. A. Moss and Major John W. Lang, *Manual of Military Training* (Menasha, Wisconsin: George Banta Publishing Company, 1921), vol. I, chap. xxvii, p. 1.

[3] *The Century. Illustrated Monthly Magazine,* vol. XLVII (December, 1893), p. 316.

[4] *Military Training in High Schools of the United States* (2nd edition, Civilian Military Education Fund, 1938), p. 3.

1900 over 10,000 boys, or nearly five per cent of the male enrollment of our secondary schools, were engaged in some form of
military training.[5] After 1900, martial enthusiasm was at the ebb,
and during the next fourteen years there was actually a slight
decrease in the number of schoolboy cadets. In 1914, only 9,532
students were registered in the military units of some eighty-two
secondary institutions.[6] Then, with the outbreak of war in Europe, the tide turned once again, and by 1918 over 112,000 high
school boys, or one in every seven, were engaged in drill activities.[7]
New York State had even gone to the length of making military
training compulsory for all boys between the ages of sixteen and
nineteen.[8]

From the Armistice to 1939 there was another lull in the agitation, but as the Second World War began to press closely upon
America, demands were renewed for the training of high school
youth. A bill to foster military education in the public schools of
New Jersey was presented to the State Legislature in the spring
of 1941.[9] One year later the New Jersey Veterans of Foreign Wars
adopted a resolution calling for compulsory military training for
all high school juniors and seniors.[10] Such proposals, not by any
means confined to this one state, were similar to those which were
made with great frequency during the years immediately preceding our entrance into the First World War. Our experience in
1917–1918 was, therefore, not peculiar to that conflict. Then, as
in 1898, an increased interest in the problem was followed by a
sharp rise in the number of schoolboys in uniform. It is also evident that with the end of armed conflict the public lost its enthusiasm for military training in the public schools.

[5] *Biennial Survey, 1916–1918* (Bureau of Education Bulletin, 1919, No. 88), pp.
127–128. In 1900 the male enrollment in high schools was 216,207.
[6] *Ibid.* Total male enrollment in 1914 was 541,486. Less than two per cent of
the boys were engaged in military drill. For an excellent study of military education in the public schools between 1862 and 1914, see Margaret M. Gearhart,
Military Instruction in Civil Institutions of Learning, 1862–1914 (unpublished
thesis, University of Iowa, 1928).
[7] *Ibid.* Total male enrollment in 1918 was 704,856. At least 112,683 boys in
1,267 high schools were registered in drill units.
[8] Ping Ling, "Military Training in the Public Schools," *The Pedagogical Seminary,* vol. XXV (September, 1918), pp. 255–256.
[9] *New Jersey Educational Review,* vol. XIV (April, 1941), p. 190. This bill was
numbered "A-161."
[10] *New York World-Telegram,* June 29, 1942.

1. Attitude of the War Department, 1914–1917

Popular agitation for military training has not been entirely spontaneous. For instance, between 1914 and 1917 the War Department did its best to awaken American citizens to the urgent need for preparedness. As early as 1914 Congress was asked to provide money for the "Plattsburg Camps" in which civilians, both boys and men, were given military training.[11] In 1915 the Secretary of War renewed this request, and recommended that the enlisted strength of the regular army be increased, by recruiting if possible, by compulsion if necessary.[12] At the same time the Chief of Staff proposed a universal military program based on the Australian and Swiss models, but this was rejected by the Secretary of War on the grounds that this type of program must operate in the public schools, over which, in America, the federal government had no authority.[13]

It was not until the spring of 1916 that Congress responded to these requests. Through the first piece of legislation of its kind enacted since 1901, the size of the army was increased to 186,000 men; the National Guard was reorganized and federalized; the authorized enrollment at West Point was doubled; and provisions for the training of reserve officers were greatly expanded. The army at once set out to secure the necessary recruits. A "Safety First" train toured the country, recruiting officers distributed large quantities of literature, and the civilian training camps were thrown wide open at government expense. At the same time, conscious that it must compete with private industry in the employment of men, the War Department began to prepare educational programs for the vocational training of its enlisted personnel.[14]

All this was still short of what the War Department believed were minimum requirements for adequate national defense. What

[11] "Report of the Secretary of War," *Annual Report of the War Department* (1914), vol. I, p. 13.
[12] "Report of the Secretary of War," *Annual Report of the War Department* (1915), vol. I, pp. 31, 38, 171.
[13] *Ibid.*, p. 34.
[14] "Report of the Secretary of War," *Annual Report of the War Department* (1916), vol. I, pp. 24–26, 33–37. This legislation was popularly known as "The National Defense Act." See *U. S. Stat. at Large*, vol. XXXIX, part 1.

they really wanted, as the Chief of Staff made quite clear in a statement to the House Committee on Military Affairs, was a program of universal, compulsory military service.[15]

The War Department knew, however, that most Americans were not yet ready for such a step. Officially, the military leaders committed themselves to a program which in 1916 looked forward to an eventual army of 1,500,000 men. Of this number, 500,000 were to be trained and ready for immediate action, another 500,-000 were to be available for service within ninety days of the outbreak of war, and a third group of the same size was to be available when needed. "To prepare for this task," the Chief of Staff pointed out, "requires us to use every available means of educating the young as to their future duties as citizens." This education, he added, "can be partially given in the public schools." As proof that the proposal to use the schools was not a "theoretical scheme," the report described the "Steever" or "Wyoming System," already in operation in a number of public high schools. "There is every reason," Major General Scott concluded, "why the 'Wyoming plan' should be taken up by every high school in the country."[16]

2. Military Training in the High Schools, 1916–1917

As has been indicated, from the Spanish-American War to the outbreak of the European conflict in 1914, the number of boys enrolled in cadet units had remained practically constant, varying only a few hundred between the figures of 9,000 and 10,000. The concern of many Americans over the war abroad and our lack of preparedness, the defense measures taken by private groups and by Congress, and the recommendations of the War Department, had an immediate effect. Within two years, or by the end of 1916, our schoolboy soldiers had increased from 9,000 to 25,000; or, to put it differently, four out of every one hundred high school boys were receiving military training.[17]

---

[15] "Report of the Chief of Staff," *Annual Report of the War Department* (1916), vol. I, p. 160.

[16] *Ibid.*, p. 174.

[17] The enrollment rose from 9,532 in 1914 to 24,433 in 1916. Total enrollment of boys in high school during these years increased from 541,486 to 660,641. *Biennial Survey, 1916–1918* (Bureau of Education Bulletin, 1919, No. 88), p. 128.

The National Defense Act of June 3, 1916 provided two methods for stimulating military education in the public schools of the country. One provision authorized the establishment of a Reserve Officers Training Corps, the Junior Division of which was open to high school students. Full equipment and the necessary instructors were to be available to those institutions which applied for membership. It was required that the schools furnish a minimum enrollment in each unit of at least one hundred physically fit male students fourteen years of age or over, and an agreement that the course of study stipulated by the War Department would be followed for three hours per week with full credit for the students.[18] A second provision of the Act authorized the federal government to issue "such arms, tentage, and equipment as the Secretary of War shall deem necessary for proper military training." This equipment was to go to those schools which had in operation a course of military training prescribed by the War Department. Requirements as to number of students and detail of officers were essentially the same as those under the R.O.T.C. program.[19]

The first high school unit was established at Leavenworth, Kansas, on January 29, 1917, but was discontinued the following October when the War Department withdrew all regular army officers from the high schools.[20] In the case of Leavenworth, military training did not cease, however, for the high school maintained its cadet corps intact, shortly thereafter affiliating it with the newly organized High School Volunteers of the United States.[21] Schools entering the H.S.V.U.S. hoped to take advantage of the War Department's offer of equipment and instructors authorized by the National Defense Act. Inability to secure the regular army

[18] *U. S. Stat. at Large,* vol. XXXIX, part 1, pp. 191–193. The Senior Division of the R.O.T.C. divided the work for schools and colleges into two major courses, the basic and advanced, each of two years' length. Students entering either course agreed to complete the full two years of work. The advanced course also carried the requirement of six weeks in an army camp, but the student was rewarded by "commutation and subsistence" for the entire two years, full army pay and subsistence while in camp, and the commission of second lieutenant upon successful completion of the work. The Junior Division offered only the basic course. Other requirements were the same for both divisions.

[19] *Ibid.,* p. 197.

[20] *Military Training in High Schools of the United States. R.O.T.C.* (2nd edition, Civilian Military Education Fund, 1938), p. 5.

[21] *Ibid.*

officers was a sharp blow to the schools, but by one means or another the military activities were continued. Sometimes retired officers were placed in charge of the work; in many instances the athletic teachers served as directors.

The H.S.V.U.S. was sponsored by the editors of *Everybody's Magazine*. This group of men performed a service similar to that of the Grand Army of the Republic in the years preceding the Spanish-American War. The opening shot in the nation-wide publicity campaign was fired by George Creel in an article written early in 1916. This was called "Wyoming's Answer to Militarism: Five Years of Training Schoolboys to Think True, Live True—and Shoot True."[22] Since it was the "Wyoming System" which was urged upon "every high school" by the War Department, and since a large part of the military training of the war years was actually conducted along these lines, it might be well at this point to outline briefly the sort of military education provided in the Wyoming schools.[23]

Creel, in describing the work of the Cheyenne schools, went back to its origins in 1911. At that date, Lieutenant Edgar Z. Steever was assigned by the War Department to duty as inspector-instructor of the organized militia of the state. Finding time heavy on his hands, Steever proposed to form a cadet corps in the high schools of Cheyenne. Strong opposition at once developed. In Creel's words, the objections raised in 1911 were typical of *"all* opposition to such ideas."[24] Labor unions saw in the schoolboy corps merely another form of the state militia which had been used all too frequently in the past to break strikes; parents and preachers were afraid that military ideals would be instilled in the minds of their children and that militarism would be imposed upon the nation. Educators professed to fear the destruction of individual initiative and the undermining of a sense of personal responsibility.[25]

Lieutenant Steever met all these objections with an organiza-

[22] *Everybody's Magazine*, vol. XXXIV (February, 1916), pp. 150–159.

[23] For a more detailed description of the "Wyoming System," see Colonel L. R. Gignilliat, *Arms and the Boy. Military Training in Schools and Colleges* (Indianapolis, Indiana: The Bobbs-Merrill Company, 1916), pp. 224 ff.

[24] Creel, "Wyoming's Answer to Militarism," *Everybody's Magazine*, vol. XXXIV (February, 1916), p. 151.

[25] *Ibid.*, pp. 151–152.

tion that was voluntary rather than compulsory; that stressed physical training and education in citizenship by means of organized athletics for all, rather than purely military drill. Winning the consent of the Cheyenne School Board and the approval of the parents, before long Steever had his program in operation throughout the city schools with practically one hundred per cent participation. Within a few months he had the added satisfaction of seeing it inaugurated in other schools throughout the state. Boys who volunteered were organized in squads of eight, with weak and strong youngsters carefully distributed through each group. Each squad elected its own leader. Competition was carried on within the schools and on a state-wide basis. A major activity was known as "wall-scaling." The boys were required to run fifteen yards to an eight and a half foot barrier and, carrying their rifles, get over it in the shortest possible time. So proficient did they become at this activity that in the second inter-city meet held in the spring of 1915 a squad from Casper, Wyoming, won in the amazing time of six and one-fifth seconds.

There was more than this, of course, to the program. The boys drilled, held target practice with rifles borrowed from the War Department, and spent two weeks in summer camp learning to read maps, signal, make and clean camp, and conduct other military activities. Scholarship was not neglected. Squads sought to attain the highest group ratings, and achievements were posted weekly on the bulletin boards. Nor was the social life forgotten. Each squad selected a girl sponsor from among their classmates and with her help staged dances and entertainments of various sorts. Probably the high spot of each year was the dress parade and exhibition held for the benefit of the townspeople.[26]

Steever's work won wide approval. Creel, whose enthusiasm was overwhelming, reported that by the end of 1915 every city of Wyoming had either established a cadet corps or was preparing to do so, and that inquiries were pouring in from all over the state.[27] In his article he quoted favorable comments from prominent groups and individuals. Attributed to the principals of Wyoming's schools was the remark: "Since the organization of the

26 Creel, "Wyoming's Answer to Militarism," *Everybody's Magazine*, vol. XXXIV (February, 1916), pp. 153–156.
27 *Ibid.*, p. 156.

cadet corps, truancy is no longer a problem, nor do our boys quit school for a premature entrance into industry. School life has been made interesting, and we have no trouble in keeping them for the complete course." The judges of the juvenile courts are reputed to have said: "We are the doctors, but Lieutenant Steever is the sanitarian. We prescribe, but he prevents. There used to be about eight per cent of delinquency among high school boys, but the self-discipline and self-restraint of the cadets have wiped it out." The warden of the state penitentiary claimed that "If Lieutenant Steever gets them, I don't." Major-General Leonard Wood was particularly pleased:

> Give these Steever cadets three months in a training-camp for the purpose of coordinating what they have learned, and familiarizing them with the work in the mass, and you will have as fine and effective a body of troops as ever took arms in defense of a country. The high school training gives the boys the sound physical base that is the first essential to any rational plan of national preparedness. It teaches the important lessons of abstinence and self-mastery, and forms the invaluable habits of discipline and cooperative effort. Above all, it grounds them in the fundamentals of military science and training, lifting them high above the raw volunteers who are the despair of officers in a crisis.[28]

Creel himself was in favor of universal military training. He proposed that every high school boy in the United States be required to prepare himself for the defense of his country. While in school, the boys would be trained under the "Wyoming System." Immediately upon graduation, they would spend three months in camp, as Major-General Wood had suggested. For the next two years, they would spend two weeks each summer in camp; and for each of the following three years, ten days in camp would be required. This program, as Creel pointed out, would provide continuous training from high school to the age of about twenty-five, and would insure a large body of trained reserves in time of war. It was to be compulsory, although Creel did not like that word. To require military training of all high school boys was really not compulsion, he insisted, "but merely *majority enforcement* of such action as *majority agreement* deems necessary

---

[28] *Ibid.*, pp. 156–158.

for the advance and protection of the nation, the state, the city, and the individual."[29] Not all Americans could agree that the issue of compulsion could be resolved so easily.

It was interesting that Creel, later to have charge of America's propaganda machine, should have been the first to arouse widespread concern over the idea of high school military training. His article appeared in the February, 1916, issue of *Everybody's Magazine*. Letters at once poured in to Howard Wheeler, the editor, from readers eager for more details. How, some asked, did one go about starting such a program in a school system? What help would the federal government give? Wheeler, already actively campaigning for universal military training,[30] decided to capitalize upon this widespread enthusiasm. Adopting the title of the High School Volunteers of the United States, he started at once to organize military training in the public schools of the nation.

The publicity campaign was formally launched in July with a letter of endorsement from the Secretary of the Interior, Franklin K. Lane.[31] Similar letters from Governor Charles S. Whitman of New York, and Newton D. Baker, Secretary of War, were given wide circulation.[32] A prominent lecturer, Edward Amherst Ott, was appointed chairman of a field organization; with fellow lecturers on the Chautauqua program he was soon spreading the news of the movement through the East and Middle West. By November he was able to report strong interest. Requests for information were reaching him from as far west as California, where the leaders of the Lyceum circuit were arranging their winter schedule.[33] Within six months the movement had become full-fledged. *Everybody's Magazine* had contributed space in its New York office as headquarters for the organization, the magazine had become the official organ, bronze buttons had been purchased and were being distributed to the members, and Steever had begun the preparation of a manual telling how to organize and carry on the work. The first chapter of this manual was finished and dis-

[29] *Ibid.*, p. 159.

[30] *Everybody's Magazine*, vol. XXXIV (February, 1916), pp. 147–149.

[31] *Ibid.*, vol. XXXV (October, 1916), p. 501.

[32] *Ibid.*, vol. XXXV (September, 1916), pp. 288–289.

[33] Edward Amherst Ott, "The Wyoming Idea in Full Swing," *Everybody's Magazine*, vol. XXXV (November, 1916), pp. 627–629.

tributed before November, 1916;[34] the entire bulletin was completed by the following May.[35]

As has been indicated, it was during these months that Congress authorized the War Department to detail officers and to issue equipment to those schools which wished to conduct military training.[36] The leaders of the H.S.V.U.S. were quick to point out that this aid by the federal government would relieve the schools of all expense, thus enabling many of the poorer districts to establish units of schoolboy soldiers.[37]

Up to this point, the army had done little more than to express verbally its desire to see military training carried on in every high school of the country. Now, in January, 1917, it took definite steps to implement its recommendations. Orders which would have sent Captain Steever[38] to the Philippines were countermanded,[39] and on the first of the year he was assigned to headquarters at Culver Military Academy in Indiana. From here, assisted by a staff of four commissioned officers and sixteen sergeants, he was to organize the "Wyoming System" in the schools of Chicago, Kansas City, St. Louis, "and such other centers as he could reach."[40]

Steever's first move was to call a conference of all educators and citizens interested in the work. On January 29, 1917, forty-eight delegates assembled at Culver. They came from twenty-three cities located in seven states, and proceeded to become charter members of an association pledged to work for the extension of the Steever program.[41] Plans were then drafted for the regimental organization of the cadet corps. These were carried out with such speed that a month later the First and Second Regiments of the H.S.V.U.S. were able to march in President Wilson's second in-

[34] Ibid.

[35] Ibid., vol. XXXVI (May, 1917), p. 620.

[36] See supra, p. 97.

[37] Everybody's Magazine, vol. XXXV (November, 1916), pp. 695–696.

[38] Formerly Lieutenant Steever.

[39] The editors of Everybody's Magazine claimed that they had "carried the first line of trenches" in securing this reversal of army orders. Vol. XXXVI (January, 1917), p. 113.

[40] Ibid., vol. XXXVII (August, 1917), p. 143.

[41] Ibid., vol. XXXVI (April, 1917), pp. 492–493, and (May, 1917), p. 620. This organization was known as "The Association of High Schools Giving Military Training."

augural parade.[42] Further progress was in evidence by the spring of 1917. At this time over 600 cadets from 112 towns and cities gathered at the First National Encampment of the H.S.V.U.S.[43] The movement was at this promising stage in its development when the United States declared war upon Germany.

3. The Effect of Our Entrance into the War upon Military Training in the High Schools

With our entrance into the war, a blow was struck at military training in the public schools. Officers could no longer be spared as instructors for the colleges, public, and private schools.[44] Even Captain Steever, busy in the summer of 1917 organizing the cadet work in the schools of Chicago, was abruptly ordered to report to Des Moines, Iowa, for other duties. The value of the "Wyoming System" for actual military purposes is perhaps reflected by the fact that the order for Steever's withdrawal came in the midst of "High School Volunteer Week," with several thousand boys assembled in Chicago for exhibition and drill.[45] Moreover, when Steever requested three additional weeks in Chicago for the purpose of training physical education teachers to carry on the work, the War Department was unwilling to grant him the necessary time. Only insistent efforts by the leaders of the H.S.V.U.S., including a special trip to Washington, induced the army to grant a few days' stay in order that Steever might provide for the continuation of his work. The reluctance with which the army consented to this delay is revealed in a report by the editors of *Everybody's Magazine:*

But when all the facts of the H.S.V.U.S. idea, the working out of it, and the results that had been obtained since January 1st, 1917, were laid before the authorities at Washington, and when it was demonstrated that the influence of H.S.V.U.S. training has made for better habits, higher ideals, truer patriotism, and more earnest purpose among the boys in the schools where it has been tried, the War Department late in July gave its approval . . .[46]

[42] *Ibid.*, vol. XXXVI (June, 1917), p. 719.

[43] *Ibid.*, vol. XXXVII (July, 1917), p. 126. The Encampment lasted two weeks. Ten states were represented.

[44] "Report of the Adjutant-General," *Annual Report of the War Department* (1917), vol. I, p. 168.

[45] *Everybody's Magazine*, vol. XXXVII (August, 1917), p. 142.

[46] *Ibid.*, vol. XXXVII (September, 1917), p. 334.

Such was the attitude of the military leaders in the summer of 1917. Active support ended. Although the services of retired officers enabled the War Department to continue the R.O.T.C. program in the colleges,[47] the Junior Division, in 1917 still largely on paper, was almost forgotten.

This is not to say that military training in the public schools of the country ended. Actually, it continued to expand during the war years. The mail reaching the headquarters of the H.S.V.U.S. "swelled enormously" in the summer of 1917 as realization dawned upon local schoolboards that it was now up to them to carry on the work.[48] But the active support of the War Department was for all practical purposes at an end, and the movement which in the early months of 1917 had held the promise of becoming a nation-wide program under federal auspices now depended upon private organizations for its very existence.

These local groups resorted to various expedients to overcome opposition and place military training in the public schools. In Cleveland, Ohio, for example, the Board of Education virtually railroaded a cadet corps into the city school system. On March 12, 1917, they adopted a resolution to introduce drill into the schools. Copies of this resolution were sent to leading educators throughout the country, with a plea for similar action in other cities.[49] A series of meetings was then held to explain to the citizens of Cleveland why such action had been taken. The public was warned, however, that " 'There must be no debate or questions at any meeting.' " In spite of strenuous protests,[50] the cadet corps was established with almost ninety per cent of the 5,000 high school boys enrolling voluntarily.[51] Encouraged by this generous support from the boys, the following winter the Board of Education took the further step of making the drill compulsory.[52] This forceful action by the Cleveland educational authorities is better

[47] "Report of the Adjutant-General," op. cit., pp. 168–169.
[48] Everybody's Magazine, vol. XXXVII (October, 1917), p. 479.
[49] "Public Schools and the National Crisis," The Survey, vol. XXXVII (March 24, 1917), p. 723.
[50] "Protest by Cleveland Settlement," The Survey, vol. XXXVIII (April 7, 1917), p. 24.
[51] Everybody's Magazine, vol. XXXVI (May, 1917), p. 620.
[52] When Schoolboards Run Amuck. Opinion No. 396 of Attorney General John G. Price of Ohio. . . . (Pamphlet, Washington, D. C.: Reprinted by American Union Against Militarism, no date), p. 11.

understood when it is remembered that the President of the Board, Edward Bushnell, was an active leader in the H.S.V.U.S.[53]

The influence of private individuals was sometimes exerted with greater subtlety. Birmingham, Alabama, probably offers a more typical illustration of how military drill was incorporated into many school systems. In this city, the movement was started by E. G. Evans, a soldier who had been discharged from the army for physical disability. Reading in *Everybody's Magazine* of Steever's work in Wyoming, he decided to organize the school-boys of Birmingham. When the superintendent of schools refused to have anything to do with the proposal, and when vigorous opposition developed in civic groups, Evans announced that the cadet corps would have no connection with the public educational system. His first call for volunteers drew almost one hundred boys within twenty-four hours; by the end of a month over half of the boys in the city were enrolled and in uniform. Rifles of ancient vintage were procured and sections of the barrels were sawed off to make them lighter. A public parade and exhibition were staged to demonstrate the effectiveness of the training. Opposition appears to have melted away. The Board of Education passed resolutions endorsing military drill and offering credit for the work, a parade ground was donated by the city, and drill was officially started in every high school in Birmingham.[54] Publicity had accomplished as much as Cleveland's dictatorial tactics.

This nation-wide campaign was rewarded with increasing success. A few states actually adopted legislation which, in one way or another, encouraged military training, although only one state, New York, made such work compulsory for all boys between the ages of sixteen and nineteen. Cities in practically every state of the Union provided either obligatory or elective courses in military education for high school boys.[55] Before the war ended, over 112,000 students in 1,267 of the nation's secondary schools were enrolled in cadet units.[56] Over one third of these

[53] *Everybody's Magazine*, vol. XXXVI (May, 1917), p. 619.
[54] *Ibid.*, vol. XXXIX (August, 1918), p. 104.
[55] Ping Ling, "Military Training in the Public Schools." *The Pedagogical Seminary*, vol. XXV (September, 1918), pp. 252–254. Arizona, Indiana, Louisiana, Michigan, New Hampshire, Oklahoma, and Oregon had such legislation. New York stood alone in the rigor of its law.
[56] *Biennial Survey, 1916–1918* (Bureau of Education Bulletin, 1919, No. 88), p. 127.

were members of the H.S.V.U.S.;[57] the remainder were organized as independent cadet corps of the sort familiar to Bostonians for over half a century.

The resolution adopted by the school authorities of Pueblo City, Colorado, may be considered as typical of the provisions made by those cities which established military training as part of the regular educational work:

Resolved that Central High School maintain a prescribed course of military training extending through two years of the high school course. Such training to be open to all boys as a voluntary and elective study, provided that when elected, the study shall be continued for at least one year and shall not be dropped in that time except by permission of the school management for adequate reasons.

The high school will give credit for military training to the extent of one unit of the total requirements for graduation, one half unit per year, provided, further, that such credit shall be given on condition that the course in military training consist of not fewer than two hours a week for not fewer than thirty weeks of a school year and the conduct of a camp for not less than two weeks each school year.

The actual teaching of the military training shall be done by a regular teacher in the school. When possible, the teacher shall be the teacher of physical education. This work shall be done, when such arrangements are feasible, under the direction and supervision of an officer of the regular army detailed for that purpose. The teacher shall make such preparation for this work as may be directed by the Board of Education.[58]

Military drill units were confined almost entirely to the larger city systems. Since more than half the youth of the nation lived in rural areas, this situation was disturbing to those who were in favor of military training for all school children. Various attempts were made to organize the boys and girls who lived on the farms and in the villages of the country. In the Northwest, for example, an organization known as the Farm Boy Cavaliers of America was started by Professor D. D. Mayne of the University of Minnesota. By 1918, "troops" had been formed in half a dozen of the Western states, and the movement was spreading. The organization was modeled on the medieval Chivalric Order, with the boys classed as Knights, Squires, and Pages. The girls, known

[57] *Everybody's Magazine*, vol. XXXVIII (May, 1918), p. 72.
[58] Ping Ling, *loc. cit.*, pp. 254–255.

as Home Cavaliers, were termed Novices, Damoiselles, and Ladies. Each Cavalier was expected to utilize a plot of ground on his father's farm to raise hogs, poultry, sheep, cattle, horses, and crops. But although these boys were formed into "troops," the element of military training was practically nonexistent, and schoolboy soldiers continued to be largely a product of the cities.[59]

As the months passed, the exercises performed by the cadet organizations began to take on a much more martial character. The Chicago high schools proposed to prepare the girls as Red Cross nurses and first aid workers, the actual instruction to be given by the women teachers.[60] To aid in the boys' program, orders were placed with the Rock Island Arsenal for 3,000 army rifles with bayonets and scabbards, 200 gallery practice rifles, 240 sabers and belts, 3,000 "pup" tents, and enough haversacks, canteens, cups, knives, forks, and spoons to outfit 3,000 cadets.[61] All this took place before we entered the war. A year and a half later, Chicago reported as successfully accomplished the following activities:

1. Prepared a thorough, practical course, on the competitive plan, in bomb and grenade throwing, using Mill's bombs, and grenades, like those that fly from trench to trench in France—but dummies—made by the boys themselves in the school foundries and manual training rooms. . . .
2. Organized a course in semaphore signaling. . . .
3. Five hundred boys are studying telegraphy in high school, and a special course of H.S.V.U.S. training has been organized for these boys.
4. Wall-scaling competitions were held in February and competitions in the war game will be held soon. . . .
5. Preparations are being made for the National H.S.V.U.S. week in Chicago on a truly war scale. . . .
6. The volunteers were mobilized to help the Chicago Post Office when it was swamped by the Christmas avalanche. . . .[62]

This emphasis on the purely military aspects of the training went much further than the sponsors of the H.S.V.U.S. desired. As early as the fall of 1917, the editor of *Everybody's Magazine* expressed concern over the situation. "Our answer to militarism," he warned, "would be drowned in the clash of hundreds of thousands

59 *Everybody's Magazine*, vol. XXXVIII (February, 1918), p. 88.
60 *School and Society*, vol. V (January 20, 1917), p. 75.
61 *Army and Navy Journal*, vol. LIV (February 3, 1917), p. 717.
62 *Everybody's Magazine*, vol. XXXVIII (April, 1918), p. 93.

of bayonets, unless the spirit, the idea, behind every touch, every word we send out to the youth of the land is for Good Citizenship —better citizenship and all that it means in the burning light of these days. This is the Greater Task."[63] A year later, just before the war ended, he wrote with even more discouragement: "The larger results we have aimed at have not been achieved. *There is little understanding among the high schools of the place of military training in their work, of the possibilities of it, and of the necessity of uniformity in it, and of the real need of a national organization of the schools.* The work in most of the schools is dealt with largely from the military point of view, and little attempt is made to coordinate it with the rest of the educational scheme. Then, too, the spirit of localism exists everywhere, and the schools are not inclined to take the national viewpoint in this work."[64] Despite efforts to redirect the training into channels of greater educational value, the editor of the sponsoring magazine was unable to change the situation, and in 1919 he abandoned his leadership of the H.S.V.U.S.[65] Mill's bombs and grenade-throwing were apparently more than many of the earlier supporters of the movement had bargained for when they urged that every schoolboy be given military training as preparation for citizenship.

Throughout 1918, however, the cadet corps prospered, and the army, which in the summer of 1917 had withdrawn its support, now showed a renewed interest in the educational system. To coordinate military needs with educational activities, the Committee on Education and Special Training was set up by the War Department. A Civilian Advisory Board was appointed to assist the army officers in this work.[66] Attention was at first confined to the colleges and to the vocational training of drafted men, and for several months little thought appears to have been given to the problems of the secondary schools. This situation was rectified in the summer of 1918 with the creation of a Secondary School Division within the Committee on Education and Special Training.

[63] *Everybody's Magazine,* vol. XXXVII-B (November, 1917), p. 110.
[64] *Ibid.,* vol. XXXIX (October, 1918), p. 103.
[65] *Ibid.,* vol. XLI (September, 1919), p. 113.
[66] *Committee on Education and Special Training. A Review of Its Work During 1918* (By The Advisory Board, War Department, 1919), Part I, pp. 11–12.

Major Meras, Chairman of this new division, saw at once that "the demand for military training in secondary schools is not being met." Consequently, during the last three months of the war he spent much time in considering measures which would enable the public schools to cooperate more effectively with the military machine. Efforts were made to increase the equipment available for cadet training, and some 25,000 rifles were released by the War Department for this purpose.[67] The lack of army personnel to serve as instructors in the schoolboy organizations was met by two expedients: arrangements were made for the admission of Canadian officers to the United States to serve in this capacity,[68] and a number of public schools were instructed to apply to the nearest college for the part-time detail of officers from the Student Army Training Corps.[69] A further step was taken when A. B. Meredith, Assistant Superintendent of the Schools of New Jersey, was appointed to the committee as an expert consultant on secondary schools. It had been increasingly evident that neither the army officers on the Secondary School Division nor the civilian members of the Advisory Board, most of whom were college men, were competent to plan public school policies. It was hoped that Meredith's appointment would solve the problem.[70]

But nothing reveals more clearly the importance which the public schools were beginning to assume in the minds of the military leaders than a recommendation by the Committee on Education and Special Training that secondary school teachers whose work was considered essential be given exemption from the draft.[71] Immediately upon the adoption of this new policy by the War Department, the Commissioner of Education sent a letter to all principals and superintendents offering them advice as to why and when teachers should be deferred.[72]

[67] "Minutes of the Joint Meeting of the Committee and Advisory Board," September 18, 1918. Committee on Education and Special Training. MSS., World War Division, War Department Records.

[68] *Ibid.*, Minutes for October 9, 1918.

[69] *Ibid.*, Minutes for November 13, 1918.

[70] *Ibid.*, Minutes for November 6, 1918.

[71] *Ibid.*, Minutes for September 25, 1918; *infra*, pp. 212–214. For a statement of the War Department's policy, see *School and Society*, vol. VIII (October 21, 1918), p. 468. For the action taken by one large city, New York, see *School and Society*, vol. VIII (September 28, 1918), p. 376.

[72] *School and Society*, vol. VIII (October 26, 1918), pp. 492–493.

That army officials were contemplating much more extensive use of the public schools is indicated by several additional recommendations by Major Meras. Acting upon his suggestion, the War Department in the fall of 1918 admitted boys from Honor Military Academies[73] to the Officers Training Camps.[74] The recommendation that high school boys be permitted to enter the Students Army Training Corps, and that special "cramming courses" be provided to expedite this process,[75] was still under consideration by the military authorities when the war ended. Finally, the renewed interest of the army in the military training of schoolboys was revealed in measures being taken to organize the Junior Reserve Officers Training Corps as authorized by the National Defense Act of 1916.[76]

After the Armistice, the Commission on Education and Special Training turned its attention to the R.O.T.C. work, and during the winter of 1918–1919 vigorous efforts were made to establish training units in the schools and colleges. Once again the War Department displayed enthusiasm over the idea of training schoolboys. "It cannot be said," the report of the Committee stated, "that a system which enabled large numbers of boys to acquire military training before they reached eighteen would not make an important contribution to the military preparedness of the country." Moreover, the report went on, there can be "no more effective way of arousing popular interest and support for the country's military needs than by enabling boys of the less privileged classes (to enroll) in the national training corps."[77] So a cycle was completed, and the army had reverted to its policy of 1916. Popular enthusiasm for martial problems had subsided, and the military leaders were forced to plead with the public to maintain what they believed to be an adequate army. The American schools offered excellent avenues of approach to the public.

The postwar efforts of the War Department were only partially

[73] "Honor Schools" were institutions which had been inspected by the army and had been given high ratings for their military training programs.

[74] "Minutes of the Joint Meeting of the Committee and Advisory Board," September 25 and October 2, 1918, *op. cit.*

[75] *Ibid.*, Minutes for September 25, 1918.

[76] "Annual Report of the Chairman of the Committee on Education and Special Training to the Chief of Staff," July 9, 1919. MSS., World War Division, War Department Records, pp. 27–35.

[77] *Ibid.*, p. 33.

successful. A wave of apathy to all things of a military nature swept the country during the 1920's and 1930's, with violent opposition developing in certain quarters. Only during the last six or seven years of the 1930's did the Junior R.O.T.C. make any really substantial gains.[78]

4. Arguments for and against Military Training in the Public Schools

As we have seen, military training was not brought into the public schools without strong opposition. When the movement began to exhibit signs of real vitality during the years 1916 and 1917, scores of articles in advocacy or opposition swelled the volume of periodical literature. A certain amount of the opposition was hushed when we entered the war. Professor William H. Kilpatrick, for example, who in the previous months had lectured extensively against such training on the grounds that it had little educational value and was actually harmful, abruptly terminated his lecture engagements when we took up the sword.[79] Other critics continued to protest.

The decline in outspoken opposition was to some extent offset by the fact that a number of the most ardent prewar proponents of schoolboy training now transferred their attention to more pressing issues. George Creel, who in 1916 had fired one of the most telling shots in behalf of the "Wyoming System" of military training in the public schools,[80] went out for much bigger game in the spring of 1917. Nothing short of universal obligatory military service would satisfy him.[81] This also appears to have been

[78] On December 29, 1919, the War Department announced the establishment of 50 high school units of the R.O.T.C. By September 30, 1934, there were 61, an increase of only 11 in 15 years. By 1937, three years later, there were 90 Junior units, a gain of 29 in three years. "War Department Bulletin No. 43." MSS. World War Division, War Department Records; *Military Training in High Schools of the United States. R.O.T.C.* (2nd edition, Civilian Military Education Fund, 1938), pp. 5, 13–15. For an interesting debate on the War Department's responsibility for this unusual growth in recent years, see "Mr. Bishop Versus Mr. Johnson. A Lively Exchange Concerning Our April Article: 'The R.O.T.C. Knocks at the High-School Door,'" *The Clearing House*, vol. XII (January, 1938), pp. 281–283.

[79] Interview with W. H. Kilpatrick, New York, April 9, 1941.

[80] See *supra*, p. 98.

[81] "Four Million Citizen Defenders. What Universal Military Training Means in Dollars, Duty, and Defense," *Everybody's Magazine*, vol. XXXVI (May, 1917), pp. 545–554.

the position of many of the army officials. The War Department's recommendations of 1916 calling for military drill in every high school were not repeated in the following two years. Instead, the country was urged to adopt compulsory training in time of peace as well as in time of war.[82] This attitude was reflected in the military journals.[83] The files for the war years contain hardly a reference to the military training of schoolboys, but there is repeated emphasis on the need for obligatory service. Pointing out that the Selective Service Act was only a "makeshift," the *Infantry Journal* requested legislation that would require all boys to undergo a thorough course of training as soon as they reached the age of twenty-one.[84] This attitude is not, of course, difficult to understand. With a full-scale war on their hands, military leaders could not be expected to exhibit much enthusiasm for the military training of adolescents.

The principal arguments advanced for the introduction of military training into high schools stressed its physical, disciplinary, and civic values. In addition, it was sometimes claimed that such training would develop manly habits and good manners, inculcate a respect for labor and a love of country, and even reduce crime. It was, in the words of Newton D. Baker, "the best investment in citizenship" the country could make.[85] Young Franklin Delano Roosevelt, Assistant Secretary of the Navy, wanted his boys to have such training.[86] Typical were the views of one prominent educator and psychologist, President G. Stanley Hall of Clark University: "We must admit," he wrote, "that all these [cadet organizations,

[82] "Report of the Chief of Staff," *Annual Report of the War Department* (1917), vol. I, p. 139.

[83] See the *Infantry Journal:* Editorial, "Universal Military Service and Training," vol. XIII, Part 2 (April, 1917), pp. 669–670; S. B. M. Young, "Universal Military Training," vol. XIV (November, 1917), pp. 322–324; Theodore Roosevelt, "Universal Military Training," vol. XIV (January, 1918), pp. 542–543; H. H. Sheets, "Universal Military Training Legislation Imperative Before Demobilization," vol. XV (January, 1919), pp. 537–540. See also the *Army and Navy Journal:* vol. LIV (May 12, 1917), p. 1184; vol. LVI (November 30, 1918), p. 456.

[84] Editorial, "Looking Ahead—A Military Policy Needed." *Infantry Journal,* vol. XIV (September, 1917), pp. 222–223.

[85] Joseph H. Odell, *The New Spirit of the New Army. A Message to the "Service Flag" Homes. With an Introduction by Newton D. Baker* (New York: Fleming H. Revell Company, 1918), p. 8.

[86] Franklin D. Roosevelt, " 'On Your Own Heads,' " *Scribner's Magazine,* vol. LXI (April, 1917), pp. 413–416; John T. Flynn, *Country Squire in the White House* (New York: Doubleday, Doran and Company, Inc., 1940), pp. 100–101.

the Boy Scouts, and physical education programs] lack something of the spirit of rigid discipline, subordination and splendid *esprit de corps* which actual soldiering gives and which heaven knows our callow, shambling American adolescents need, especially now when so many fathers are called away, so that boys are growing wild and slightly criminal, for want of a touch of the real military spirit which has a unique power that physical culture never can attain to make men out of hobble-de-hoys."[87]

Although those who favored military training in the public schools did have strong support, the fact remains that only during the years filled with the war spirit were they able to make much headway. This in itself is a valid reason for believing that they were far outnumbered by their opponents.[88] The general viewpoint of the opponents of the program may be summarized in the words of one educator. "I am opposed," he wrote, ". . . because it is a snare as a method of attaining preparedness for national defense, and a delusion as a means of common school education. . . . *In the name of Jehovah and the little red schoolhouse on the hill, keep your hands off the American boy until he is at least nineteen years of age!*"[89]

The value of the program as physical training was vehemently denied by the physical education directors.[90] Although it is obvious that this group had a bias in favor of their own physical education work, the truth is that they were supported by a number of the country's leading educators. In the winter of 1916–1917, a committee was formed to promote in the legislature of every state a measure officially entitled "a bill to uphold national vitality through the establishment of physical education and training in the public schools of the state." These were the words of Dr. Dudley A. Sargent, head of the physical education work at Harvard University. This committee, headed by the name of John Dewey, conducted a vigorous campaign.[91] The American

[87] "Some Educational Values of War," *Pedagogical Seminary*, vol. XXV (September, 1918), pp. 305–306.

[88] Winthrop D. Lane, "Teaching and Military Training," *The Survey*, vol. XXXVI (July 15, 1916), p. 418.

[89] Edward B. Degroot, "Physical Education Versus Military Training in Secondary Schools," *American Physical Education Review*, vol. XXII (May, 1917), pp. 302–304.

[90] See the files of their journal, the *American Physical Education Review*.

[91] See *infra*, p. 121; *School and Society*, vol. V (February 18, 1917), p. 170.

Physical Education Association placed itself on record as opposed to all military training of schoolboys. It did admit that the "Wyoming Plan," the Boy Scouts, the Camp Fire organizations, and other youth movements were beneficial "insofar as they emphasize athletic and group games, physical training and outdoor activities." On the other hand, the Association stated that "we strongly disapprove of the military aspect as represented by the manual of arms and the cadet uniforms."[92] Herman J. Koehler, Master of the Sword at West Point, as early as 1896 had protested against military drill for young boys. "The use of the musket," he wrote, "as a means of physical development for anyone, be he man or boy, is worse than worthless. It is, in my opinion, positively injurious."[93] Later, in a manual prepared by Koehler and fellow-officers and adopted for use by the army, competitive games and calisthenics were emphasized, with the manual of arms given a subordinate place.[94] Sargent claimed that military drill was responsible for "the physical peculiarities, deficiencies, and deformities which existed in a large number of boys coming to Cambridge from the public schools of Boston."[95]

Not all army men agreed that military training had physical values for high school boys. Captain Walter L. Bouve, testifying before the Massachusetts' Military Commission in 1915, stated that the schoolboys became so disgusted with the monotony of the drill exercises that they later refrained from joining the militia. He urged that no military work be carried on in the public schools, but that one month in summer camp be required of the boys.[96] Colonel L. W. V. Kennon, writing in the *Infantry Journal,* claimed that military training in the schools was superficial and failed to reach more than a small number of America's youth. He preferred a six-month period of training after the boys had reached the age of eighteen. But, since the army did not need so

[92] *American Physical Education Review,* vol. XXI (October, 1916), pp. 429–432.
[93] N.E.A., *Proceedings,* 1917, p. 787.
[94] *Extracts from Manual of Physical Training. As Issued by the War Department for Use in the United States Army. . . . Adapted from the regulations in force in the New Armies* (latest edition, New York: National Military Publishing Company, 1917).
[95] *The Reference Shelf* (New York: H. W. Wilson Co., 1926), vol. IV, No. 3, p. 158.
[96] Editorial, "Military Training vs. Physical Education in Schools and Colleges," *American Physical Education Review,* vol. XX (November 20, 1915), p. 535.

many reserves, Colonel Kennon suggested that those drafted should be chosen by lot.[97] Other examples might be cited to show that not all army men shared the War Department's enthusiasm for military training in the high schools.

To many educators, the alleged disciplinary and civic virtues of military training were ridiculous. President David Starr Jordan of Leland Stanford University was one of these. Militarism, he wrote, "is blind, ignorant, insistent, and contemptuous of the values of human freedom." He had no sympathy with the viewpoint attributed to General Thomas O'Ryan, in 1916 a member of the Military Training Commission of New York State. "We must get our men so that they are machines," O'Ryan is reputed to have said, "and this can be done only as a process of training. We have to have our men trained so that the influence of fear is overpowered by the peril of an uncompromising military system, often backed up by a pistol in the hands of an officer. . . . The recruits have got to put their heads into the military noose." President Jordan insisted that "only that training which develops individual initiative is worthy of the name of discipline. Collective discipline impairs individuality. The good citizen of America is not a chattel sheltered by a state he does not control."[98]

That many of the advantages claimed for military training were largely illusory was the opinion of other influential groups in the country. Commissions appointed by the legislatures of both Massachusetts and New Jersey to investigate the value of such training turned in adverse reports.[99] The labor unions were antagonistic.[100] The National Grange revealed its disapproval.[101] The American Union Against Militarism conducted a strenuous campaign to prevent militarism from sweeping the country and to keep military drill out of the public schools.[102] The Department of Superintend-

---

[97] *Infantry Journal*, vol. XIII, Part 2 (January, 1917), pp. 385–386.

[98] David Starr Jordan, "Military Training in American High Schools," *The Reference Shelf*, vol. IV, No. 3, p. 150.

[99] *Report of the Special Commission on Military Education and Reserve* (Boston: Wright and Potter Printing Co., 1915); *Report of the Commission on Military Training and Instruction in High Schools. To the Legislature, Session of 1917* (Trenton: MacCrellish and Quigley Co., 1917).

[100] Gignilliat, *Arms and the Boy*, p. 138.

[101] "Swinging Around the Circle Against Militarism." *The Survey*, vol. XXXVI (April 22, 1916), p. 96.

[102] *Ibid.*, pp. 95–96; and vol. XXXV (January 1, 1916), p. 370.

ence of the National Education Association accepted with almost complete unanimity a resolution presented by its Committee on Military Training in the Public Schools; this resolution called for physical education but emphatically rejected military drill.[103] The Bureau of Education, in response to numerous requests, published a study of military training in foreign countries, and reported that it was not generally regarded as a successful substitute for physical education.[104] The National League of Teachers Associations, claiming to represent 20,000 teachers, took a firm stand against universal military training.[105] John Wanamaker, who for many years had conducted a drill organization made up of employees of his store in Philadelphia, objected to military training in the Philadelphia schools on the grounds it was an expensive and useless fad.[106] Ernest Thompson Seton, pioneer in the Boy Scout movement, resigned as Chief Scout because he felt that the organization's original interest in "trees, flowers, and woodcraft has given place to military drill and thus has robbed it of its ideals."[107]

Since military training failed to gain headway in the public schools before 1914, and immediately declined after the war, it would seem reasonable to conclude that the opposition was firmly established, and that only the popular alarm during the years from 1914 to 1918 permitted the advocates to advance their program. The fact that the number of schoolboy soldiers began to increase with the outbreak of war in Europe, and rose sharply when we entered the conflict, would appear to support this conclusion.

[103] N.E.A., *Proceedings*, 1917, pp. 778–790.

[104] W. S. Jesien, "Military Training of Youths of School Age in Foreign Countries" (Bureau of Education Bulletin, 1917, No. 25), p. 481.

[105] "Universal Military Training," *The Survey*, vol. XL (July 27, 1917), p. 481.

[106] "Merchant Prince Opposes Military Training in High Schools" (Pamphlet. Reprint of an article in the Philadelphia *Public Ledger*, June 12, 1918, in the files of the Committee on Militarism in Education, Jane Addams Peace Collection, Friends Historical Library, Swarthmore College).

[107] "Again the Boy Scouts and Militarism," *The Survey*, vol. XXXV (December 25, 1915), p. 342.

CHAPTER V

HEALTH AND WELFARE

To those who think at all, health is the most important subject in the curriculum.

—*Willis A. Sutton, Superintendent of Atlanta Schools, 1929*[1]

It is no longer merely the voice of the philanthropists crying in the wilderness the doctrine of the individual's right to abundance of life; it is the Nation in its hour of crisis demanding the fullest physical capacity of all its men, women, and children. The truth is pounded home with every succeeding engagement on land and sea that the conservation of human life is now a part of practical affairs, something to receive its place in the everyday consideration of those responsible for national progress. In war's terrible markets human life is the basic legal tender. Money, munitions, ships, and all the other essentials for the prosecution of war are but promissory notes.

—*P. P. Claxton, Commissioner of Education, 1918*[2]

1. Physical Training

One result of the demand for military training in the public schools was a quickened appreciation of the value of physical training.[3] That the nation needed youths who were sound in body, all agreed; differences of opinion arose only over the methods which would most surely provide physically fit young men and women. In the years from 1914 to 1917, much energy was expended in a discussion of the relative merits of military versus physical training. It was clear that the debaters themselves frequently confused the two types of training. The most ardent exponents of military training often claimed for it values which were in reality derived only from the physical training activities incorporated into the military work.[4]

[1] N.E.A., *Proceedings*, 1929, p. 547.

[2] *Annual Report of the Commissioner of Education* (1918), p. 33.

[3] Thomas A. Storey and Willard S. Small, *Recent State Legislation for Physical Training* (Bureau of Education Bulletin, 1918, No. 40), p. 5.

[4] *Mind and Body*, vol. XXV (February, 1919), p. 435.

This confusion was natural, for much of the interest in both military training and physical education sprang from the same source, namely, a demand for preparedness. Numerous illustrations, drawn from a past as remote as that of ancient Sparta's, could be offered in support of the writer who claimed that "When warlike and marauding nations preyed upon others, physical education was used for military purposes."[5] One educator defined the problem quite clearly when in 1916 he remarked: "Just now our country is trying to get back to an ancient principle—namely, that one of the elements of education means training the youth of the land for national defense. The idea started two thousand years ago and is what true physical education means in the last analysis." He then proposed a system of physical training that delayed military exercises until the boys were over eighteen years of age.[6] Another school of thought was represented by that educator who, while admitting "a recognized national need for physical fitness," urged that "the preferable means" for securing it was through athletics. It is significant that he included in his program such exercises as hand-grenade throwing for high school boys.[7] Meanwhile, the man in the street saw only the necessity for preparedness; how he got it was, in many cases, a matter of little concern.

More immediately effective in arousing popular enthusiasm for physical education were the revelations of the army medical examinations given to the drafted men. During the three years prior to our entrance into the war, the United States Army had been able to accept only twenty-four per cent of the 400,000 men applying for enlistment at the recruiting stations,[8] yet these facts apparently did not excite any widespread comment from the public. When, however, 2,753,922 men between the ages of twenty-one and thirty-one were examined in the first draft, the nation was shocked to discover that almost fifty per cent[9] had physical

[5] Jesse Feiring Williams, *A Text-Book of Physical Education* (Philadelphia: W. B. Saunders Co., 1931), p. 35.

[6] Randall Warden, "Physical Training Versus Military Training," N.E.A., *Proceedings*, 1916, p. 686.

[7] Edward P. Gilchrist, "Socialized Athletics," *School and Society*, vol. VII (May 18, 1918), pp. 598–599.

[8] F. L. Kleeberger, "Athletics and the War Game," *School and Society*, vol. VII (May 11, 1918), p. 541.

[9] 46.82 per cent.

defects. More than half of these defects[10] were so serious as to cause rejection by the army. To make it worse, many of the men who were accepted had to be assigned to special "developmental battalions" before they could be classified as first-line soldiers. The public alarm was not surprising in view of the fact that one out of every three men finally called into the armed forces had some physical defect.[11]

Figures of this sort became powerful weapons in the hands of those who advocated physical training. That probably thirty to forty per cent of the men turned down by the military authorities had remediable defects, which could have been corrected in childhood, was a strong argument for greater attention to the health of school children. With such data it was easy to claim that the 5,000,000 boys of high school age should be given adequate physical training, that at the very minimum the 750,000 boys actually enrolled in secondary schools should be given every opportunity to develop into those physically fit leaders which the nation so desperately needed. After all, it was emphasized, these boys were a national asset, and physical education was nothing more than a necessary measure of preparedness.[12] President Sisson of Montana State University stated before a group of educators that for the "vast majority" of pupils, physical education did not exist. "We teachers are living in a fool's paradise," he warned, "if we think such a condition is going to be tolerated much longer. The fiery crucible of the war era is trying all things, and will choose and reject ruthlessly."[13] Such arguments, used with telling effect during the war years, soon bore fruit.

English school men had taken advantage of a similar interest in the problem of health to incorporate into their educational law a number of comprehensive and far-reaching measures; the same procedure was followed in this country.[14] Before 1915, only three

10 24.96 per cent of the total number examined.

11 Ellwood P. Cubberley, *Public Education in the United States* (Boston: Houghton Mifflin Company, 1934), pp. 615–616.

12 W. S. Small, "Physical Education in the High Schools in the Present Emergency," N.E.A., *Proceedings*, 1918, p. 181; A. C. Strange, "Preparedness Through Physical Education," N.E.A., *Proceedings*, 1917, pp. 525–528.

13 N.E.A., *Proceedings*, 1917, p. 282.

14 Storey and Small, *Recent State Legislation for Physical Education* (Bureau of Education Bulletin, 1918, No. 40), p. 5.

states[15] had enacted laws calling for some form of physical training; during the war years, eight additional states by legislative enactment adopted a system of compulsory physical education for the school children.[16] Nor was this the complete picture, for when the war ended six other states were considering laws of a similar nature.[17]

The initial impulse, in most instances, had been an interest in military training which took the form of bills requiring such drill of high school boys. Investigation and deliberation convinced the legislators that military training was of less value than a sound system of physical education, even for military preparation, and bills calling for physical training were therefore introduced. New Jersey made the inclusion of military drill optional with the local school districts;[18] New York actually changed from a system of military training to a broader program of physical education.[19]

These new physical education laws called for far more than the mere substitution of calisthenics for military drill. The New York statute called for " (1) individual health examination and personal health instruction (medical inspection); (2) instruction concerning the care of the body and concerning the important facts of hygiene (recitations in hygiene); and (3) physical exercise as a health habit, including gymnastics, elementary marching and organized supervised play, recreation, and athletics."[20] New Jersey's law was even more comprehensive:

Such a course shall be adapted to the ages and capabilities of the pupils in the several grades and departments and shall include exercises, calisthenics, formation drills, instruction in personal and com-

[15] North Dakota (1898), Ohio (1904), and Idaho (1913); T. A. Storey, W. S. Small, and E. G. Salisbury. *Recent State Legislation for Physical Education* (Bureau of Education Bulletin, 1922, No. 1), p. 5.

[16] Illinois (1915), New York (1916), New Jersey (1917), Nevada (1917), Rhode Island (1917), California (1917), Maryland (1918), and Delaware (1918). Nevada's law made physical training compulsory for only high school students. Storey and Small (Bureau of Education Bulletin, 1918, No. 40), *op. cit.*, pp. 5–7.

[17] *Ibid.* These states were Massachusetts, Connecticut, Ohio, Nebraska, Pennsylvania, and Colorado.

[18] *Report of the Commission on Military Training and Instruction in High Schools. To the Legislature, Session of 1917.*

[19] *New York's Sober Second Thought. Being the 1919 Report of the New York State Reconstruction Commission on Military Training under the Welsh-Slater Acts of 1916* (Reprinted in full by the American Union Against Militarism. Washington: no date), 15 pp.

[20] Storey and Small (Bureau of Education Bulletin, 1918, No. 40), p. 9.

munity health and safety and in correcting and preventing bodily deficiency, and such other features and details as may aid in carrying out these purposes, together with instruction as to the privileges and responsibilities of citizenship, as they relate to community and national welfare, with special reference to developing bodily strength and vigor and producing the highest type of patriotic citizenship, and in addition, for female pupils, instruction in domestic hygiene, first aid, and nursing. To further promote the aims of this course any additional requirements or regulations as to medical inspection of school children may be imposed.[21]

These two states, together with California, in 1916 and 1917 enacted laws which were the broadest in purpose and the most definite in character of all such laws adopted during the war period. Their programs came closest to meeting the principles suggested as desirable by the authorities in the Bureau of Education. These federal officials reminded all who were interested that "the object of a State law for physical education is to secure the development of the potential physical capacity of the boys and girls of the State; to make them physically, morally, and socially fit for the duties of citizenship and the joy of wholesome living." The Bureau added a warning to the effect that too much must not be expected of the public educational system, since it was only one of the many agencies concerned with the development of healthy citizens.[22]

It was gratifying to find eight states during the years from 1915 to 1918 taking such definite steps for the physical development of their youth; nevertheless, the advocates of physical education did not rest on their laurels. Early in 1917 a group of prominent educators formed The Committee for Promoting Physical Education in the Public Schools of the United States, opened headquarters in Washington, and began to press for the adoption by the various states of a "model" bill, drafted by Dr. Dudley A. Sargent of Harvard.[23] New organizations began to appear; the Boston Society for Physical Education, for example, was organized in the late fall of 1918.[24] A conference of school men, meeting in Philadelphia in May, 1918, adopted resolutions calling for a

21 *Ibid.*, p. 9.
22 *Ibid.*, p. 15.
23 *American Physical Education Review*, vol. XXII (February, 1917), p. 113.
24 *Ibid.*, vol. XXIII (December, 1918), p. 557.

complete system of physical education for the state of Pennsylvania.[25] The American Physical Education Association chose for the topic of its annual convention "Physical Education and the War."[26] The National Security League issued *A Manual of Physical Training* for use during the school year of 1918–1919.[27] The National Education Association's Commission on the Reorganization of Secondary Education stressed health as "fundamental among the objectives of education," and prepared a special bulletin on *Physical Education in Secondary Schools.*[28] The Association also formed a National Committee on Physical Education, and in the fall of 1918 called upon the Playground and Recreation Association of America to establish a National Physical Education Service. This service was to provide "organizing machinery through which the influence of all interested agencies might be directed toward the securing of state and national legislation for physical education." The organization was created and went into action immediately; magazine articles, press releases, speeches, and conventions were used to stimulate public enthusiasm. In spite of all these efforts, however, it was reported that as late as the winter of 1918–1919 there had been "no effective, hearty promotive work on the part of the teachers of the country."[29]

Not the least important of the meetings devoted to the topic of physical welfare was the special conference called by the Commissioner of Education. In February, 1918, a group of the nation's leading educators, representing nineteen national organizations interested in health, met at Atlantic City to decide how they could best promote an adequate system of physical education for all youth. After extended discussion, the conference adopted a resolution calling for (1) "a comprehensive thoroughgoing program of health education and physical education" for all boys and girls of elementary and secondary school age, both urban and rural, in the United States; (2) legislation similar in purpose and scope to the New Jersey and New York laws for every state in the union; (3) legal authority and financial support to make it possible for

[25] *Ibid.*, vol. XXIII (May, 1918), p. 325.
[26] *Ibid.*, vol. XXIII (March, 1918), pp. 173–174.
[27] *Mind and Body*, vol. XXV (September, 1918), pp. 193–201.
[28] (Bureau of Education Bulletin, 1917, No. 50).
[29] E. Dana Caulkins, "The Promotion of Physical Education Through State Legislation," N.E.A., *Proceedings*, 1919, p. 320.

the United States Bureau of Education to influence and supervise a nation-wide program of health and physical education; (4) a Congressional statute, based upon the principles embodied in the Smith-Hughes Act, which, through federal grants of money, would provide an opportunity for every state to carry on its own program of physical education.[30]

A bill embracing these and other recommendations, referred to by its friends as "the most comprehensive and important educational measure that has ever been put before Congress," was introduced in the Senate on October 10, 1918.[31] Although the bill was never enacted into law, the agitation of which it was merely one by-product did have tangible results. By 1918 the Commissioner of Education was able to report that "physical training, systematically taught this year for the first time in many schools, will be more effective next year. It has already enlivened the schools, created new enthusiasms, and contributed to the welfare of the children and teachers."[32] The eight states that adopted legislation during the war years to provide compulsory physical education for school children were joined, in the period from 1918 to 1921, by seventeen others.[33]

Less tangible, but perhaps in the long run of much greater importance, was the quickened interest of the public in problems of health and physical efficiency. As one commentator remarked: "His Honor, Mr. Average Citizen, is coming to realize what physical educators have long talked, namely that a basis of health and normal physical development must rest beneath any successful program for human betterment." Organizations such as the Boy Scouts were "received with a new popular enthusiasm," and those agencies concerned with the health of the nation's children were in

[30] *American Physical Education Review,* vol. XXIII (December, 1918), pp. 179–180. Present at the conference were Doctors Wood, Sargent, McKenzie, Storey, and Crampton. Representatives attended from the College Directors Society, the Bureau of Child Hygiene, the Town and County Nursing Service, the Committee of Physical Education of Secondary School Principals, the Child Helping Department of the Russell Sage Foundation, the Life Extension Institute, the Southern Sociological Congress, the Social Hygiene Society, the American Posture League, the War Department Training Camp Activities, the American Medical Association, and the American Federation of Labor.

[31] *Mind and Body,* vol. XXV (January, 1919), pp. 410–411.

[32] *Annual Report of the Commissioner of Education* (1918), p. 33.

[33] T. A. Storey, W. S. Small, and E. G. Salisbury, *Recent State Legislation for Physical Education,* p. 5.

a "stronger position than ever before."[34] It was more than wishful thinking that led the editors of the *American Physical Education Review* to state that "the war has focused the attention of America upon the physical education of its people."[35]

2. *Welfare: The Children's Bureau*

But more than physical training was needed if we were to develop a nation of healthy, vigorous people. For many years before World War I the public had been becoming increasingly aware of the fact that there is more to healthful living than merely taking exercise. Our interest in physical education had started in the 1830's and 1840's with the introduction of German gymnastics and military drill into the country. This interest was re-enforced in the 1870's by the Swedish gymnastics, and until the twentieth century physical training enthusiasts devoted most of their attention to calisthenics.[36] About 1900 emphasis began to be placed on free play and athletics, and by 1917, as we have seen, we were viewing health problems from a wider perspective.

Many influences had entered American life to encourage this broader viewpoint. The great educational reformers, among them Pestalozzi, Froebel, Herbert Spencer, G. Stanley Hall, John Dewey, Edward L. Thorndike, and William H. Kilpatrick, had all stressed the value of physical activity, play, and recreation in education.[37] Science and medicine had made many contributions, particularly since the Civil War. Bacteria had been discovered and isolated; knowledge about causes and control of children's diseases had been greatly extended; and much progress had been made in sanitary science and preventive medicine.[38]

American schools were slow to respond to these developments. Medical inspection and health supervision were started in a number of European countries nearly a generation before they were adopted by any American school system. Argentine and Chile

---

[34] E. Dana Caulkins, "The Promotion of Physical Education Through State Legislation," *op. cit.,* p. 319.

[35] Editorial, vol. XXII (December, 1917), p. 499.

[36] Cubberley, *Public Education in the United States,* p. 606.

[37] James E. Rogers, "Education for Leisure—Abstract." N.E.A., *Proceedings,* 1929, p. 545; see also Fred E. Leonard, Pioneers of Modern Physical Training (2nd edition, New York: Association Press, 1915).

[38] Cubberley, *Public Education in the United States,* p. 607.

instituted compulsory medical inspection in 1888; Japan in 1898. Boston, in 1894, adopted the first system of medical inspection for school children in the United States. By 1911, as many as 411 cities and twenty states had made provisions for such services, and 415 school nurses were at work.[39]

This movement had been led by the medical profession. In 1916, for example, The Rockefeller Foundation announced the establishment of a School of Hygiene and Public Health at The Johns Hopkins University for the training of public health officers.[40] The University of Cincinnati opened a School of Nursing and Health in the same year.[41] Those interested in the advancement of a health program, and there were, of course, many educators among this group, were encouraged by these and measures of a like nature. Before we entered the war, emphasis had begun to shift from the detection of disease to its prevention, and from remedial procedures to the preservation of health.

Determined that the war should not interrupt this work, and that we should profit by the experience of others, the Children's Bureau initiated in 1917 a thorough investigation of child welfare in the warring countries. It was clear that the entire health program in Europe had been retarded during the opening months of the war. Doctors, nurses, teachers, playground supervisors, and other health officers had been called into the armed forces. Activities of both public and private welfare agencies were further curtailed by a shortage of funds, for the public was inclined to devote its time and money to work of a more dramatic type. In two respects, however, the experience of Europe offered encouragement: first, it was apparent that the problems of health in wartime were similar to those encountered in time of peace, only they were aggravated by the war to unusual proportions; second, it was gratifying to know that in most European countries the early policy of neglect had been reversed, and measures for the protection of mothers, babies, and young children had increased since the war began.[42]

[39] *Ibid.*, pp. 607–608; C. Morley Sellery, "Present Day Trends of School Health Service," N.E.A., *Proceedings*, 1931, p. 555.

[40] "A Great Step in the Progress of Health," *The Nation*, vol. CII (June 29, 1916), p. 690. [41] *Science*, vol. XLIV (July 28, 1916), p. 126.

[42] Mary Elizabeth Titzel, "Building a Child-Welfare Program in War Time," *The American Journal of Sociology*, vol. XXIV (January, 1919), pp. 411–412.

Armed with data drawn from these studies of Europe in wartime, the Children's Bureau began a battle to safeguard the health of American children. These efforts were supported by a public which had suddenly become health conscious as a result of the draft revelations. It took little argument in 1917 to persuade people that the time to prevent physical disabilities was in childhood. Moreover, it was obvious that the old system of medical inspection was not in itself enough. We needed positive measures; school physicians, nurses, and clinics; corrective physical exercises; and a comprehensive program of health education for both children and adults.[43]

The Children's Bureau had already prepared the ground for such a campaign. Established in 1912 with orders to "investigate and report . . . upon all matters pertaining to the welfare of children and child life among all classes of our people," it had been the first agency in the world to consider "as a whole the conditions, problems, and welfare of children."[44] From its inception, the Bureau had been directed to a wide range of problems. These included "infant mortality, the birthrate, orphanage, juvenile courts, desertion, accidents and diseases of children, employment, and legislation affecting children in the several States and Territories." In 1916 it was given the added responsibility of enforcing the Federal Child Labor Act.[45]

The statistical record of the Bureau indicates in a general way the rate and extent of its expansion. From an initial appropriation of $25,640 in 1913, expenditures had grown to more than $300,000 in 1916; during the last year of the war they reached a total of nearly $750,000.[46] The same story is revealed in the rapid growth of both correspondence and publications. In 1916, 60,095 letters were handled;[47] three years later the number had increased to 94,337.[48] Publications sent out from Washington totalled 330,737 copies in 1915–1916;[49] more than 400,000 in 1916–1917;[50]

[43] C. Morley Sellery, "Present Day Trends of School Health Service," loc. cit., pp. 555–556.

[44] The Children's Bureau: Yesterday, Today and Tomorrow (Children's Bureau, 1937), p. 1.   [45] Ibid., p. 3. See infra, pp. 176 et seq.

[46] Ninth Annual Report of the Children's Bureau (1922), p. 9.

[47] Fourth Annual Report of the Children's Bureau (1916), p. 26.

[48] Seventh Annual Report of the Children's Bureau (1919), p. 5.

[49] Fourth Annual Report of the Children's Bureau (1916), p. 25.

[50] Fifth Annual Report of the Children's Bureau (1917), p. 28.

612,000 during 1917–1918;[51] and almost 3,000,000 in 1918–1919.[52] This last figure does not include more than 7,500,000 weighing cards distributed during the special campaign carried on during 1918–1919.[53]

Nor are the activities of the Children's Bureau fully revealed in the statistics of expenditures, correspondence, and publications. Following the example set by its chief, Julia Lathrop, the Bureau's agents and friends throughout the country worked indefatigably to bring health problems to the attention of the public. Speeches before educational organizations, women's clubs, and civic associations; press releases; articles in magazines; and the personal work of millions of volunteers all served to make the American people health conscious.

Prior to our entrance into the war, the Bureau had concentrated upon infant welfare. The work took the form of "Baby Week Campaigns." Inaugurated by Chicago in 1914, the plan was at once adopted by a number of other cities. "Baby Week" was dedicated to the welfare of infants, and was featured in each city by lectures, baby-health conferences, contests, school programs, parades, plays, distribution of pamphlets, leaflets, and other printed material for the care of babies. These publicity campaigns were so successful that the General Federation of Women's Clubs decided to cooperate with the Children's Bureau in a nation-wide "Baby Week" to be held in the spring of 1916. The program was endorsed by the President, the Secretary of Labor, and leading state and municipal officials throughout the country. The United States Reclamation Service gave space in an issue of the *Reclamation Record* for an appeal to women to take an active part in the campaign. The Commissioner of Indian Affairs urged the employees of the Indian Service to assist. The United States Public Health Service contributed educational materials for free distribution. The Office of Home Economics in the Department of Agriculture prepared a special bulletin on *Food for Young Children*. The National Congress of Mothers and Parent-Teachers Associations cooperated. Many other organizations, including schools, libraries, civic associations, state boards of health, the press, and

[51] *Seventh Annual Report of the Children's Bureau* (1919), p. 6.
[52] *Sixth Annual Report of the Children's Bureau* (1918), p. 25.
[53] *Seventh Annual Report of the Children's Bureau* (1919), p. 9.

state universities and agricultural colleges took part in the work. As a result of this publicity, several thousand American cities, towns, and rural communities organized and celebrated "Baby Week." The Children's Bureau reported that "towns where the one logical obstacle to a celebration existed, namely, a shortage of babies, held celebrations nevertheless for all children under school age." It was estimated that at least half of the 14,186 incorporated cities, towns, and villages of the nation had taken part in the campaign. Millions of Americans were awakened to the importance of health. One small North Dakota village reported: "If any other rural club thinks it cannot hold a baby examination, refer them to us, for it wakes up a township better than a presidential election."[54] Plans were made by the General Federation of Women's Clubs and the Children's Bureau to repeat the campaign in 1917.

Meanwhile, the United States entered the war and, as has been described, the health program was immediately accelerated. In June, 1917, members of a number of organizations met in New York City to hold an informal discussion of child welfare in wartime. Before disbanding they adopted several resolutions. Public health nurses and physicians were urged to look upon their activities as war service. Graduates of the public schools were encouraged to take up nursing. Communities were asked to train volunteers to assist the public health nurses and the welfare workers. The extension of all "sound recreational facilities" was advocated. Finally, it was suggested that the Council of National Defense organize a national committee to keep in touch with the problems of child welfare.[55]

In response to demands of this sort, a Woman's Committee was created in the Council of National Defense. Its job was to cooperate in the war program of the Children's Bureau.[56] By the spring of 1918 an organization had been established with about 17,000 local units and an estimated membership of 11,-000,000 women.[57] It was this organization, backed by women's

[54] *Baby-Week Campaigns* (Rev. edition, Children's Bureau Bulletin No. 15, 1918), pp. 9–15.

[55] *Fifth Annual Report of the Children's Bureau* (1917) pp. 26–31.

[56] *Plan for Organization to Carry Out Program for the Children's Year, April 6, 1918–April 6, 1919.* National Archives (Bureau of Education, 106–111).

[57] Children's Bureau, *Yesterday, Today and Tomorrow*, p. 40.

clubs, civic associations, public schools, and other interested groups, that insured the success of the child welfare campaign of 1918.

It was decided to dedicate the second year of the nation's participation in the war to the children, and the Bureau urged the public to make it "in fact as well as in name, a Children's Year throughout the country."[58] President Wilson gave the campaign his hearty support. "Next to the duty of doing everything possible for the soldiers at the front," he wrote, "there could be, it seems to me, no more patriotic duty than that of protecting the children, who constitute one third of our population."[59] He reinforced this official endorsement with a special allotment of $150,000 from his war emergency fund.[60]

The program opened on April 6, 1918, with a campaign to protect the health of mothers, infants, and young children. This was, in large part, a continuation of the prewar activities of the Bureau, and the experience gained in the earlier campaigns proved invaluable. The excellent organization of the Children's Year program is revealed in the materials released for publication. One leaflet, for example, contained directions for conducting the weighing and measuring test with which the campaign opened. In it was told how to set up child health centers, how to administer the test, how to secure publicity, how to enlist volunteer aid, how to keep the records, and where and how to secure equipment and examiners. Instructions were sufficiently detailed to include the warning that "examiners should wash their hands before examining each child."[61]

Although most of the work was done by volunteer laymen, in many cases skilled supervisors had charge of the activities. Thousands of children were given not only the weighing and measuring tests, but complete physical examinations as well. One far western state reported that over 40,000 children had received such attention, with the tabulations revealing remediable

[58] *Save 100,000 Babies. Get a Square Deal for the Children* (Children's Bureau, Children's Year Leaflet No. 1, 1918, Bureau Publication No. 36), p. 2.

[59] *Sixth Annual Report of the Children's Bureau* (1918), p. 25.

[60] Children's Bureau, *Yesterday, Today and Tomorrow,* p. 45.

[61] *April and May Weighing and Measuring Test. Part 1. Suggestions to Local Committees* (Children's Bureau, Children's Year Leaflet No. 2, 1918, Bureau Publication No. 38), p. 2.

defects in forty-seven per cent of them. In addition to the regular channels of publicity, a number of unusual devices were used to interest the people. Cleveland sent a motor clinic throughout the city. Michigan used a similarly equipped interurban car to reach the rural communities. Boston built a "Children's House" on the Commons. This was, according to the official claim, "a fine model of a type which could be modified, built, and equipped by school boys and girls in any town or country neighborhood."[62]

A second major activity of the Bureau centered in its efforts to prevent the injurious effects of child labor. High wages and the urge to be doing something to further the war lured thousands of children from the schools into industrial or farm labor. But the Bureau's responsibilities did not end with the enforcement of the federal child labor statute. The studies of Europe in wartime had revealed not only a sharp increase in the employment of children, but a marked deterioration of health and an alarming rise in juvenile delinquency.

Students of the European problem offered a number of explanations for this situation. An abnormal demand for child labor, the requisitioning of school buildings for military purposes, and a relaxation of school attendance laws all tended to keep children from the classrooms. Customary authority was weakened by the withdrawal of male teachers from the schools, a diminution of the police forces, the departure of older brothers for military service, and the absence of both parents from the home. Restraining influences of peacetime were relaxed as church activities, club work, evening schools, and welfare enterprises were interrupted. In the feverish war atmosphere, the children amused themselves by reading vicious literature, watching sensational motion pictures, or aimlessly wandering about the streets.[63]

Although in 1918 only a few studies were available to measure the effect of the war upon juvenile delinquency and health in the United States, the Children's Bureau was convinced that we, too, had reason for concern. Even the rural areas were faced with

[62] *Sixth Annual Report of the Children's Bureau* (1918), p. 24.

[63] *Juvenile Delinquency in Certain Countries at War. A Brief Review of Available Foreign Sources* (Children's Bureau, Dependent, Defective, and Delinquent Series No. 5, Bureau Publication No. 39, 1918), pp. 7–8, 16. This was corroborated in studies made by Paul V. Kellogg, editor of *The Survey*, who examined conditions in Canada. Quoted in *School and Society*, vol. CXXXIV (July 21, 1917), p. 74.

these problems.[64] The public was reminded that the same social and economic conditions which had brought an increase of juvenile delinquency to the belligerent countries of Europe were present in this nation. In view of this situation, it was particularly disturbing that we had paid little heed to the preventive measures which the other countries had discovered to be so important. The Bureau officials warned that "the war is inflicting a positive injury not only on the delinquents themselves but on other children and on the community as a whole."[65]

To control juvenile delinquency and to protect young children from industrial exploitation and from broken health, three major campaigns were carried on, in addition to the enforcement of the child labor statute. One of these campaigns sought to secure adequate financial support for the families of men in the armed forces. Immediately upon our entrance into the conflict, studies were initiated by the Children's Bureau to determine just what provision was being made in other countries to protect the wives and children of the fighting men. The first report, prepared under great pressure, was transmitted to the President on August 29, 1917. It revealed that "alone among the belligerent countries studied the United States is making no allowance whatever for the families of men in active service; the United States permits but does not require an allotment of pay."[66] It was further revealed that practically every European country had increased its allowances since the outbreak of war. England, in fact, had made special provision for men with financial obligations incurred before they entered the service. Assistance was given to enable such men to pay for furniture or real property; rents, taxes, loans, and mortgages; and for children's schooling.[67]

This report of the Children's Bureau was given wide publicity, and served as the basis for a law enacted in October, 1917. Men

[64] Kate Holladay Claghorn, *Juvenile Delinquency in Rural New York* (Children's Bureau, Dependent, Defective, and Delinquent Series No. 4, Bureau Publication No. 32, 1918), p. 15.

[65] *Juvenile Delinquency in Certain Countries at War, op. cit.*, p. 24.

[66] *Governmental Provisions in the United States and Foreign Countries for Members of the Military Forces and Their Dependents* (Children's Bureau, Miscellaneous Series No. 11, Bureau Publication No. 28, 1917), p. 27. The countries studied included Austria, Germany, France, Italy, The Netherlands, Russia, Switzerland, Great Britain, and the British Colonies.

[67] *Ibid.*

who entered the service with families dependent upon them were required to make allotments from their pay for the benefit of their families; to this the United States added a further allotment which varied in relation to the nearness of kin and the number of dependents. The service men and their families were also protected by war risk insurance which provided death benefits and payments in the event of partial or complete disability. In addition, provision was made for the re-education, at national expense, of those men who returned maimed or disabled to civilian life. The Federal Board for Vocational Education was put in charge of this program of re-education.[68]

A second campaign was known as the "Back-to-School Drive." Strongly supported by governmental officials and educational authorities, the Children's Bureau urged civic associations to make special efforts "to see that all children under 14 are in school and that they are enabled to come there suitably clad and fed and able to secure the full advantages of school."[69] Reports indicated that forty-five states, New York City, the District of Columbia, and Hawaii entered vigorously into the campaign.[70]

A number of methods were used to induce children to return to school. The Bureau attempted to raise scholarships. Pointing out that it cost $120 to keep a child in school for one year, the federal authorities asked local civic associations to provide at least one scholarship for each of the 281,000 schoolhouses in the country.[71] Greater help was probably furnished to the campaign by visiting teachers, vocational training courses, and vocational guidance and placement committees. In some localities, continuation and part-time schools provided a partial answer to the problem.[72] The money value of education was not neglected; those who advanced this argument attempted to state in precise terms the increased earning power that resulted from each additional year of education.[73] A vast amount of publicity was devoted

[68] Frederic L. Paxson, *Recent History of the United States. 1865 to the Present* (Boston: Houghton Mifflin Company, 1937), pp. 522–523.

[69] *Fifth Annual Report of the Children's Bureau* (1917), p. 26.

[70] *Seventh Annual Report of the Children's Bureau* (1919), p. 9.

[71] *National School Service*, vol. I (December 15, 1918), p. 9.

[72] *Seventh Annual Report of the Children's Bureau* (1919), p. 9.

[73] See, for example, the study by A. Caswell Ellis, *The Money Value of Education* (Bureau of Education Bulletin, 1917, No. 22); also *School Increases Earning Power*, *National School Service*, vol. I (January 1, 1919), p. 16.

to the campaign, both by the Children's Bureau and the Bureau of Education.[74] Julia Lathrop, Chief of the Children's Bureau, was gratified at the response. To illustrate the whole-hearted support given to the drive by volunteer groups, she cited the case of one small community. In this town the teachers supplied the local child welfare committee with a list of approximately seventy children at work on permits; all but one were persuaded to return to school.

The drive had started on October 17, 1918. When the Armistice was declared, less than a month later, the children were requested to remain in school for still another reason. This was expressed on a poster that was widely displayed. It read: "Children Back in School Means Soldiers Back in Jobs." On February 1, 1919, a follow-up campaign was started with a "Stay-In-School Drive."[75]

A third and final major campaign was conducted by the Children's Bureau as part of the "Children's Year" program. This was an effort to secure better recreational facilities for children. It was carried out with the same meticulous attention to detail which the Bureau had displayed in its other wartime activities. In a special bulletin containing suggestions as to organization and procedure, the federal officials gave their reasons for inaugurating the campaign:

The Recreation Drive aims to promote the games which increase physical adeptness and skill, which train the eye, and develop the ability to respond instantly not only to the direction of the leader but to the need of the game. One purpose of the Drive must be to implant in the minds of the children the idea that keeping themselves fit is patriotic, and that they are serving their country when they make themselves stronger. Indiana has adopted for the Recreation Drive the slogan, "For a Stronger America."[76]

The drive culminated in the fall of 1918 with a "Patriotic Play Week." Success was guaranteed from the outset because of the generous support received from a score of national organizations. The Women's Committee of the Council of National Defense, the

[74] The attitude held by the Commissioner of Education and given wide circulation in the educational press is revealed in a statement quoted in *School and Society*, vol. VII (April 6, 1918), p. 404.

[75] *Seventh Annual Report of the Children's Bureau* (1919), p. 9.

[76] *Patriotic Play Week. Suggestions to Local Child-Welfare Committees.* (Children's Bureau, Children's Year Leaflet No. 4, Bureau Publication No. 44, 1918), p. 3.

Department of Agriculture's extension agents, and The Playground and Recreation Association of America were perhaps the most important of the cooperating agencies. Among the other groups active in the campaign were the Junior Red Cross, the Boy and Girl Scouts, the American Folk Dance Society, and the garden clubs of the Bureau of Education.[77] As a result of the recreation drive, sixteen states reported that "many new playgrounds" had been started.[78]

When "Children's Year" came to an end, the leaders had every reason to feel pleased with the success of the program. The educational results were probably the most important. Millions of adults had learned that there is a relationship between height, weight, and age, and that thousands of children were undernourished and had physical defects which, in many cases, were remediable. Millions realized for the first time that child welfare is an important national problem. The awakened interest was revealed in the distribution of over 18,000,000 posters, dodgers, leaflets, and miscellaneous publications of the Children's Bureau. All this material went out only upon request; none was broadcast.

There was, however, more tangible evidence of the success of the program. California's experience may be cited as typical. In this one state, 53,462 children had been weighed and measured; 40,000 of this number had been given complete physical examinations by qualified medical men. No less than seventeen county health centers were established, and ten county health nurses were employed. Legislative action was taken to provide dental hygienists for children, and a divsion of school hygiene was created in the State Board of Health.

Similar results were noted in other parts of the country. Before the campaign started, only seven states had child hygiene divisions; in 1918, four additional states were added to this list; during 1919, when the full effects of the publicity were felt, seventeen more states established agencies for the protection of child health. From twenty-four states came reports of new health centers; the city of New Orleans alone recorded twenty-nine new health centers. The demand for public health nurses was greater

77 Ibid., pp. 3–4.
78 Seventh Annual Report of the Children's Bureau (1919), p. 12.

than the supply. One New England state set as its goal a public health nurse in every town, and provided free scholarships for any girls who wished to take the necessary training for such a career.[79] The health services now provided by our public schools owe their existence, in large part, to the movement which was started in the World War years.

3. Welfare: The United States Public Health Service

The one federal agency specifically charged to look after the health of the nation was the United States Public Health Service. The history of this organization dates back to 1798, at which time Congress enacted measures providing for the relief of sick and disabled seamen. Out of this beginning grew the Marine Hospital Service in the Treasury Department. In 1902 the name of this organization was changed to The United States Public Health and Marine Hospital Service; this was shortened in 1912 to the United States Public Health Service. In the minds of some people, these changes and the expansion of activities foreshadowed the eventual establishment of a Federal Department of Health in the President's Cabinet.[80]

The prewar services of this organization were extensive. By 1916 it was operating fifty-six quarantine stations on our own coasts and twenty-six other stations in our insular possessions. A hygienic laboratory had been established in Washington with a staff of thirty-seven officers and technical assistants. A training school had been established for the service. In addition, the federal health authorities exercise the right to inspect all biological laboratories both here and abroad before permitting them to sell viruses, serums, and other medical supplies in the United States. The problem of sanitation was eliciting an increasing amount of attention.[81]

With the war came new responsibilities. The health of troops in camp had to be safeguarded, and the civil areas around the camps required careful attention. In this aspect of its work, the

[79] *Seventh Annual Report of the Children's Bureau* (1919), pp. 10–12.

[80] George M. Price, "The Nationalization of Public Health. War Program of the United States Health Service," *Survey*, vol. XLI (October 19, 1918), pp. 62–63.

[81] Ezra Kimball Sprague, "The United States Public Health Service," *The Outlook*, vol. CXII (August 16, 1916), pp. 911–913.

Public Health Service cooperated closely with the Army, Navy, Bureau of Sanitary Service in the Red Cross, and the state and local health officers. After the Armistice, the return of millions of troops to American shores made necessary a vast expansion in the facilities of the quarantine stations.[82]

All this, however, was in a sense merely the expansion of previous activities. The officials of the Service believed, as had the educators and medical men at the Atlantic City health conference, that we needed "a nationalization of public health activities by the federal government through a far-reaching and comprehensive control of disease prevention, sanitation, and public health education." These officials were convinced that health problems could be handled efficiently only on a nation-wide scale. Their belief that local health agencies were utterly inadequate was confirmed by the draft rejections and by the inability of the local organizations to deal with the problems raised by the influenza epidemic of 1918–1919.[83]

Like so many other organizations, the Public Health Service eventually reached the conclusion that the schools must play an increasingly important part in the health education of the American people. Particularly troublesome was the rural situation. As Surgeon-General Blue expressed it: "If military preparedness is desired, it is of prime importance that the physical efficiency of our rural population, the bone and sinew of the race, be raised and maintained at its maximum." In order to determine what methods would best serve to raise health standards in the rural areas, the Service conducted a number of field surveys. Certain areas were selected for study; houses were visited and sanitary conditions observed; an effort was made to educate the people through lectures, distribution of literature, and the aid of prominent people in each neighborhood. Finally, a follow-up system was developed in which each house was revisited, improvements were noted, and attempts were made to stimulate further interest. These surveys confirmed earlier conclusions that the health of country children was inferior to that of boys and girls living in

82 John W. Trask, "The Work of the United States Public Health Service in Relation to the Present War," *The American Journal of Public Health*, vol. VII (December, 1917), pp. 987–991.
83 Price, *loc. cit.*, p. 63.

the cities. Malnutrition, diseases of the lungs, heart, eyes, ears, and throat were much more frequent in the rural areas. "Many of these defects," one physician noted, "are attributable to unsanitary conditions in the little red schoolhouse." One immediate result of the surveys was an increased emphasis upon school hygiene.[84]

Convinced that public health education was the "most effective single weapon" to combat disease, the Public Health Service made a special effort to reach the public school teachers. The pages of the *National School Service* were used to advertise its leaflets.[85] Thousands of toothbrushes were distributed in the rural areas, and boys and girls were taught the proper methods for cleaning teeth.[86] The mobilization of health services made necessary by the influenza epidemic in the fall of 1918 also did much to awaken the public to the need for safeguarding health.[87] In these ways, and in cooperation with other agencies, the Public Health Service contributed to the health education of the American people.

4. Welfare: The Bureau of Education

Other federal organizations took an active part in the health crusade. The Junior Red Cross, a quasi-public agency, offered considerable support. In September, 1918, it issued a special teacher's manual, one chapter of which was devoted to a discussion of "education in health."[88] Before the war ended, plans had been worked out for a systematic campaign in the winter of 1918–1919. This started with efforts to introduce courses in first aid and home nursing into the high school. In January, 1919, the Junior Red Cross distributed a thirty-two page pamphlet containing suggestions for "personal health and community sanitation."[89]

Even Creel's propaganda organization helped to publicize the health campaign. Through the medium of the semi-monthly

---

[84] Sprague, *loc. cit.*, p. 913.

[85] *National School Service*, vol. I (November 1, 1918), p. 6.

[86] "Uncle Sam as a Doctor," *St. Nicholas*, vol. XLIV (December, 1916), p. 168.

[87] "The United States Public Health Service and the Influenza Epidemic," *Science*, vol. XLVIII (November 15, 1918), pp. 487–488.

[88] *Junior Red Cross Activities. Teachers Manual* (Washington: The American Red Cross, Department of Development, Junior Membership), 1918.

[89] *National School Service*, vol. I (January 15, 1919), p. 9.

teachers' magazine, *National School Service,* messages and prepared materials from the Public Health Service, the Children's
Bureau, and the Junior Red Cross were brought to the attention
of the teachers. Lessons were inserted on the care of teeth and
proper habits of eating and sleeping.

It was the Bureau of Education, however, that bowed only to
the Children's Bureau in its efforts to safeguard the physical well-
being of school children. Throughout 1917 and 1918 it collabo-
rated with the Child Health Organization in a partnership that
grew constantly closer.

Early in the war, the New York Academy of Medicine had
established a Committee on the Wartime Problems of Childhood. This organization was at first concerned principally with the
steady increase of malnutrition due to the rising cost of living and
an ignorance of food values. Further investigation convinced the
committee that there were larger issues to be faced. It felt that
because of the war health was "the most in danger of all our
national resources," and that the "army of twenty million school
children has as yet received very scant consideration." The committee affiliated with the National Child Labor Committee. Its
publicly avowed purpose was to awaken Americans to their obligation to safeguard the health of children.[90]

The Bureau of Education was the logical organization through
which to reach the public schools. It was located in Washington
at the very heart of our war effort. It had extensive contacts with
parent-teacher associations. Its Division of Home Economics had
already done considerable work with the problem of proper feeding. So there began that close association that was to continue
throughout the entire war.

For the first year, the Bureau of Education gave generous publicity to the health program and its mailing lists, and franking
privileges were made available to the Child Health Organization.[91]
By October, 1918, a more effective arrangement had been developed. The Child Health Organization maintained its New York
City offices as headquarters for research, and for experimental and

[90] L. Emmett Holt, "An Announcement of the Child Health Organization," MSS.
(Undated). National Archives (Bureau of Education, 106–20).

[91] F. K. Lane to L. E. Holt, February 26, 1918. National Archives (Bureau of
Education, 106–20).

demonstration work. It also paid the salary of Miss Sally Lucas Jean, who, with W. S. Small, Child Hygiene Specialist of the Bureau of Education, was in charge of the Bureau's health activities. The Bureau of Education, for its part, agreed to pay Miss Jean's traveling expenses; to handle all field work, conferences, and advisory services; to publish as much as possible of the health literature in the Government Printing Office; and to continue to use the franking privileges for the distribution of literature.[92] The two organizations made a splendid team. At the New York end were facilities and specialists to carry on research; the Washington organization was equipped to distribute the educational materials to the public.

In reviewing the health and welfare activities of the war years, it is clear that there was much overlapping of effort. Fortunately for the success of the campaign, all interested agencies agreed that it was essential to awaken the public to the vital problem of child welfare. This agreement as to purpose led to close cooperation in the conduct of the publicity program. Moreover, the war had forced attention upon matters of physical well-being, and the public was in a receptive frame of mind. While it is impossible to estimate the influence of the health crusade upon subsequent developments in the public schools, it could hardly have been coincidental that the postwar years witnessed an astonishing advance in this phase of our educational program.

[92] Correspondence between F. K. Lane and L. E. Holt. October, 1918. National Archives (Bureau of Education, 106–20).

CHAPTER VI

FOOD AND FINANCE

Food will win the war!—*Wartime slogan, 1917–1918*

Little Jack Horner will sit in a corner
With meals his good mother has planned.
She'll feed her whole brood with the choicest of food,
Which she in her wisdom has canned.—*Publicity of the National
War Garden Commission, 1918*

1. The Food Problem in 1917

Napoleon anticipated one of the basic problems of total war when he asserted that "an army marches on its stomach." By 1917 the intimate relationship between food, health, industrial production, and civilian morale had become quite clear. An adequate supply and distribution of foodstuffs was a prerequisite to victory. Will Irwin, one of whose wartime jobs was keeping track of Allied morale, registered his "opinion" that "the pinch and fear of hunger might have turned the delicate balance, in that critical spring of 1918, to a German triumph on the west and a lost or drawn war. Had the Food Administration fallen into hands less trained and competent," he added, "had it been boggled or muddled and delayed—then disaster, even before we drew our sword fully from its scabbard. When in May, 1917, Hoover began establishing a policy and building a machine in advance of official sanction, he was getting a start for a hard, close race with starvation and defeat."[1]

Food and troops! These, declared the Allied Nations, were their most urgent needs in the spring of 1917.[2] Since the outbreak of war in the harvest months of 1914, European farmlands had been stripped of millions of workers and devastated by the march of armies. Conditions in the conquered countries had become

[1] Will Irwin, *Herbert Hoover: A Reminiscent Biography* (New York: The Century Company, 1928), p. 205.
[2] *Ibid.*, p. 188.

desperate; the belligerents had resorted to stringent rationing.[3] Upon the United States, nearest of the sources of supply, fell the burden of feeding Europe, but the attraction of high industrial wages had drawn workers from the farms, and by 1917 the shortage of labor was acute.

Herbert Hoover, successful administrator of Belgian Food Relief,[4] was promptly called upon for assistance. Early in April he was asked to determine the immediate needs of the Allies; a few weeks later he was brought from Europe to organize agricultural production and food conservation for an "all out" war effort. Working through the Food Administration, established in August, 1917, after weeks of furious senatorial debate, within a few months Hoover had organized our chaotic efforts into a smoothly operating machine of production and distribution that was pouring an adequate supply of meats, fats, grain, and sugar into Europe.[5]

Like George Creel, Hoover urged cooperation rather than coercion. He was "food administrator," not "dictator," and he never failed to correct, from the President down, those who addressed him by the latter term. The American people were to be volunteers, not conscripts, in the battle for food. "My idea," he explained to the Senate committee which was considering the Food Administration bill, "is that we must centralize ideas but decentralize execution." Out of this concept was hatched that vast program of publicity and propaganda which reached down to the last home in the smallest village in the United States.[6]

This is not to say that Hoover carried the entire burden of increasing production, or to suggest that the wartime effort was a new departure in federal policy. The history of American agriculture was, up to the end of the World War, a history of constantly expanding farmlands. For half a century before 1917 the federal government had followed a deliberate policy of increasing the productivity of the nation's acreage. This policy was implemented by such measures as the Morrill Act of 1862 which gave free lands to individuals for farms, and land grants to the states

[3] Charles Lathrop Pack, *The War Garden Victorious. Its War-Time Need and Its Economic Value in Peace* (Philadelphia: J. B. Lippincott Company, 1919), pp. 5–7.

[4] In his biography, Will Irwin presents an extremely favorable view of Hoover's relief work among the Belgians.

[5] Irwin, *Herbert Hoover*, pp. 188–190.   [6] *Ibid.*, pp. 193–210.

for the establishment of agricultural colleges; by the 1887 provision for agricultural experiment stations; and by the Smith-Lever Act of 1914 which started extension work upon a systematic basis among the farmers of the country. These activities were conducted under the direction of the Department of Agriculture. Irrigation projects, administered by the Bureau of Reclamation in the Department of the Interior, had been fostered since the turn of the century. The war on pests and the search for better seeds, fertilizers, and farming methods had been vigorously pursued.

Perhaps less familiar to the average urban dweller was the growth of agricultural education in the secondary schools in the years immediately preceding the war. In 1913–1914, for example, Vermont had only four schools employing a specially trained agricultural teacher; in 1914–1915 there were nine; in 1915–1916 there were fifteen; and during 1916–1917 the number increased to twenty-three.[7] In the entire United States, by June, 1916, more than 2,100 public high schools were giving agricultural instruction to about 41,000 pupils; during the following year the number of schools and pupils more than doubled. This increase was the result of the prewar efforts of vocational education enthusiasts,[8] but it was further stimulated by the urgency of the food situation in 1916 and 1917.[9] The impetus given to education of this type by

[7] C. L. Lane, "Agricultural Instruction in the High Schools of Six Eastern States" (Bureau of Education Bulletin, 1918, No. 3), p. 62.

[8] A. C. Monahan and C. H. Dye, "Institutions in the United States Giving Instruction in Agriculture" (Bureau of Education Bulletin, 1917, No. 34), p. 23.

[9] H. N. Goddard, "Results Achieved in Secondary Agricultural Schools and Methods Pursued in Actual Practice," N.E.A., *Proceedings*, 1917, pp. 603–617. The paper contained a report of agricultural education being given as of June 30, 1916:

Number of public high schools teaching agriculture   2,175
Number of public high schools teaching agriculture primarily:
  As informational subjects   1,521
  As vocational subjects   566
Number of persons teaching agriculture:
  Male   2,007
  Female   247
  Number of these with any special training in agriculture   1,021
Number of students of secondary grade studying agriculture   41,055
Number of schools using school land for instructional purposes   392
Number teaching through home-project method   337
Number in which instruction consists wholly of classroom work   416
Number in which instruction consists of classroom work, with laboratory
  exercises and observation on neighboring farms   1,064

the publicity of the war years bore some fruit in the postwar period,[10] yet it is well to bear in mind that much of the war activity was hastily improvised, poorly organized and administered, and had little, if any, lasting value.

2. Increasing Production: Schoolboys as Farm Laborers

In reply to its urgent appeals to the farmers to double production, the Massachusetts Public Safety Committee received this rejoinder: "If you want us to raise more food you must find an available labor supply which we have been unable to discover." Further investigation disclosed not only the truth of this contention, but also the alarming fact that high costs of seed and fertilizer, combined with the scarcity of labor, were leading most farmers to plan a curtailed program.[11] This shortage of farm workers was not, of course, confined to Massachusetts. As the draft began to take effect and industrial production commenced to soar, the situation became serious. One county, for example, with 2,000 farms lost over 400 boys through the draft alone.[12]

A possible solution presented itself in an estimated 250,000 to 300,000 boys over sixteen years of age enrolled in the high schools,[13] and movements to mobilize these schoolboys for farm service sprang up spontaneously in all sections of the country. By the first week in May, 1917, the Public Safety Committee of Massachusetts had asked all school officials to cooperate, the aid of county agricultural agents had been secured, and thousands of circulars and labor contract forms had been distributed among the farmers. Before the end of the month over 500 boys had been released from school work, 200 more were to go on June 10, nine camps had been established for the boys, and three more were in the course of development.[14]

From all over the country came reports of similar activities. The New York City Board of Education stated on May 9 that 250

[10] Thomas H. Briggs, "Secondary Education," *Biennial Survey, 1916–1918* (Bureau of Education Bulletin, 1919, No. 88), p. 219.

[11] W. I. Hamilton, "Mobilizing Boys for Farm Labor," *School and Society*, vol. I (June 16, 1917), pp. 714–715.

[12] "Minutes of a Conference in the Office of the Commissioner of Education," February 15, 1918. National Archives (Bureau of Education, 106–13).

[13] *Ibid.*

[14] Hamilton, *loc. cit.*, p. 716.

boys had been placed on farms, and that a camp at Newburgh had been established.[15] In New Jersey all schoolboys over fourteeen who could secure their parents' permission were excused by the Department of Education to work on the farms of the state; by the end of May, the educational authorities claimed that 6,332 boys had already started farm work and that 2,722 more were available.[16] Within two weeks of our entry into the war, authorization was given to the 200 school boards of Cook County, Illinois, to close immediately all grades above the sixth in rural schools. At the same time, plans were made to release on April 16 over 6,000 boys sixteen years of age and older from the high schools of Chicago. In this case it was stipulated that they must take a pledge to work on the farms of Cook County or to enter some employment by which the food supply of the nation might be increased. All pupils so excused from school were to receive full credit for the entire semester's work.[17] Reports of this sort are typical of those received by state superintendents of education during the spring weeks of 1917.[18]

In general, the farm work was organized along three different lines. Far from typical, but perhaps most interesting, were the cooperatives carried on by the boys themselves. The Froh-Heim Farm Club in New Jersey is an example of this relatively rare type of enterprise. On April 30, 1917, fifty-eight boys from fourteen to twenty years of age, drawn from the high schools of Plainfield, Bloomfield, and South Orange, began to plant an eighty-acre vegetable farm on the estate of Grant B. Schley at Far Hills, New Jersey. With a $20,000 advance from their benefactor, two trained agricultural instructors from Rutgers College to direct the work, and a Y.M.C.A. secretary to supervise their social life, the boys had everything in their favor. In addition to a dormitory, they were provided with washrooms, hospital, cooperative camp store, savings bank, and recreational facilities such as a baseball field, running track, three tennis courts, and a swimming pool.

Nearly nine hours of their daily program was devoted to farm

15 *School and Society*, vol. V (May 26, 1917), p. 614.

16 *Ibid.*, vol. VI (August 18, 1917), p. 196.

17 *School and Society*, vol. V (April 21, 1917), p. 465.

18 The reports of city and state superintendents of education, and the files of educational periodicals, contain numerous references to this school-to-farm movement.

labor. All routine work except cooking and washing dishes was done by the boys. They followed a regular schedule:

4:45	Colors	12:00	Farm duty
5:00	Breakfast	5:00	Recall
6:15	Inspection of bunks	5:30	Dinner in uniform
6:30	Drill	6:15	Drill
7:15	Farm duty	6:45	Sunset
11:00	Lunch (served in the field)	7:00	Recall
		8:30	Taps

For this work the boys received free board and one dollar a week for spending money. All profits from the camp were divided among the boys at the end of the summer.

This was farming *de luxe* for the sons of wealthy parents. It would have been attractive to boys of all classes. There were other experiments of a similar nature, but they were few and scattered, and their contribution to the sum total of the war effort was obviously negligible.[19]

Much more prevalent was the central camp plan. In these situations, the boys lived in dormitories under strict supervision, received their board and a monthly wage, and went out each day to work on the surrounding farms. Their daily routine was regulated in the same manner as that of the Froh-Heim Farm Club. Expenses were met by a prearranged daily wage collected from the farmers by the directors of the camps.[20]

The usual arrangement, however, was for the boys to work as typical farm hands. Those in rural areas usually lived at home and worked on their own or neighboring farms. City boys boarded on the job. In these cases the boys themselves usually negotiated for their wages.

Valuable as much of this work undoubtedly was, criticism was widespread and frequently justified. Many of these early programs were ill-advised and badly organized. An undertaking at Bernardsville, New Jersey, illustrates this point. Here the high school was closed two weeks early and the building was turned into a dormitory. Some fifty schoolboys were enrolled in the "camp," but to the chagrin of the directors there was no farm

[19] *School and Society,* vol. VI (August 18, 1917), pp. 196–197. This is the summary of an investigation conducted by the National Child Labor Committee.
[20] *Ibid.*

work available. Those in charge had assumed that the boys were needed. They were mistaken. The farmers did not feel that the inexperienced boys could give them service worth $1.80 a day, and for several weeks the "war work" consisted of mowing lawns for the neighbors, pruning trees, trimming shrubs, and pulling weeds from the town roads. As an investigator from the National Child Labor Committee remarked, "This work was only temporary, of course, 'to keep the boys busy until farm work could be found,' but it does not increase food production; nor does it appeal to boys who have left school with the distinct idea of serving their country."[21]

This same investigator reported a much more serious problem, that of the exploitation of child labor. Lack of proper supervision was in large part responsible for this situation. Frequently the school authorities made no preliminary investigations, with the result that many children were overworked and underpaid. In one instance, a fifteen-year-old boy, slight in build and weighing only 113 pounds, was worked from five in the morning to eight at night; for his labor he received room, board, and two dollars monthly.[22] The evidence indicates that lack of supervision with the consequent exploitation of children was widely prevalent in the summer of 1917.[23] State superintendents of education reported a variety of practices, ranging from the complete absence of supervision to the most carefully organized and administered programs. The desirable type of program was secured by one state in which the educational authorities ruled that:

The local school authorities and the parents should thoroughly investigate the conditions under which the pupil is employed in each individual case, and should be satisfied that the hours of labor, the conditions of living, the remuneration received, and all other conditions affecting the welfare of the pupils are satisfactory before releasing the pupils from school for such employment. Local school authorities are best able to pass upon all these questions, and they should take this responsibility. Girls should be released only for service on the farms

21 *Ibid.*
22 *Ibid.*
23 Thomas J. Smart, "The Policies of State Superintendents toward Students Entering Agricultural Employment during the War," *School and Society*, vol. VIII (October 26, 1918), pp. 480–487. See also vol. VI (August 18, 1917), pp. 198–199; and vol. VI (September 8, 1917), pp. 289–290.

and then only when they may be employed in their homes or so near their homes that they may be under the supervision of their parents.[24]

From an educational viewpoint, the most serious difficulties were the disorganization of the schools and the problem of credits. Many schools closed early in the spring and opened late in the fall, thus shortening their terms by a number of weeks;[25] others merely dismissed those students who pledged themselves to work on farms or to engage in some form of food production. In both cases, the question of academic credit was raised. At least six states refused in 1917 to grant unearned credits; as one superintendent remarked: "We hold it dishonest and untruthful to credit work on a farm as credit for algebra, etc." Nine states reported that credit was given when the student produced evidence of employment, showed his grades to be above passing, and did a successful job on the farm during a designated period of time. Several states left the decision as to credit in the hands of the local school authorities. Only four states placed no restrictions on the granting of credit. Bad as the situation was, with a large amount of promiscuous granting of unearned credit, the practice was not so widespread as the alarmists' cries might indicate. In 1918 there was a decided trend toward a more clearly defined policy with increased restrictions upon the wholesale dismissal of school children and the conferring of unearned credits.[26]

Was the work worthwhile? Did the boys really aid in the production of food? This was the question uppermost in the minds of many educators in the fall of 1917. A conference was held in the winter of 1918 to consider the policy of the government toward school children, and a representative of the Department of Agriculture was asked point blank if the work had any value. His reply, although qualified, was in the affirmative:

It was effective where it was well-directed. Having just come from Illinois it is fresh in my mind. A good many boys were sent out of Chicago from a trade school by a teacher, a Mr. Hays, and he con-

[24] Smart, loc. cit., p. 483.
[25] Thomas H. Briggs, "Secondary Education," Biennial Survey, 1916–1918 (Bureau of Education Bulletin, 1919, No. 88), p. 219; Alexander Thompson, "Preparedness —A Veneer or a Fundamental—Which Will Our Schools Give Our Children," N.E.A., Proceedings, 1917, p. 68.
[26] Smart, loc. cit., pp. 482–484.

sidered every individual case, both on the part of the boys and the farmer asking for help. He asked what kind of a place it was, where will the boy sleep, will he have meals with the family, etc., and he considered with the same care the young men who were anxious to go out, and he had to reject a great many.

In fact, this same representative added, "a good many" farmers testified that high school boys were better than transient farm labor in harvesting and general work.[27] Another investigator reported that the farmers were actually enthusiastic.[28]

In spite of a large amount of criticism voiced against releasing schoolboys for farm work,[29] the reaction in general was favorable. A majority of the farmers welcomed the assistance.[30] Many educators felt that this type of activity produced educational by-products of considerable value. The public developed an increased appreciation of the high school boy. City youngsters reached a new understanding of the farmer and his problems, and agricultural courses were introduced for the first time into many city schools.[31] As a result, more systematic plans were made for extending the work during the planting season of 1918.

Meanwhile, the Department of Labor, keenly aware of the scarcity of farm workers, in the spring of 1917 took steps to organize the schoolboys of America in a great federal program. These plans matured when the United States Boys' Working Reserve was established within the National Employment Service. William E. Hall was appointed Federal Director. A National Committee was appointed to assist him; this was composed of the governors of the several states, or their appointees, and the leaders of the national boys' organizations, for example, the Boy Scouts. A National Advisory Council was also created with a membership drawn from the ranks of farm management, physical welfare agencies, and transportation, finance, and child labor organizations. In charge of each state was a director responsible to the federal authorities; his work was facilitated by traveling federal organ-

27 "Minutes of a Conference in the Offices of the Commissioner of Education," February 15, 1918. National Archives (Bureau of Education, 106–13).

28 *School and Society*, vol. V (May 12, 1917), p. 558.

29 Smart, *loc. cit.*, p. 384.

30 *Report of the State Superintendent of Public Schools of the State of Maine for the School Year Ending June 30, 1918* (Maine, 1919), p. 9.

31 Briggs, *loc. cit.*, p. 219.

izers and a number of zone directors. Within the framework of this nation-wide organization, the boys of America between the ages of sixteen and twenty-one were mobilized to relieve the shortage of agricultural labor.[32]

The key men were the state directors. Success or failure depended upon their ability to stimulate enthusiasm in school men, agricultural agents, leaders of boys' clubs, women's clubs, and editors of local papers. One of the ablest of the state directors was Charles A. Parcells, of Detroit, Michigan. His methods were interesting and illustrative. To further his program, in the fall of 1918 a banquet was given to the 200 boys who had worked on the farms around Grand Rapids during the summer. In the midst of the festivities, telegrams were received from the governor and high officials of the state. The high point of the evening was reached when Parcells announced that the splendid service rendered by the boys had made them eligible to belong to the United States Boys' Working Reserve. They then arose and took the following oath of allegiance:

I do solemnly swear that I will support and defend the Constitution of the United States against all enemies, foreign and domestic; that I will keep true faith and allegiance to the same; that I take this obligation freely, without any mental reservation or purpose of evasion; and I will faithfully discharge the duties which I am about to assume.[33]

Governor Sleeper aided in the campaign by setting aside the week of March 18–23, 1918 as enrollment week; during this period over 9,000 boys were registered for service. Although many would have worked on farms anyway, it was estimated that perhaps sixty per cent were real additions to the labor supply of Michigan.[34]

Great care was taken in placing the boys. Only those over sixteen were accepted, and Junior Counselors were maintained in the local branches of the United States Employment Service with orders to make every effort to persuade those under sixteen to remain in school. Where these efforts were unsuccessful, the counselors tried to place the boy in a position which offered some promise for the future, suggesting at the same time a program of

[32] *School and Society*, vol. VI (July 14, 1917), p. 51.
[33] L. B. W., "The United States Boys' Working Reserve: Boy Soldiers of the Soil," *Michigan History Magazine*, vol. IV (January, 1920), p. 280.
[34] *Ibid.*, p. 281.

continuation schooling.[35] The names of reliable farmers were secured from reputable local officials, and application blanks were mailed to those on the approved list. For his part, the farmer was required to state on the blank the type of work required of the boy and the salary he was willing to guarantee.[36] Such, in brief, was the general procedure by which the enrollment of the federal organization was secured.

Michigan had reason to be pleased with the experiment. Over 7,000 boys were placed on farms during the summer of 1918, and it was claimed that hundreds of acres would have been plowed under if the boys' services had not been available. An estimated harvest of $5,000,000 worth of beets was credited to their work.[37]

Many other states also mobilized the schoolboys for farm service. In Maine, for example, only 600 boys registered with the Junior Volunteers during the spring and summer of 1917; in the following year the number rose to over 2,000. The farmers reported that they "were greatly pleased" with the boys' work, and the State Department of Education claimed that the students had helped to relieve the labor shortage.[38] New Jersey, to cite another instance, registered over 10,000 boys as Junior Farm Recruits during the first two months of our participation in the war.[39] Some states, like Michigan, started independently, then swung their organizations into the federal program. It appears to be true that the work was done most systematically in those nine states which did join the national organization.[40] Before the war ended, the Department of Labor claimed an enrollment of 250,000 in the United States Boys' Working Reserve.[41]

The work was further expedited by the generous support of the state colleges and agricultural schools. Many of these institutions gave short courses for high school boys before they took up their farm duties.[42] At State College, Pennsylvania, the ad-

[35] Sixth Annual Report of the Children's Bureau (1918), p. 9; Memorandum, July 10, 1918. National Archives (Bureau of Education, 107–23).

[36] L. B. W., loc. cit., p. 285.

[37] Ibid.

[38] Maine, Report of the State Superintendent of Public Schools (1918), p. 9.

[39] School and Society, vol. VI (August 18, 1917), p. 196.

[40] Smart, loc. cit., p. 385.

[41] Sixth Annual Report of the Children's Bureau (1918), p. 9.

[42] William M. Hepburn and Louis M. Sears, Purdue University: Fifty Years of Progress (Indianapolis: The Hollenbeck Press, 1925), p. 194.

vanced students in the Agricultural School were responsible for this training; later these same students took charge of farm camps composed of units of twenty-four boys.[43] Where trained instructors were not available, substitutes were used. In some cases retired farmers gave the instruction; implement dealers frequently staged demonstrations on the use of their machinery; and the county agricultural agents taught short courses in the local schools.[44] Probably the chief criticism that could legitimately be directed against all of these activities was their lack of organization, and it was along these lines that the United States Boys' Working Reserve was operating when the war ended.

3. Increasing Production:
The United States School Garden Army

Like so many of the war activities, the home garden movement had roots in the prewar years. As early as 1914 Congress took cognizance of the educational value of this new development and appropriated a small sum of money for the Bureau of Education to use in expanding home and school gardening. By 1917, 100,000 school children in about one hundred cities were doing garden work under the direction of the educational authorities.[45]

The Commissioner of Education, P. P. Claxton, was impressed with the possibilities of the work. On February 24, 1918, he transmitted to the Secretary of the Interior a detailed plan for a national program to serve, he said, "as one means of meeting the food emergency which now exists."[46] Claxton proposed to enlist all children between the ages of nine and fifteen in systematic garden work on vacant lots and in backyards. It was estimated that at least 5,000,000 of the 7,000,000 boys and girls of this age in the United States could find some available space for a garden. With one teacher-director in charge of each group of 100–150 children, a minimum of 40,000 instructors would be required. It was hoped

[43] *School and Society*, vol. VII (March 30, 1918), p. 379.
[44] Smart, *loc. cit.*, pp. 486–487.
[45] Memorandum of P. P. Claxton, June 2, 1921. National Archives (Bureau of Education, 400–25). For examples of school garden enterprises before the war, see Charles O. Smith, "Garden Clubs in the Schools of Englewood, New Jersey" (Bureau of Education Bulletin, 1917, No. 26); and J. L. Randall, "Educative and Economic Possibilities of School-Directed Home Gardening in Richmond, Indiana" (Bureau of Education Bulletin, 1917, No. 6).
[46] P. P. Claxton to F. K. Lane. National Archives (Bureau of Education, 400–25).

that parents and older brothers and sisters would assist in the work, all of which was to be done after school, on Saturdays, and during vacation periods.

The Commissioner painted a glowing picture of the expected benefits: At least $250,000,000 worth of food could be produced; raised at the point of consumption, this would release transportation facilities and an equivalent amount of produce for export to the Allied nations. The money made by the children would be invested in war bonds, and the children would benefit physically, mentally, and spiritually. The project was to be, in brief, a combination of business, education, and patriotism.

Claxton then went on to suggest a plan of organization. The Bureau of Education would conduct the work through a national director, an assistant director, fifteen stenographers, and one messenger—truly a modest request! Aid would be furnished by the Department of Agriculture, which would give bulletins and leaflets on gardening and which would ask its county extension agents to use part of their time in supervising the teacher-directors. Further help would be furnished by the Council of National Defense, which would assist in raising money in the local communities to pay the salaries of the directors. Finally, the National War Garden Commission would cooperate by donating unlimited numbers of its practical farm bulletins and by printing at cost the daily record book already prepared by the Bureau of Education.[47]

The relationship between the National War Garden Commission and the Bureau of Education was extremely close. An independent enterprise, conceived by Charles Lathrop Pack in March, 1917, the National War Garden Commission had a rapid growth. The list of members was impressive, including such names as Luther Burbank and President Charles W. Eliot of Harvard.[48]

[47] *Ibid.*

[48] Pack, *The War Garden Victorious*, pp. 1, 9. Other members were P. P. Claxton; Dr. Irving Fisher, Yale University; Fred H. Goff, Ohio; John Hays Hammond, Massachusetts; Fairfax Harrison, Virginia; Hon. Myron T. Herrick, Ohio; President John Grier Hibben, Princeton University; Emerson McMillin, New York; A. W. Shaw, Illinois; Mrs. John Dickinson Sherman, Chairman of the Conservation Department of the General Federation of Women's Clubs; Captain J. B. White, Missouri; Hon. James Wilson, former Secretary of Agriculture; Assistant Secretary of Agriculture (for the year 1917), Hon. Carl Vrooman; P. S. Ridsdale, Executive Secretary, who was also Executive Secretary of the American Forestry Association, with the Conservation Department of which the Commission was affiliated; and Norman C. McLoud, Associate Secretary.

Success was in large measure the result of an ably conducted publicity campaign. Daily garden lessons were released to the press, a short instruction book was prepared and millions of copies were distributed free, canning and drying manuals were published, and the country was plastered with posters. Among the most compelling of these posters were James Montgomery Flagg's "Sow the Seeds of Victory" and J. Paul Verree's "Can the Kaiser."[49] By the end of 1917 the Commission was prepared to claim substantial achievements. More than 3,500,000 home gardens had been planted, some 500,000,000 quarts of vegetables and fruits had been canned, and the total value of the produce amounted to about $350,000,000. To comment in Pack's own words: "Assuredly tall oaks from little acorns grow."[50]

With such claims to lend weight to Claxton's proposal of a federal program, it is not surprising that he won the hearty support of the administration. President Wilson gave a strong endorsement, expressing the hope that "this spring every school will have a regiment in the volunteer war-garden army."[51] Of more immediate importance was his contribution of $50,000 from the National Security and Defense Fund.[52]

By April detailed plans for the United States School Garden Army had been definitely worked out along the lines originally suggested by the Commissioner of Education. A national director, J. H. Francis, was appointed. Claxton, in a letter to the educational authorities of the country, explained the program and asked for their cooperation. Every member of the army was to have an insignia—the privates, for example, were to have a service bar with U.S.S.G.A. in red letters on a white background with a border of blue. Each company of not more than 150 children was to be under the direction of a teacher, and was to be officered by a captain and one or two lieutenants.[53] The school men were referred to the States Division of the Council of National Defense

49 *Ibid.*, pp. 17–21.

50 *Ibid.*, p. 23.

51 W. Wilson to F. K. Lane, February 25, 1918. National Archives (Bureau of Education, 107–23).

52 J. F. Abel to P. P. Claxton, March 9, 1918. National Archives (Bureau of Education, 400–25).

53 J. H. Francis, *The United States School Garden Army* (Bureau of Education Bulletin, 1919, No. 26), p. 5.

for teachers salaries, if these could be raised in no other way, and to the National War Garden Commission for practical garden bulletins.[54]

The response to Claxton's request was gratifying. Agricultural experts from the colleges gave freely of their time and advice.[55] Patriotic and educational associations cooperated.[56] The newspapers printed slogans, posters, editorials, lessons, and articles prepared by specialists.[57] Julius Rosenwald offered to match, dollar for dollar, funds raised by local agencies to conduct garden work among Negro children in the South.[58]

Large claims were made for the success of the movement. In July, 1918, the Department of the Interior announced an enrollment of 1,500,000 children and the cultivation of more than 1,200,000 gardens—the discrepancy between plots and workers being the number of gardens that had failed. It was stated that 20,000 acres had been converted into productive lands, releasing an equal amount of acreage for the growth of produce more important to the war effort. An estimated 50,000 teachers were reached by the educational leaflets, hundreds of thousands of parents became interested in the activities of their children, and thousands of civic associations found a new reason for existence. The average yield per acre was valued at $500. "In other words," the report concluded, "the school children of America will have this year contributed not less than $50,000,000 worth of food products to winning the war. Because this food is consumed at home or marketed in the immediate vicinity of where it is grown it is calculated that the children have given Railway Director McAdoo the equivalent of 50,000 freight cars for the transportation of coal and other war necessities."[59]

This is a glowing report of achievement, and one that receives

[54] P. P. Claxton to educational leaders, March 21, 1918. National Archives (Bureau of Education, 400–25).

[55] *School and Society*, vol. VII (March 16, 1918), p. 315.

[56] *Ibid.*, vol. VIII (November 23, 1918), p. 618.

[57] R. H. Wilson, "The War Garden Movement," *School and Society*, vol. VIII (August 10, 1918), p. 179.

[58] *School and Society*, vol. VIII (November 2, 1918), p. 529. See also correspondence between J. Rosenwald and P. P. Claxton, spring and summer of 1918. National Archives (Bureau of Education, 400–25). An accounting of April 12, 1919, revealed that Rosenwald was called upon for only $3,299.25.

[59] *Ibid.*, vol. VIII (August 31, 1918), p. 254.

ample corroboration in the files of periodicals and the pages of the press for the months of 1918. Under the stimulus of the drive. lawns, tennis courts, and golf links were torn up; backyards and vacant lots were covered with a mantle of bean, pea, and tomato plants; and many of the waste places of the nation were transformed into radish and potato patches. But beneath the records lies another story. One gets a hint of it in the Interior Department's own report, where it is stated that 300,000 gardens "failed from various causes."[60] Since this was one fifth of all the projects, the waste in seeds, time, and fertilizer must have been enormous. Moreover, if the memories of those who played a small part in the direction of the children may be trusted, many of the "successful" projects were a monument to the director, not to the boys or girls who proudly wore the badges.[61]

No less cogent was the criticism made by President Charles W. Eliot of Harvard. "I have just read with mortification," he wrote to Claxton, "the circular about school gardens headed 'Memorandum for the Press,' dated April 8, 1918. It is hysteria and gross exaggeration from beginning to end. . . . Should not all persons connected with education do their best to prevent the issue of all such senseless announcements and exhortations?" Eliot particularly objected to the emphasis upon financial profits to be derived from the war gardens. The President of Harvard "ventured to doubt the computation" that fifteen dollars' worth of food had been produced for every dollar invested. He admitted his desire to see garden projects in all the schools, but expressed the fear that if "war emotions" lured agriculture and horticulture into the institutions by specious promises of financial profits, the garden movement would be doomed. President Eliot insisted that such projects could be no more profitable in terms of dollars and cents than the industrial arts had proved to be—and their contribution in this respect had amounted to nothing.[62] It is

60 *Ibid.*

61 Robert T. Hance, "School Gardens," *School and Society,* vol. VIII (October 26, 1918), pp. 497–99. The writer expressed doubt as to the educational value of activities not fully planned and executed by the pupils. Those who wish corroboration of Hance's contention that the adult directors frequently did all the work, need only consult their own memories or the memories of their friends who took part in the war garden movement of 1918.

62 Correspondence between C. W. Eliot and P. P. Claxton, April 18–27, 1918. National Archives (Bureau of Education, 400–25).

interesting to note that he lived to see the whole school garden program collapse in the post-war years.

The most serious criticism of the garden activity came from the Department of Agriculture. From the first intimation of Claxton's plans the Department was afraid that the program would encroach upon the extension work being conducted under the Smith-Lever Act. While Claxton's plans were still maturing, the Secretary of Agriculture wrote a letter of warning:

> The Department is planning to put on an extensive campaign for the promotion of this work, and would be pleased to cooperate with you wherever such cooperation is practicable. You will realize that the Department approves this problem from the point of view of food production, and that its educational phases are of secondary importance.[63]

This letter initiated a bitter conflict between the two federal agencies.[64] The basic issue was one of jurisdiction, the Department of Agriculture claiming that for a number of years it had been doing exactly this sort of work through its boy and girl farm clubs. Claxton sharply replied that it was the very success of the garden enterprise which aroused the jealousy of the Agricultural Department; he later contended that it was this same jealousy which was responsible for the blocking of further appropriations for the U.S.S.G.A. a little over a year after the war had ended.[65] Although there was truth in Claxton's charge, there were other reasons for the cessation of the school garden work. With the signing of the Armistice, the food situation was no longer so acute; moreover, there was no war spirit to stimulate the people, and they were reluctant to tear up tennis courts and spend their week ends with hoe and spade for the sake of an occasional basket of home-grown string beans.

The Department of Agriculture was especially incensed at the close relationship between the Bureau of Education and the independently operated National War Garden Commission. This

[63] D. F. Houston to P. P. Claxton, January 31, 1918. National Archives (Bureau of Education, 400–25).

[64] Correspondence between the Bureau of Education and the Department of Agriculture, 1918. National Archives (Bureau of Education, 400–25).

[65] Memorandum of P. P. Claxton, June 2, 1921. National Archives (Bureau of Education, 400–25).

annoyance was expressed with some heat by the Assistant Secretary of Agriculture in a letter to Claxton:

The circulation of [their] literature is most unfortunate. That is a private undertaking without responsibility but its name conveys the impression to the lay mind that it is an official function. The work is not conducted with the necessary care and I have reason to believe that the miscellaneous distribution of its propaganda may do more harm than good. Indeed, I feel that it is a serious mistake for any function of government to give official recognition to any ill-considered undertaking of this kind, and that the Department of Agriculture and the Agricultural Colleges in all the states of the Union are the best sources of information on agricultural subjects, including gardening. . . .

[It] would be unthinkable for the Department of Agriculture to institute any activity concerning public education without suggestion or full approval of the Bureau of Education, and I cannot help thinking that the Bureau of Education should hesitate to undertake any agricultural activity without the suggestion or approval of the Department of Agriculture.[66]

The controversy continued throughout the spring, summer, and fall of 1918. Finally, on November 13, after a number of conferences, the two parties to the dispute agreed to divide the work. This solution was embodied in a memorandum which, it was hoped, would so clarify the problem that further duplication of effort would be obviated. It was agreed that "all subject matter involved in practical instruction and advice on gardening by any public agency should be such as is approved by the Department of Agriculture and the Agricultural College." This statement was, of course, a blow at Pack's National War Garden Commission. So at last, with the war ended, the vexatious problem of privately prepared agricultural literature was finally resolved. It was also agreed that garden work in the grammar grades of cities, towns, and villages was a recognized function of the public school system. The Bureau of Education was given a free hand in this area of activity, and its agents were to represent the federal government in developing the program through the state and local organizations. On the other hand, the Commissioner of Education promised to make no further efforts to induce school men to extend the work of the U.S.S.G.A. He did, however, reserve the right

[66] March 23, 1918. National Archives (Bureau of Education, 400–25).

to consider and to act favorably upon voluntary requests from superintendents, boards of education, and teachers. For its part, the Department of Agriculture agreed to confine its activities to the rural areas, with the one reservation that if city children applied for admission to its own boys' and girls' clubs, they would be received.[67]

Although the conference closed with a warm promise to stand together "solidly for conditions that will bring dignity, strength, and a fuller recognition to the most fundamental and universally important of the great arts"—meaning, of course, agriculture— the marriage of the two organizations was short-lived. Disputes continued, ending in 1919 with the complete disintegration of the United States School Garden Army.[68] It is unfortunate that in this work, as with so many of the wartime enterprises, hasty organization and failure clearly to define policy brought only friction and ultimate disaster.

4. Conserving Food

While it was important to increase the production of foodstuffs, it was no less vital to conserve. The leadership of the conservation program was assumed by the Food Administration. Even before the division was officially established, Hoover began to outline his plans. On June 9, 1917, he asked the Commissioner of Education to meet in conference to discuss means by which the Bureau could cooperate in the conservation of food.[69] Four days later Claxton submitted a rough draft of his proposals. It was necessary, he pointed out, to reach all those who used food in the home. This included at least 50,000,000 men and women. These adults, Claxton wrote, "must be instructed in as clear and definite a way as possible. To reach all of these with printed bulletins is practically impossible. Some millions of them cannot read; more millions do not read. I can think of only one means by which

[67] Memorandum of Understanding Between the United States Department of Agriculture and the Department of Interior Relating to the Organization of School Children for Home Garden Work, November 13, 1918. National Archives (Bureau of Education, 400–25).

[68] Correspondence between the Bureau of Education and the Department of Agriculture, spring of 1919. National Archives (Bureau of Education, 400–25).

[69] H. Hoover to P. P. Claxton, June 9, 1917. National Archives (Bureau of Education, 106–18).

all of them can be reached," he concluded, "and that is through the agency of the schoolhouse."[70]

With funds limited and the cost of printing high, Claxton suggested that the Food Administration start its campaign with the teachers in attendance at the summer schools. Through the teachers trained in these schools and in the teachers' institutes which met for a week or more in the summer, fall, and early winter, instruction in food conservation might be carried to millions of children and their parents. If a short course were prepared, the Commissioner stated, the Bureau of Education would be glad to give it the widest possible publicity among school men.[71]

Hoover acted upon this proposal with his characteristic energy. Working under his direction, domestic science experts immediately rushed to completion a ten-lesson course, copies of which were forwarded to the summer schools. In spite of the haste with which it had been carried on, the enterprise was evidently a success. Several hundred thousand students took the course in the summer of 1917.[72] Later, in the fall, the executive officers of twenty-two of the large summer sessions met at Ann Arbor, Michigan, and voted "unanimously and enthusiastically" to continue the work in the summer of 1918.[73]

Meanwhile, three courses of a more extensive nature were being prepared. These were released week by week during the spring semester of 1918 to more than 700 colleges, normal schools, and state educational institutions. Over 40,000 teachers were reached. The courses were repeated in 150 summer sessions.[74] Through these teachers the food message was carried to millions of homes.

[70] P. P. Claxton to H. Hoover, June 13, 1917. National Archives (Bureau of Education, 106–18).

[71] Ibid.

[72] School and Society, vol. VI (September 8, 1917), p. 291.

[73] Maxcy R. Dickson, The War Comes to All: The Story of the United States Food Administration as a Propaganda Agency (unpublished doctoral dissertation, George Washington University, 1942). This study is based upon the extensive files of the Food Administration in the National Archives.

[74] Dickson, op. cit. "The first course, 'Food and the War,' comprised fifteen lectures," wrote Mr. Dickson. "It was open to all students and gave a general survey of the world's food problems in its geographic, economic, and nutritional aspects and the effects of the war. The second course, 'Fundamentals of Food and Nutrition in Relation to the War,' was a course of forty-eight lectures open to students taking Course I, but primarily for juniors and seniors. The third was a laboratory course of sixty-four hours on the use and conservation of foods. It was open only to students taking Courses I and II."

The preparation and distribution of instructional materials was a cooperative enterprise. Charles H. Judd, in 1917 Director of the School of Education of the University of Chicago, gave an interesting version of the beginning of this work:

> Mr. Hoover invited me to come to Washington and said he wanted to carry on propaganda for the Food Administration in the schools. I told him I was glad to undertake to develop a broad social understanding in the schools but was not interested in specialized propaganda. Mr. Hoover accepted my view.
>
> I then called his attention to the fact that there was a federal agency related to public education. I said that in my judgment any work with the schools should be a joint enterprise. He accepted this view and put me in contact with Secretary Lane. I went, of course, to Mr. Claxton of the then Bureau of Education.[75]

The organization that was eventually set up within the Food Administration for the purpose of reaching the educational institutions was headed by the Schools and College Division. Each state chose, with the approval of the Governor, a Director of School and College Activities. In addition, every school and institution of higher learning was requested to select a School or College Food Administrator to serve as chairman of a committee of faculty and students. To aid in the collection of suitable materials for instruction, an experimental laboratory was set up in cooperation with the Office of Home Economics of the Department of Agriculture. This laboratory was directed by representatives of the Agricultural Department and the Food Administration; the experiments were conducted by a small staff of scientifically trained investigators. In this way data were assembled. The publications were distributed through the cooperation of the Women's Committee of the Council of National Defense, the Department of Agriculture's extension agents, the Bureau of Education, and the Creel Committee.[76]

Publications circulated by these organizations ran into millions of copies. One extremely important series, *Lessons in Community and National Life,* written by Charles H. Judd and Leon C. Marshall, has already been discussed,[77] and attention has been

[75] C. H. Judd to the author, May 14, 1941.
[76] Dickson, *op. cit.*
[77] See *supra,* pp. 65–69.

directed to the conservation courses given to teachers in colleges, normal schools, and summer sessions.[78] A growing demand for suitable material for public school teachers led to the publication of a booklet called *Food Guide for War Service at Home.* This was prepared by two teachers and a representative of the Department of Agriculture.[79] The Bureau of Education compiled a volume of nearly eighty recipes under the title of *The Preparation and the Preservation of Vegetables.*[80] A number of leaflets were written specifically for use by school children. *Young America's Part* was issued in the spring of 1918; a few months later a laboratory manual called the *Use and Conservation of Food* was distributed in the public schools. This was one of a series which also included *The Little Book of Food and Winning the War: How the Little Folks Held the Line.*[81] When it is remembered that this enumeration by no means exhausts the list, and that the Department of Agriculture had in circulation a large number of both prewar and emergency leaflets, the sheer volume of conservation literature poured into the schools during the war years is seen to be impressive. While much of it came in for a generous share of criticism,[82] either because it was inadequate or because it misrepresented the facts, there is no doubt that the material was widely used. Indeed, the historian for the Food Administration states that these public school activities were among the most important and fruitful of the entire conservation program.[83]

Among the most active of those who participated in the food conservation campaign were the home economics teachers and the extension agents of the Department of Agriculture. As in the case of agricultural education, training in the household arts had been developing rapidly before the war.[84] Where in 1900 only twelve normal schools had introduced home economics courses,

[78] See *supra*, p. 159.

[79] Katherine Blunt, Frances L. Swain, and Florence Powdermaker (New York: Charles Scribner's Sons, 1918).

[80] Henrietta W. Calvin and Carrie A. Lyford (Bureau of Education Bulletin, 1917, No. 47).

[81] Dickson, *op. cit.*

[82] Dickson, *op. cit.*

[83] William C. Mullendore, *History of the United States Food Administration, 1917–1919* (California: Stanford University Press, 1941), p. 92.

[84] Isabel Bevier, *Home Economics in Education* (Philadelphia: J. Lippincott, 1924), pp. 169–174.

by 1914 work of this nature was being offered in practically all public normal institutions; and between this date and our entry into the war, the movement became even more widespread.[85] The special responsibility that rested upon the shoulders of this trained group of home economics teachers was called to their attention in a bulletin issued by the Bureau of Education in the summer of 1917:

Teachers of home economics can reach into the homes of the patrons of the public schools and aid in extending a knowledge of food conditions. They can explain the reasons why American families are asked to modify some of their food habits. They can raise food economy to the plane of patriotic service. They can assist families in matters of economy, so that better living conditions can be maintained. Of course, all home economics teachers will alter laboratory practices so as to conform to present food conditions, but they may do much more; they may carefully make plain the reasons why America with her abundance of food material asks her people to select carefully, use wisely and waste not one particle.[86]

The home economics teachers fully lived up to the demands laid upon them. In Oakland, California, for example, the household arts department of the public school system gave instruction in cooking well-balanced meals, distributed thousands of practical recipes to homes, utilized the school kitchens to demonstrate efficient cookery practices to the parents, offered courses in camp cooking to the boys, and taught dietetics in connection with classes in home nursing.[87] These are typical of the activities carried on by home economics teachers throughout the country.

The children, too, lived up to expectations. They helped to preserve fruits and vegetables in school kitchens and at home. They operated demonstration booths in public places.[88] They participated in the inevitable poster and essay contests.[89] They took part in the various conservation campaigns. In brief, they were propaganda agents, carrying to every home in the land the

[85] Mary G. Barnum, "The Normal Schools and the Demand for Education in the Household Arts," N.E.A., *Proceedings*, 1917, p. 397.

[86] *School and Society*, vol. VI (November 10, 1917), p. 558.

[87] *Report of the Superintendent of Schools, 1917–1918* (Oakland, California: Published by the Board of Education, 1919), p. 143.

[88] *Sixty-fourth Annual Report of the Board of Education for the Year Ending June 30, 1918* (Chicago, 1919), p. 139.

[89] Oakland, California, *Report of the Superintendent of Schools* (1918), p. 143.

message of conservation. This, indeed, was Hoover's conception of the part school children should play in the war effort.[90] To him, as to so many other leaders in American life, they were little more than "catalytic agents"[91] whose function was to precipitate patriotic action in the adults. Hoover went so far as to propose that the schools put aside the regulation three "R's" for the duration of the war and devote at least one quarter of their time to food work.[92]

It was in this capacity of propaganda agents that the pupils visited the homes of America to secure the signatures of parents and friends to the "food pledge." A signature was a promise to follow Hoover's requests, and entitled the signer to display a window poster as evidence of his patriotism. The State of Oregon turned in signatures from ninety-two per cent of all families. That this amazing exhibition was not entirely the result of spontaneous enthusiasm is revealed in the report of one county superintendent of schools. This zealous educator required that every home in the county be visited by the school children and "signed" or placed on record "with the reasons for failure." He was extremely proud of the enforced persistence of the teachers and pupils, remarking that "This is the most important work that the schools have ever been called upon to 'put over,' and a true measure of their practical efficiency. . . ."[93] All school men did not, of course, share these views, and it was against just such a "misuse" of the schools that men like Judd obdurately set their faces.[94]

While the overlapping of jurisdiction and the duplication of effort and published materials were disheartening, the record reveals the story of a successful conservation campaign. Although C. L. Pack's exuberant claim that 1,450,000,000 jars of fruit and vegetables had been preserved in 1918 is difficult to accept,[95] there can be no doubt that substantial achievements resulted from Hoover's efforts. Much energy was expended in attempts to

[90] C. H. Judd to the author, May 14, 1941.

[91] This peculiarly apt term was employed by James R. Mock to describe the attitude of many leaders in regard to the proper function of the schools in wartime. Interview, Washington, December 10, 1940.

[92] Dickson, op. cit.

[93] Oregon, Twenty-third Biennial Report of the Superintendent of Public Instruction (1918), p. 6.

[94] See supra, pp. 67–68.

[95] The War Garden Victorious, p. 23.

stimulate patriotic ardor, yet the activities were also educational in the best meaning of the term. "It is safe to say," concluded one observer, "that the people of the United States, as a whole, learned more of food, its classes, uses, and cost than they had learned in five years before."[96]

5. Saving Money and Scrap

Conservation efforts did not stop with food. During the war the Waste Reclamation Division salvaged such scrap as metals, leather, paper, horse-hair, bags, tinfoil, and peach pits to the value of $1,650,000,000.[97] The Treasury Department raised $21,-477,000,000 in loans from the American people. This was particularly gratifying, for the government had asked for only $18,500,-000,000 in four Liberty and one Victory Loan drives, and now accepted even less money than was subscribed.[98] During this same period, the Junior Red Cross collected $3,700,000 in dues from the school children; in addition, it furnished to the armed forces more than 15,000,000 articles, such as surgical dressings, furniture, and games valued at over $10,000,000.[99] Money was also raised for such organizations as the Y.M.C.A. and Belgian Relief, and for such projects as the adoption of refugee children in Europe.

While it is true that the Treasury Department offered its bonds at attractive rates of interest—the first issued paid 3.5 per cent; the last, 4.75 per cent[100]—this is by no means a complete explanation of the unusual success of the campaigns, and of course it had no connection with the other drives for salvage and relief. As in the case of Hoover's equally successful campaigns for food conservation, much of the credit belongs to the boys and girls in the public schools.

The money subscribed by the children was in itself impressive. No figures are available for the country as a whole, but the following examples will illustrate the extent of the financial contribu-

96 Bevier, *Home Economics in Education,* p. 174.
97 *National School Service,* vol. I (March 15, 1919), p. 1.
98 *National School Service,* vol. I (May 1, 1919), p. 16.
99 *The Work of the American Red Cross During the War. A Statement of Finances and Accomplishments. For the Period July 1, 1917 to February 28, 1919* (Washington: American Red Cross, 1919), pp. 15, 25. See *infra,* pp. 193–194, for further details concerning the articles produced by the Junior Red Cross.
100 *National School Service,* vol. I (May 1, 1919), p. 16.

tion of the children. In one year, the pupils of the public schools of Maine bought over $500,000 worth of thrift stamps.[101] Incomplete returns from West Virginia showed that, by October 1, 1918, the children had purchased over $600,000 worth of war stamps and bonds.[102] The pupils of the Chicago schools invested more than $1,432,315 in War Savings Stamps during 1918.[103] This was, on the whole, a remarkable demonstration of patriotic effort.

The children made their major contribution, however, in the service they rendered as publicity agents. It was generally agreed that, as one educator expressed it, "the schools did their most effective work by furnishing a means of carrying the plan and responsibility to parents and patrons."[104] Another educational authority observed that "The need for popular subscription to the Liberty Loans was presented most effectively in many homes through the pleading questions of school children."[105]

Various methods were used to stimulate the interest of the pupils and, through them, to reach the parents. The War Savings Division of the Treasury Department assumed the leadership of the publicity campaign. One of its major activities was the preparation and distribution of propaganda materials. A series of twenty "Thrift Leaflets" was written in cooperation with the Department of Agriculture. These were designed to induce people to save not only money, but all materials useful in wartime, such as fuel, food, clothing, and electricity. The topics treated included *How Shall We Choose Our Food, Thrift on the Farm, Business Methods for the Home, Saving Fuel in Heating, Taking Care of Your Clothing, Teaching Thrift to Young Children,* and *Is Thrift Worth While, Mr. American? Then Buy War Savings Stamps.* The Treasury Department also published a *Textbook for Speakers on Thrift Stamps and War Savings Bonds.*[106] In this bulletin the

---

[101] Maine, *Report of the State Superintendent of Public Schools* (1918), p. 9.

[102] *Biennial Report of the State Superintendent of Free Schools of West Virginia for the Two Years Ending June 30, 1918* (Charleston, West Virginia, 1919), p. 20.

[103] *Sixty-Fifth Annual Report of the Board of Education for the Year Ending June 30, 1919* (Chicago, 1919), p. 28.

[104] West Virginia, *Biennial Report of the State Superintendent of Free Schools* (1918), p. 20.

[105] *Seventy-Third Annual Report of the Commissioner of Public Schools of Rhode Island* (Albany, New York: Hamilton Press, 1918), pp. 5–6.

[106] Treasury Department, National War Savings Committee (Washington: Government Printing Office, 1918).

war-savings plan was explained by the Chairman of the National War Savings Committee. The Secretary of the Treasury, William G. McAdoo, gave reasons for our declaration of war. Suggestions on how to plan a thrift talk and illustrative data were supplied. Part of the booklet contained model speeches for those who wished to address school children, city audiences, church congregations, or groups apathetic to the war effort.

Bulletins of a similar nature were published by the Creel Committee for the use of the Junior Four Minute Men in the public schools.[107] Creel's organization also opened the pages of its teachers' periodical for the publicity of the Treasury Department. This committee was without doubt one of the most effective channels through which to reach the schools.

In addition to the usual appeals to teachers and the ever-present poster and essay contests, a number of unusual devices were employed to excite enthusiasm. In New Jersey, for example, the State Department of Education prepared special lessons in mathematics. These were built around the topic of Liberty Bonds. Pupils were asked such questions as:

1. The first issue of Liberty Bonds was for $2,000,000,000, but the public subscribed for $3,000,000,000. By what per cent was the first issue oversubscribed?

8. How much would a man have to invest in Liberty Bonds to pay his daughter's college expenses from the income if the expenses average $400 each semester?

The State Department also recommended that committees of pupils be formed in every school to visit the local post office or bank and find out about thrift stamps and war bonds.[108]

The success of the campaigns depended to a great extent upon the vigor shown by the leaders in each state. In Oregon, the State Director of the War Savings Campaign called a meeting in every schoolhouse on June 28, 1918, to celebrate President Wilson's "National War Savings Day." He also secured permission

107 The third and fourth of these *School Bulletins* were published as supplements to *National School Service*, vol. I (September 15 and November 15, 1918).

108 *Annual Report of the State Board of Education and of the Commissioner of Education of New Jersey with Accompanying Documents for the Year Ending June 30, 1918* (Somerville, New Jersey: The Unionist-Gazette Association, 1919), pp. 21–22, 29.

from the educational authorities to organize the school children into what he called "Junior Rainbow Regiments." Each regiment enrolled 1,000 pupils. To become eligible for membership, a child had to sell at least fifty dollars' worth of thrift stamps. By the end of June, 1918, five regiments had been formed, the last with 1,300 members. It was estimated that these 5,300 children alone had sold over $500,000 worth of bonds, and that the total raised in the state school system was $2,500,000.[109]

So it went throughout the nation, with state after state vieing for the honor of selling the most bonds. The Superintendent of Public Schools in Idaho proudly stated that "Madison County had the distinction of being the first county in the United States to report an enrollment of one hundred per cent of its school children for thrift stamps."[110] His words were echoed by a fellow educator in a neighboring state who claimed that ninety-five per cent of Colorado's school children had invested in war savings stamps or Liberty Bonds.[111]

These drives to conserve food, save money, and salvage scrap were of fundamental importance in the war effort. They involved, as one authority pointed out, "stupendous savings in the staples of food supply, the zealous conservation of mineral and forest resources, the introduction of effective war prohibition, and the growing of home gardens—in a word, the practice of thrift in all phases of home and national life."[112] They were successful because they were well-organized and because they received an enormous amount of excellent publicity. But there was another reason for the exceptional results achieved in the conservation campaigns. One and all, they lent themselves to the movement for thrift education which had been developing rapidly before we entered the war.

The thrift movement had its roots in Germany, where school

[109] Oregon, *Twenty-third Biennial Report of the Superintendent of Public Instruction* (1918), pp. 7–8.

[110] *Third Biennial Report of the State Board of Education and Board of Regents of the University of Idaho* (Boise, Idaho, 1919), p. 58.

[111] *Twenty-second Biennial Report of the State Superintendent of Public Instruction for the Official Biennium Ending November 30, 1918* (Denver, Colorado: Eames Brothers, 1919), p. 9.

[112] Carobel Murphey, *Thrift Through Education* (New York: A. S. Barnes and Company, 1929), p. 13.

savings banks were started early in the nineteenth century. These soon spread to other countries of Europe, but the United States remained indifferent to this development. We were too busy with the exploitation of our resources during the nineteenth century to become concerned over problems of conservation. By 1900, however, we had reached a point where capital for further expansion was badly needed, and we were ready for any plan that would tap the individually small but collectively large resources of the masses. Such a plan was ready and waiting.

In 1885, J. A. Thiry, a school teacher of Long Island City, New York, started a school savings bank. He kept track of the pupils' small accounts by means of stamps. The idea was sound, and in 1890 the Stamp Savings Society of Boston was launched. In this case, the social workers tapped the savings of the poor by distributing the stamps through the "neighborhood houses." The plan spread into other states.[113] Before the World War broke out, Massachusetts had enacted a law providing for compulsory thrift education in the public schools, and laws in New York, New Jersey, California, and Minnesota made provision for the correlation of school and local savings banks.[114] It was this program that formed the basis for the successful thrift stamp plan inaugurated by the Treasury Department in 1917.

A second influence entered the movement for thrift education when certain social agencies began to take an interest in conservation. The Y.W.C.A., for example, in 1913 established a Thrift and Efficiency Commission to encourage thrift education among women. The following year, the American Society for Thrift was started in Chicago.[115] The president of this society, Mrs. W. Straus, was one of the leaders of the Thrift Congress which met in San Francisco in the summer of 1915. From her came the first public suggestion ever enunciated that thrift should be taught in the public schools. As a direct result of her efforts, ably supported by David Starr Jordan and other delegates to the Thrift Congress, the leaders of the National Education Association were encouraged to support the movement.

---

[113] Mildred W. Walter, *Thrift Education Through School Savings* (Report No. IV of the Research Department of the Women's Educational and Industrial Union of Boston, 1928), pp. 7–8.

[114] Murphey, *op. cit.*, p. 12.   [115] *Ibid.*

The National Education Association immediately organized a Committee on Thrift Education, which thereafter met regularly at the annual convention of the Association. Many educators became enthusiastic. Careful studies were carried on, essay contests were held to awaken interest, and in 1918 the Committee issued two bulletins which attracted wide attention: *Agricultural Preparedness and Food Conservation,* and *Financing the War Through Thrift—Reconstruction Through Conservation.*[116] These activities did much to advance the teaching of thrift in the schools.

A third and compelling motive for this type of education was, as has been indicated, the war itself. Those federal agencies concerned with problems of conservation seized the opportunity to cooperate closely with the thrift organizations. Largely as a result of these efforts, the public attitude toward thrift began to change. Before the war, a large number of Americans looked upon the practice of thrift somewhat contemptuously, but in 1917–1918 conservation measures of all sorts were vested with a new dignity.[117] It was patriotic to save. Many people believed, as one student put it: "The practice of thrift furnishes foundations for the best kind of character training. Children can be readily taught the dignity of labor; the moral and economic value of earning and saving; reasons for the elimination of waste; the need for health and strength; the proper employment of the leisure hour, and the necessity for conserving our natural resources."[118]

There were, in addition to its value as "character training," other and more substantial reasons for the practice of thrift. Many institutions—for example, building and loan associations, insurance companies, and savings banks—saw in this type of education an opportunity for immediate and direct financial gain. In the postwar years they brought strong influence to bear upon the educational system to incorporate thrift into the curriculum.[119] The Treasury Department also continued to support the work, even after the war had ended. Indeed, in 1919 the federal govern-

[116] Arthur H. Chamberlain, *Thrift Education. Course of Study Outline for Use in Years One to Eight Inclusive* (2nd edition, The American Society for Thrift, 1928), pp. 3–5.

[117] Murphey, *op. cit.,* p. 15.

[118] Chamberlain, *op. cit.,* p. 5.

[119] Murphey, *op. cit.,* p. 14.

ment launched its most extensive thrift campaign. Courses of study were released for elementary schools,[120] secondary schools,[121] and teacher-training institutions,[122] with the objective of developing a "habit of economy in our national life."[123]

Those responsible for the conservation campaigns could look back upon their efforts with satisfaction. People had been encouraged to increase production; they had also learned to consume more wisely and to save more carefully. As for the schools, striking advances were made in the development of thrift education. This work furnished a precedent for our present courses in consumer and safety education.

[120] The following pamphlets were issued by the Savings Division of the Treasury Department: *Thrift in the Schools. Outline of a Course of Study for Elementary Schools* (Washington, 1919); *Outline Suggested for Teaching Thrift in Elementary Schools* (Washington, 1919); *Ten Lessons in Thrift* (Washington, 1919); *Learning How to Save* (Washington, 1919).

[121] For the secondary schools, the Treasury Department published *Fifteen Lessons in Thrift* (Washington, 1919); and *Thrift Day Program for Use in Elementary and High Schools* (Washington, 1920).

[122] Leaflets distributed to teachers included *Outline of Lessons to Teach Thrift in Normal and Training Schools for Teachers* (Washington, 1919); and *Teaching the Simple Principles of Economics. For Normal and Teacher-Training Schools* (Washington, 1920).

[123] *National School Service,* vol. I (May 1, 1919), p. 9.

CHAPTER VII

LABOR SUPPLY AND THE PRODUCTION OF ARTICLES FOR THE WAR EFFORT

At the beginning of the war, when first the shortages of labor became apparent, a raid was made upon the schools, a great raid, a successful raid, a raid started by a large body of unreflecting opinion. The result of that raid upon the schools has been that hundreds of thousands of children in this country have been prematurely withdrawn from school, and have suffered an irreparable damage, a damage which it will be quite impossible for us hereafter adequately to repair.—*H. L. Fisher, President of the English Board of Education, statement made during the First World War*[1]

More than in time of peace, we should fight now against the obstacles in the way of school attendance. . . . We must do even the impossible in order that the children who will replace tomorrow the generation mowed down by the war may be perfectly well prepared for the duty imposed on them by the sacrifice of their elders.—*French Ministry of Public Instruction, warning given during the First World War*[2]

1. Effect of the War upon Child Labor

To produce and to conserve foodstuffs, it had been necessary to call upon the boys and girls of America. But industry, too, faced its problems, and it was only natural that eyes should be turned hopefully toward the classrooms of the nation. The schools were in a position to make three contributions to the industrial effort: they contained a potential supply of badly needed labor; they had facilities for training skilled workmen; the manual training and domestic science equipment was available for the production of certain simply finished goods for camps and hospitals.

Foremost of the difficulties which confronted industry during

[1] P. P. Claxton, "Europe's Educational Message to America," *School and Society,* vol. VIII (September 14, 1918), p. 312.

[2] *Back-To-School-Drive* (Children's Bureau, Children's Year Leaflet No. 7, Bureau Publication No. 49, 1918), p. 3.

the war was the shortage of manpower, and it was here that the schools could help. Indeed, for many years, a number of manufacturers had looked upon the child life of the country as little more than a vast reservoir of cheap, unskilled labor, and the war only served to confirm their belief. On the other hand, this attitude was revolting, to many of their fellow industrialists, to large sections of the public, and, of course, to professional educators. When the National Association of Manufacturers argued that secondary and higher education was apt to infect the students with "Bolshevism," and that the pupils should therefore be put into trade schools, John Dewey registered a vehement protest. "The moral is evident," he wrote. "The sooner the children leave school . . . the more they will be protected from these dangerous bolshevistic college professors, and the less dangerous will they be to twenty per cent or more annual dividends in the textile industries of the United States, and hence less dangerous to the future of America."[3]

High wages and soaring prices accompanied the wartime demand for labor. Some children were forced to leave school in order to help their parents provide food and shelter for the families; others were drawn into factories by the lure of good pay. After our declaration of war upon Germany, those pupils who left school could defend their actions by a third argument, namely, that it was patriotic to fight on the industrial battlefront. Even by 1916 the situation had become sufficiently serious to call for comments and warnings from educators.[4]

It is difficult to present any precise figures to reveal the effect of the war upon school enrollment,[5] but the available data point to only one conclusion. According to the Bureau of Education, enrollment in the elementary schools continued to increase during 1917 and 1918, rising, however, only one and one half per cent instead of what was considered the normal two and one half per

[3] Curti, *Social Ideas of American Educators*, p. 530.

[4] The Compulsory Education Department of Chicago, Illinois, for example, reported the high cost of living as responsible for pupils "in increasing numbers" leaving school to enter gainful employment. *School and Society*, vol. V (January 20, 1917), p. 75. Comments of this nature were voiced with greater frequency as the nation moved closer to war.

[5] The statistics of the Bureau of Education are not easily broken down for comparative purposes, and no studies are available to contrast conditions in rural and urban areas or in different sections of the country.

cent.[6] The high schools were more directly affected. Here the increase fell off sharply, with a gain of two and one half instead of the anticipated ten per cent. Moreover, the new students were almost all girls; the number of high school boys was actually less than in the previous school year of 1916–1917.[7] Since city schools were most affected, it may be permissible to conclude that greater opportunities for employment in the urban areas were largely responsible for this situation.[8] Further analysis of these figures throws more light upon the picture. With a secondary school enrollment of approximately 1,600,000 in 1918,[9] the normal increase of ten per cent would have added about 160,000 pupils. Since, however, only about twenty-five per cent of the expected increase actually materialized, there were somewhere around 120,000 pupils, nearly all boys, who failed to enroll in 1918.

Many of these boys probably went into industry;[10] others enlisted in the armed services. On this point, an officer from one of the naval recruiting stations in Portland, Oregon, made an interesting observation before the National Education Association in the early summer of 1917. He spoke with pride of the rising rate of schoolboy enlistments.

When the war began for us, numerous high schools throughout the state patriotically release their pupils, giving them certain credits. Thirteen boys came from a high school in Sheridan. Those thirteen were accepted. It was my first experience to accept thirteen men in a row for the navy. Since then I have accepted thirty-seven consecutively. It was the volunteer system in time of actual need, causing the very best to go to the front. High school and college men are the rule now, not the exception as before.[11]

---

[6] By "normal" the Bureau of Education meant the curve of expectancy based upon the enrollments of previous years.

[7] This applied only to the first three grades of high school. The fourth year did not show an actual decrease in enrollment.

[8] *Annual Report of the Commissioner of Education* (1918), p. 6; *School and Society*, vol. VII (February 2, 1918), p. 134; Chicago, Illinois, *Sixty-fourth Annual Report of the Board of Education* (1918), p. 188; *Report of the School Board of the City of Springfield, Massachusetts, 1918* (Springfield, Massachusetts: Press of Springfield Printing and Binding Company, 1918), p. 9; *Twentieth Annual Report of the Superintendent of Schools, 1918* (New York, New York: Board of Education, 1919), p. 184.

[9] *Biennial Survey, 1916–1918* (Bureau of Education Bulletin, 1919, No. 88), p. 59. The exact number was 1,645,171.

[10] *Back-To-School-Drive, op. cit.*, p. 3.

[11] N.E.A., *Proceedings*, 1917, p. 554.

Many school men considered it their patriotic duty to provide workers for the nation's wartime effort. As George D. Strayer, Chairman of the N.E.A. Commission on the National Emergency in Education, wrote in 1918: "There is a popular notion that boys and girls can be of more use to their country in going to work than in staying in school."[12] Although the temporary release of boys and girls to work on farms in the spring and fall of 1917 and 1918 helped to disrupt the schools,[13] it was the permanent withdrawal to accept positions in industry that particularly disturbed a large number of educators. Their concern is reflected in the educational journals and in the reports of city and state superintendents of education.

2. Enforcement of the Federal Child Labor Law

Although, as the Commissioner of Education pointed out, American educational institutions "suffered much less than the schools of most other countries engaged in the war,"[14] even in this nation conditions were bad enough to alarm thinking people. Consequently, measures were taken immediately upon our entry into the war to prevent the United States from falling into the initial errors of the European countries.

Studies by the Children's Bureau helped to arouse the public to the urgencies of the situation.[15] They revealed that in a number of nations, notably Australia, New Zealand, and Canada, standards of school attendance and the protection of child labor had been fully maintained. These examples, the Bureau urged, should furnish direction for our own endeavors. Less encouraging were reports from other countries, principally from England, France, and Italy. Here there had been a marked relaxation of prewar standards. Indeed, in each of the latter countries the war had produced strikingly similar results. The outbreak of hostilities had been followed by a "period of widespread unemployment accompanied by tremendous pressure in the few industries which were immediately necessary for war supplies." In many places, labor

---

[12] "The Emergency in Secondary Education," *School and Society*, vol. VIII (August 31, 1918), p. 269.

[13] See *supra*, pp. 145 *et seq.*

[14] *Annual Report of the Commissioner of Education* (1918), p. 6.

[15] See *supra*, pp. 130–131.

restrictions had been sharply relaxed, schools closed or their activities curtailed, children employed in dangerous or heavy industry, and the hours of labor greatly lengthened. As a result, health problems had emerged, juvenile delinquency had increased, and, significantly enough, production had slumped. With these conclusions the Children's Bureau issued a warning: "The point which does stand out unmistakably from the foreign experience is the general realization that the labor standards achieved in time of peace are none too high to promote the efficiency of work, the intensity of output, and the general level of health which are absolutely essential to the nation's welfare in wartime."[16]

While publicity helped, the major weapon of the Children's Bureau was the Federal Child Labor Act, signed by the President on September 1, 1916, and effective one year from that date.[17] This was obviously not a war measure. It seems, in fact, reasonable to conclude that the movement to improve the status of children received considerable impetus from the studies of James and Thorndike in the field of psychology, the work of G. Stanley Hall in the problems of childhood, and the developing philosophy of John Dewey. At about the time that these educators were making their contributions to a new understanding of the importance of childhood, the "muck-raking" books began to roll from the press. In these volumes men like Jacob Riis and John Spargo painted vivid word pictures of the bestial conditions under which many children were forced to labor.

Out of such beginnings in the early years of the twentieth century emerged a rapidly increasing interest in child welfare. The organization of the National Child Labor Committee in 1904,[18] and its subsequent efforts to draw the attention of the public to the glaring evils of child labor; the debates on the Beveridge-Parson child labor bill of 1906–1917;[19] the careful investigation and nineteen volume report of the Bureau of Labor extending over the years 1907–1913;[20] and the untiring work of the newly

[16] Anna Rochester, *Child Labor in Warring Countries. A Brief Review of Foreign Reports* (Children's Bureau Publication No. 27, 1917), pp. 7–13.

[17] *Congressional Record*, 64 Cong., 1 sess., p. 12,845.

[18] *Congressional Record*, 59 Cong., 2 sess., p. 1,869.

[19] See the *Congressional Record, op. cit.*, for a history of these debates.

[20] Samuel M. Lindsay, "National Child Labor Standards," *The Child Labor Bulletin*, vol. III (1915), pp. 25–26.

established Children's Bureau—all these are but highlights in the battle for the improvement of child welfare.

The progress of this campaign was reflected in the platforms of the political parties. Although the Republicans in 1908 did pledge themselves to an effort "to lighten the burdens and increase the opportunity for happiness and advancement of all who toil,"[21] it was not until 1916 that the two major parties made definite commitments. Then, with the passage of the Owen-Keating bill a strong possibility, both Democrats and Republicans pledged their full support to a federal child labor statute.[22]

Against this long background of agitation and publicity, the first federal statute went into effect just five months after the United States had entered the war. Upon the Children's Bureau fell the full responsibility for its enforcement. A Child Labor Division was created at once by the Secretary of Labor and was provided with administrative officers, an office force, and a field staff of inspectors. President Wilson expressed his satisfaction with these accomplishments and voiced his hope that the new law would establish "irreducible minimum standards" for child labor.[23]

To secure public support for the act, the Children's Bureau directed appeals to civic associations urging that a "special effort be made locally to see that all children under fourteen are in school and that they are enabled to come there suitably clad and fed and able to secure the full advantages of school."[24] The field agents in the drive worked under the direction of the Child-Welfare Section of the Women's Committee of the Council of National Defense. Early in 1917, even before the act went into effect, a letter was released to all state chairmen:

> Will you help to make the Federal Child Labor Law effective?
> Will you see that no more time is wasted?
> The full benefit to be gained from the new Federal Child Labor Law cannot be secured merely by its complete enforcement. . . .
> This [adequate food, clothing, etc.] will cost money. It means sacri-

---

[21] *Platforms of the Two Great Political Parties, 1856–1928, Inclusive* (Compiled by George D. Ellis, under the direction of William Tyler Page. Washington, D. C.: Government Printing Office, 1929), p. 159.

[22] *Ibid.,* pp. 200, 211.

[23] Woodrow Wilson to W. B. Wilson, Secretary of Labor. Quoted in the *Evening Post,* New York, April 3, 1918.

[24] *Fifth Annual Report of the Children's Bureau* (1917), p. 26.

fice on the part of older people; it means taxes for more schools and better schools. . . .

No words can be too strong to express the importance of giving to the Nation's children nurture and education in the fullest possible measure as a wartime protection of our last reserves. It cannot but stir American women to know that England, after these years of war, is urging through the departmental committee on education a new law, keeping children in school until 14, allowing no exemptions and including all rural children, and thus going to far greater lengths than the United States law. . . .

Here is something to do.

Please visit your school authorities and labor officials and find out whether all the children in your community under 14 years of age are in school. If the school census and the attendance records differ, something is wrong.

Will you find out where the children under 14 are if not in school?

If you wish to help, please begin by filling in the accompanying blank as soon as practicable after September 1 and returning it to the Women's Committee.[25]

Meanwhile, the National Child Labor Committee was cooperating with a campaign of its own. Sunday, January 27, 1918, was set aside for observance as "Child Labor Day" in the churches. With the endorsement of the Commissioner of Education, the following Monday was designated as a day of observance in the schools, and special pamphlets and study outlines were distributed in an attempt to make the program more meaningful. This sort of activity, continued during the war years, contributed greatly to the success of the federal statute.[26]

It was not surprising that with such vigorous enforcement and such widespread publicity the Department of Labor could, in the spring of 1918, write in glowing terms of the achievements already secured. The Secretary of Labor noted that:

By June of the present year a well-organized system of administration had been developed which was constantly growing in efficiency. States with standards as high or higher than those of the Federal statute and with competent administering officials were working in excellent cooperation with the Government inspectors to the strengthening of both. In some states laws had been modified to make possible compliance with the certificating provisions of the new statute. In

[25] *Ibid.*, pp. 26–27.
[26] *School and Society*, vol. VI (December 1, 1917), p. 648.

others the direct issuance of certificates by the officers of the Children's Bureau was securing an orderly procedure, returning many children to school, increasing the popular educational demand for schools, and incidentally showing the parents and the public the need of physical tests for fitness for work. Cases of willful violation had been successfully prosecuted, though this was the least important aspect of the law. . . .[27]

But what of the opposition? In the debates of 1916 this had been outspoken and powerful. The cotton manufacturers of the South had been vehement in their protests against the restrictions; the spokesmen for the sugar beet industry were no less energetic in their protests; and the attitude of the National Association of Manufacturers left no room for doubt as to its wholehearted opposition.[28] It was not to be expected that the protests of these and other groups would cease with the passage of the bill, but it was surprising to find the fruits of victory speedily falling into their laps. On August 21, 1917, two weeks before the statute was to go into effect, Justice Boyd of the United States District Court of the Western District of North Carolina held the act unconstitutional and entered a decree enjoining its enforcement in the case then before him.[29] Delighted with this development, a number of the cotton manufacturers met in Charlotte, North Carolina, and there decided to push the case through to the Supreme Court at the earliest possible moment.[30] They were successful. Hearings were held in Washington on April 15 and 16, 1918, and the decision declaring the statute unconstitutional was handed down on the third of June.[31]

Not only was there an immediate restoration of lower standards in a number of states, but there was also an appreciable increase in the violation of existing state laws. For example, of fifty-three factories visited by inspectors of the Children's Bureau shortly after the law was declared unconstitutional, forty-seven were found to be violating the state law by employing 430 children under twelve years of age. In contrast, while the federal statute

[27] *Annual Report of the Secretary of Labor* (1918), p. 179.
[28] For examples of their attitude, see the *Congressional Record*, 64 Cong., 1 sess., pp. 1569–71, 3044–45, 12,135–38.
[29] *United States Reports*, vol. 247, p. 268.
[30] *The Evening Post*, New York, September 8, 1917.
[31] *United States Reports*, vol. 257, p. 269.

had been in effect, forty-nine factories in this same state were visited and only ninety-five children under fourteen had been found at work. The canning industry was the worst offender. In one state where the minimum age for employment in canneries was fourteen, the inspectors discovered 721 children under this age at work in 205 establishments. More than fifty of these were under ten years of age.[32]

With the situation rapidly growing worse in the summer of 1918, the War Labor Policies Board voted to write into all future government contracts a clause enforcing the standards of the now defunct federal child labor statute. In those instances where state requirements were actually higher than those which had been set up by the federal authorities, it was stipulated that work should be performed in full compliance with the existing state laws.[33] Since the Board represented all the principal purchasing agents of the federal government, and since by this time a majority of the workers in the United States were directly or indirectly affected by its decisions, the policy was extremely significant. The position of the War Department was formally announced to the nation on September 30, 1918, by Felix Frankfurter, Chairman of the War Labor Policies Board.[34] This action had been taken in spite of "determined opposition on the part of a substantial group of southern contractors."[35] The Children's Bureau was designated as the agency to cooperate with the various government departments in the administration of the contract provisions, and a special fund was assigned to the Bureau for this purpose.[36]

Although it was not until the end of September that the child labor clauses were actually inserted in the contract forms of any of the larger purchasing departments, leaving less than a month between the signing of the contracts and the Armistice, the indirect results of this measure by the War Department were beneficial. Certain standards were reaffirmed, the investigating and enforce-

[32] *Annual Report of the Secretary of Labor* (1918), pp. 739–741.

[33] War Department, *Report of the Activities of the War Department in the Field of Industrial Relations During the War* (Washington, D. C.: Government Printing Office, 1919), p. 52.

[34] *The New York Times,* September 30, 1918.

[35] War Department, *Report of the Activities of the War Department in the Field of Industrial Relations During the War,* p. 52.

[36] *Annual Report of the Secretary of Labor* (1918), pp. 739–741.

ment machinery of the Children's Bureau was kept intact, and federal support was added to the pressure of public opinion.[37]

The problem of child labor had, of course, a direct bearing upon the educational institutions. It was one thing to enforce the federal statute and to keep children out of industry; it was quite a different proposition to insist that the boys and girls remain in school when it was legally permissible and financially advantageous for them to engage in other enterprises. As we have seen, the Children's Bureau faced both of these issues, and in its efforts to keep children at their educational activities it was ably supported by the Bureau of Education. The Commissioner of Education, P. P. Claxton, had a deep conviction that the first responsibility of the educator during the war period was to the maintenance of educational standards. "Peace has its problems and its battles not less than war," he wrote, "and for the victory of the one no less preparation is needed than for victory in the other."[38]

With only advisory powers, the Commissioner was forced to rely entirely upon public opinion for the implementation of this policy. He was alarmed at the tendency to "abandon some of the safeguards society had placed about the labor of children" and the "persistent efforts" made in a number of states to overthrow the child labor and compulsory attendance laws. To combat this tendency, he poured a steady stream of letters into the hands of principals, students, parents, labor unions, woman's clubs, and religious organizations urging them to join in the fight for the maintenance of standards in the schools. Attached to these letters were endorsements of leading governmental officials, from President Wilson down.[39] The letters were followed by special bulletins to inform the public of the nature of the problem.[40] As a final measure, into the most troublesome states went representatives of the Bureau with personal appeals to school men and state

[37] *Ibid.*

[38] Unpublished MSS. of the Commissioner of Education (no date). National Archives (Bureau of Education, 107–22).

[39] *Annual Report of the Commissioner of Education* (1917), vol. I, p. 9.

[40] See, for example, C. L. Jarvis, *Work of Children During Out-of-School Hours* (Bureau of Education Bulletin, 1917, No. 20); Anna Tolman Smith, *Demand for Vocational Education in the Countries at War* (Bureau of Education Bulletin, 1917, No. 36); *Secondary Schools and the War* (Bureau of Education, Secondary School Circular No. 1, 1918).

authorities. In these activities Claxton was rendering substantial aid to the "Back-To-School-Drive" of the Children's Bureau. He also supported the efforts of the Children's Bureau to prove the value of education in terms of dollars and cents. Pupils read such pamphlets as *Boys and Girls Stay in School. The More You Learn the More You'll Earn; Stay in School—Education Pays;* and *The Money Value of Education.*[41] It was hoped that by arguments of this nature the pull of high wages could be successfully combatted.

The United States Boys' Working Reserve, a wartime division of the Department of Labor, also tried to keep children in school, refusing to give federal recognition to boys employed on farms or in industry who were under sixteen years of age. The United States Employment Service also sought to maintain educational standards by placing "junior counselors" in the local offices to exercise guidance and persuasion on children seeking to leave the classroom.[42]

Notwithstanding these extensive efforts, the problem remained acute. Four states—New Hampshire, Vermont, Massachusetts, and Connecticut—actually weakened their child labor laws; two others —New York and California—authorized a similar relaxation of their compulsory attendance laws. While this was disturbing, it must be noted that eleven states took steps to strengthen their child labor statutes and six improved their compulsory attendance laws.[43]

It was a difficult situation. The attraction of industry was powerful, with jobs that in 1915 had paid only five or six dollars a week paying by 1918 from three to four times that amount. "This is a high hurdle to put in front of a school door," remarked one educator. "It raises the question in the minds of the parents, as well as the children, as to whether that which the child receives in the school is actually worth as much."[44] Nor could the demands of industry be ignored, for the nation was at war and production was vital.

In this dilemma, the Commissioner of Education decided to

---

[41] See *supra,* p. 132.
[42] See *supra,* pp. 149–150.
[43] *School and Society,* vol. VI (December 22, 1917), p. 734.
[44] Frank M. Leavitt, *School and Society,* vol. VI (December 15, 1917), pp. 706–707.

put the problem before the leaders of government, industry, and the schools. A preliminary conference was held in his offices on February 15, 1918, with a number of representatives present from the different federal departments.[45] Tentative conclusions reached at this time were presented to a larger group of representatives at a second conference held at the Hotel Dennis in Atlantic City on February 26, 1918. "It is hoped," Claxton announced in opening the Atlantic City meeting, "that the discussion may result in agreement upon a formulation of policy in respect to the schools in wartime which will be acceptable to the Government Departments and to school authorities."[46] His hopes were realized, for out of this and subsequent discussions emerged a definite statement of federal policy. Signed by several of the leading governmental officials, the statement was given wide publicity in the summer and fall of 1918.[47]

The government stated clearly that it was of "very urgent concern that none of the educational processes of the country should be interrupted any more than is absolutely unavoidable during the war." The statement urged that all children continue their schooling, and that the graduates of high school go on to college "to the end that the country may not lack an adequate supply of trained men and women." The boys and girls were assured that those who followed this advice would be "preparing themselves for valuable service to the nation."[48]

In the light of this official statement of policy, it is interesting to note the comments made by the representatives gathered at the first conference in Washington. The speaker for the Civil Service Commission admitted that there was a great need for clerks, typists, and stenographers, but pointed out that the eighteen-year age limit prevented any raid upon the public schools. Whereupon Claxton observed: "Your greatest sin is not robbing the schools of pupils but of teachers, you are getting large numbers of teach-

45 "Minutes of a Conference in the Office of the Commissioner of Education," February 26, 1918. National Archives (Bureau of Education, 106–13).

46 "Minutes of the Atlantic City Conference," February 26, 1918. National Archives (Bureau of Education, 107–22).

47 *Governmental Policies Involving the Schools in War Time* (Bureau of Education, Teachers Leaflet No. 3, 1918). This was signed by the Secretaries of War, Navy, Agriculture, Labor, and Interior, as well as by the Chairman of the Civil Service Commission and the Commissioner of Education.

48 *Ibid.*, pp. 5–7.

ers." Mr. Filer, the Commission's representative, retorted that the obvious solution was to "raise the teachers' pay." He then went on to remark that the schools could do much to relieve the situation by giving special courses in typing and commercial work.[49]

The War Department denied that it had any interest in the schoolboys. When they volunteer for service "we can't refuse to accept them," Assistant Secretary of War Keppel remarked: "But we certainly don't want to emphasize a demand for boys of that age. It is much better for the nation if they stay where they are." Asked if the army wished to introduce military training into the high schools, Keppel countered with the question: "Who would be responsible for the drilling? The army is short of officers." Questioned further as to whether the War Department had any other projects which might draw the boys from school, he stated that the army might develop its own educational program to train men for certain trades that could be learned rapidly; in that event the boys might be urged to leave their regular work to take up this training.[50]

The speaker representing the navy denied that his department had any reason to raid the schools. Questioned about the Junior Navy League, he said bluntly that it had no governmental connection whatsoever. "There are two organizations, one for the navy and one for the army, and they are going to the schools trying to line up the boys for the service. . . . It is a very profitable industry. We investigated one of these organizations and were not satisfied with its financial backing and its motives." When asked who was responsible for shipyards and munition plants, Root at once admitted that many boys from fourteen to eighteen were employed as helpers in these industries. Were they useful under sixteen years of age? Claxton inquired. "Well," was the reply, "a boy of twelve can heat rivets as well as an older boy."[51]

This comment, disturbing enough for any educator, prompted one of the industrialists to make an even more alarming observa-

[49] "Minutes of a Conference in the Office of the Commissioner of Education," February 15, 1918. National Archives (Bureau of Education, 106–13), pp. 12–13.
[50] *Ibid.*, p. 12.
[51] *Ibid.*, pp. 13–16.

tion: "I am a manufacturer of explosives," he volunteered. "We use boys in loading hand-grenades for trench warfare. We take them just as young as the law allows. They usually run about sixteen. I understand a large number of boys are used in munition plants. Take a little thing like pouring powder into a hand-grenade, putting on the little cap, and passing it along, they can do that as well as a grown man. They use boys for what is known as hand punching."[52]

Equally discouraging was the statement from the representative of the Department of Labor:

It is my opinion—I am in conflict with some men in the Labor Department, and I speak unofficially in that way—but I believe there is going to be a labor shortage. I have been making surveys of railroads, and they are short 30,000 men on the eastern roads here now.

Question: They will fill them with men and boys will take the places of men?

Answer: Yes, that is what I mean. We are trying to build up a reserve of 250,000 shipbuilders. There is going to be a big demand for shipbuilders. There is going to be a demand in Bridgeport for 10,000 men in the next six months.[53]

This warning of a critical labor shortage was echoed by the spokesman for the Department of Agriculture, who reported that the scarcity of farmhands seriously threatened agricultural production. The remedy, as he saw it, was to use the schoolboys for work on the farms.[54]

An examination of these remarks reveals that the United States in February, 1918, ten months after we had entered the war, was faced with an acute problem of manpower. While each speaker had denied any wish to raid the schools, it is perfectly obvious that if the situation continued to grow worse, as it had every evidence of doing, sooner or later the school children would be called upon for more positive contributions in field and factory. Against this background, the official announcement of "Governmental Policies Involving the Schools in War Time" appears to have been little more than an expression of hope. As it was, in August the War Department dipped into the eighteen-year-old

52 *Ibid.*, p. 16.
53 *Ibid.*, p. 17.
54 *Ibid.*, pp. 3–4.

group for fighting material, and at this time had plans in process of development for the further utilization of the nation's schools.[55] In view of the evidence, it seems unlikely that the educational institutions could have been protected had the war continued beyond 1918.

3. Training Skilled Workers

It was important to protect the youth of the nation, and the measures to enforce the child labor statute and to keep children in school were designed to accomplish this purpose. But the nation was at war and it was equally important, and far more difficult, to furnish that supply of skilled labor so desperately needed by both industry and the armed forces. At this point the newly created Federal Board for Vocational Education was called into service.

It has been frequently stated that the Vocational Board was a wartime agency. The record does not support this contention.[56] For twenty years before our entry into the World War, interest in public vocational education had been growing. Organizations as different as the American Federation of Labor and the National Association of Manufacturers had appointed committees to investigate and to recommend action, and the N.E.A. in its annual conventions had devoted considerable time to a discussion of the place of vocational education in our school system. The National Society for the Promotion of Industrial Education, created in 1906 to coordinate the efforts of interested groups, had carried on extensive publicity. In addition, a number of state commissions had made investigations and had submitted reports which helped to clarify thought upon the problem.[57]

[55] See *supra*, pp. 108–110.

[56] Interview with J. C. Wright, Assistant Commissioner of Vocational Education, Washington, April 15, 1941. Dr. Wright was extremely emphatic upon this point. His statements are fully corroborated by other authorities. See I. L. Kandel, *Federal Aid for Vocational Education. A Report to the Carnegie Foundation for the Advancement of Teaching* (Bulletin No. 10, Boston, Massachusetts: The Merrymount Press, 1917); and Perry W. Reeves, *A Digest of the Development of Industrial Education in the United States* (Washington, D. C.: Federal Board for Vocational Education, 1932). An excellent summary is given by Cubberley, *Public Education in the United States* (Rev. ed.), chap. XIX.

[57] Reeves, *A Digest of the Development of Industrial Education in the United States*, pp. 2–14.

Perhaps the most influential study was the one carried on by the National Commission on Vocational Education. This group was appointed by President Wilson in 1913. The following year it submitted its first report to Congress. This report noted that in 1910 some 12,500,000 Americans were engaged in agricultural activities and an additional 14,250,000 were working at manufacturing and mechanical enterprises, but that not one per cent of all this number had had any opportunity for adequate training. The small kingdom of Bavaria had more trade schools than the entire United States. To supply the 1,000,000 new workers annually needed by industry would require the training of at least 3,000,000 pupils of high school age. In 1910, however, only 1,032,461 boys and girls between the ages of fourteen and eighteen were enrolled in high schools of any type, day or evening, public or private. The Commission warned that our national prosperity was at stake. "Since commercial prosperity depends largely upon the skill and well-being of our workers," the report stated, "the outlook for American commerce in competition with our more enterprising neighbors, under present conditions, is not very promising."[58] To rectify this situation, the Commission made certain recommendations. After some delay, resulting in part from the outbreak of war in Europe, these proposals were embodied in the Smith-Hughes Act which was signed by the President on February 23, 1917.[58]

Such, in brief, was the history of the Federal Board for Vocational Education. This board of seven men was to administer the distribution of federal funds to those states which submitted to the federal authorities acceptable programs for vocational training. A further proviso was inserted in the law to the effect that federal grants were to be matched dollar for dollar by the states. Under these general provisions, federal aid was also given for the instruction of teachers in agriculture and the mechanic arts, for the payment of salaries, and for the preparation of studies, reports, and courses of study seeking to develop and expand the program. Federal aid was limited during the first year to a total of $1,700,-000; nevertheless, by 1918 every state had signified its intention of participating and had taken steps to institute an acceptable

[58] Cubberley, op. cit., pp. 642–643.

course of vocational training in its public schools.[59] Although exact figures are not available, it was estimated that before the passage of the Smith-Hughes Act only about 25,000 pupils were enrolled in all of the vocational schools in the United States; within a year of the adoption of this legislation the number had risen to 164,000.[60] The war undoubtedly stimulated this development, yet it should be emphasized that what was happening was the acceleration of a prewar movement, not the initiation under wartime stress of a new program. Indeed, it has been argued that the distraction of administrators from long-range planning to the urgencies of immediate training in a few specialized skills needed by the army actually delayed the development of a sound industrial arts program in the United States.[61]

The first war work of the Federal Board for Vocational Education was conducted in collaboration with the War Department's Committee on Education and Special Training.[62] Desperately needed by the armed forces were thousands of men trained for certain special activities, such as welding, automobile repair work, and radio operation. It was decided to furnish the requisite training in short courses conducted in the manual training shops of the public and private educational institutions of the country. The army was to supply maintenance and to conduct military drill, the Federal Board was to administer the curricular and instructional activities. From the outset, this joint enterprise proved to be a failure. Even before the available training facilities had been adequately surveyed and the courses started, conflict between the military and civilian departments of the government became so awkward that the attempt at collaboration was abandoned and the Federal Board dropped out of the picture.[63] Each agency then developed its own training program.

[59] Cubberley, op. cit., p. 645.

[60] Reeves, op. cit., p. 15.

[61] Interview with J. C. Wright, Washington, April 15, 1941; Annual Report of the Federal Board for Vocational Education (Washington, D. C.: Government Printing Office, 1917), p. 7; J. H. Van Sickle, "Public Education in the Cities of the United States," Biennial Survey, 1916–1918 (Bureau of Education Bulletin, 1919, No. 88), p. 123.

[62] See infra, pp. 189–192.

[63] Interview with J. C. Wright, Washington, April 15, 1941; Committee on Education and Special Training. A Review of Its Work During 1918 (By the Advisory Board, War Department, 1918), Part 1, p. 14.

The civilian board carried on its work with men and boys in the second and third draft who had not yet been called up for service. Wherever available, the facilities of the public schools were utilized. "Buzzer" classes were started in spare schoolrooms, and manual training equipment was used to train automobile mechanics, welders, and machinists. There was no disruption of the normal school program, for the special instruction was given by the teachers either as extra work while the regular classes were in session or in the evenings and on Saturdays. Upon attaining a certain prescribed degree of efficiency, the men were presented with cards certifying to their achievements. It was expected that upon induction into the army the men bearing these cards would be sent to special military centers for further training in their specialties. In an effort to determine whether the War Department was making use of this premilitary training, the Federal Board asked each of the trainees to return to the Board's offices a card indicating his actual placement in the military organization. As these cards began to reach the federal authorities, it became clear that the program was far from successful. Men with cards certifying to their proficiency in skills urgently required by the army were frequently assigned to entirely different work. The difficulties faced by the army officers were, of course, enormous, and it is easy to understand why they found it impossible to place all men in those positions for which they were best qualified. Forced to expand within a few months from a peacetime footing of about 100,000 men to an active force of more than 4,000,000, it is not surprising that the army made mistakes. Yet the fact remains that cooperation between the military authorities and the Federal Board for Vocational Education was never very close, with the result that the procurement of skilled men was impeded. Nevertheless, when the war ended about 65,000 men and boys were enrolled in the special classes being conducted under the direction of the Federal Board for Vocational Education.[64]

It is clear that the wartime activities of the Board were in hardly more than an experimental stage of development, with the public schools playing but a negligible part. On the other hand, it should be remembered that the Board had been created less than two

[64] Interview with J. C. Wright, Washington, April 15, 1941.

months before our entry into the conflict and was faced with the extremely difficult task of organizing its work in the confusion of the war effort. The Director, C. A. Prosser, thought in terms of the effective training of every man, woman, and child for national service in war or in peace. "Liberty," he found time to write in 1918, "means efficient service, and efficient service means doing something well, and that ability comes to an individual or a nation only as a result of training and practice."[65] That the plan of training developed by his organization in 1918 was fundamentally sound is revealed by the fact that in 1939 it was dug out of the files and was used as a guide in the construction of our present defense training program.[66]

Meanwhile, the army was developing its own program. The work was under the direction of the Committee on Education and Special Training. Created by General Order No. 15, on February 10, 1918, this committee of three members was designated to survey the need for skilled men in the various branches of the service, to determine how these needs could be met, to represent the War Department in its relations with the educational institutions of the country, and to administer the training courses. Associated with the Committee was a special civilian advisory board appointed by the Secretary of War. In charge of the training activities was C. R. Dooley, head of the Educational Department of the Western Electric and Manufacturing Company.[67]

Dooley completely decentralized the organization, thus relieving the authorities in Washington of an endless amount of administrative detail. Ten educational directors were appointed, each with full responsibility for the administration of the program in his own district. The country was then scoured for vocational

[65] "Training for Citizenship Through Service," *School and Society*, vol. VIII (September 7, 1918), p. 273.

[66] Interview with J. C. Wright, Washington, April 15, 1941. Curiously enough, it was a representative of the War Department, General Frank McSherry, who was responsible for this revival of the old program. Invited in 1939 to Dr. Wright's offices to look over the World War records of the Board's activities, his enthusiasm was kindled by the possibilities of the 1918 work, and he urged its adoption by the War Department. Collaboration between the vocational education and the military branches of the federal government was much closer during the months before and after our entry into the Second World War.

[67] *Committee on Education and Special Training. A Review of Its Work During 1918* (By the Advisory Board, War Department, 1918), Part 1, pp. 11–14.

training facilities. Once a school had been selected, its equipment approved, and the course of study and number of students agreed upon, the army officers moved in. Under their direction, arrangements were made for housing, maintenance, and sanitation. Contracts for board and housing were then sublet and training was started. The educational directors remained in their respective districts to smooth out difficulties and to improve the system.[68]

All types of schools were chosen for this work. By the fall of 1918, thirteen colored and 144 white institutions were in operation. It is an interesting commentary upon the status of vocational education in the United States in 1918 that only twenty of the high schools were utilized by the army.[69] Each institution conducted that type of training for which it appeared to be best fitted. Three of the St. Louis high schools, for example, set up courses in blacksmithing, machine shop practice, woodworking, and automobile repairing. With their manual training shops thus occupied for war purposes, the regularly enrolled high school students attended classes which met before and after school hours and on Saturday mornings.[70] In addition to similar courses, Oakland, California, provided in its public schools training for oxy-acetylene welders and cutters, ignition experts, radio operators, and Morse telegraphers.[71]

Obviously, thorough training in these skills could not be secured in three weeks, and emphasis was placed upon teaching the men to do well one highly specialized job. Automobile mechanics were trained to work on ignition systems, chassis, or engines—not on the entire car.[72] Machinists were taught to run either a lathe, a planer, or a shaper.[73] Yet even after 320 hours of this specialized instruction, not all men were turned back to the army as "experts." Many were listed as "journeymen," able to do ordinary work, or as "apprentices," who, although showing aptitude for the job, still required training.[74]

[68] Ibid.
[69] Ibid., p. 19.
[70] Sixty-Fourth Annual Report of the Board of Education of the City of St. Louis for the Year Ending June 30, 1918 (St. Louis, Missouri, 1918), pp. 157–158.
[71] Oakland, California, Report of the Superintendent of Schools (1918), p. 273.
[72] Ibid., p. 273.
[73] St. Louis, Missouri, Sixty-Fourth Annual Report of the Board of Education (1918), p. 161.   [74] Ibid., p. 160.

The lack of qualified teachers seriously impeded the program. Although many of the regular manual training instructors gave their spare time to assist in the work, a number of the teachers were skilled mechanics taken from the local garages and machine shops.[75] Indeed, upon the completion of the first courses, the better students were frequently retained as instructors.[76] Nor was the equipment all that could be desired. In some cases the army furnished old Liberty engines;[77] automobile dealers lent much equipment;[78] and a number of the schools opened free automobile clinics where cars were repaired for the mere cost of parts.[79] Finally, the courses were not well planned. The work had been started so hastily that the Committee did not have time at first to prepare manuals for instructional purposes, even assuming that in the early stages it knew exactly what it wanted to do. As a result, the schools were simply told what skills the army needed and the precise duties the men would be required to perform; with this information to serve as a curriculum, the instructors worked out their own courses of study. Here, of course, was the point at which the educational directors could and did render valuable service, and by the end of the war they had improved and considerably standardized the instruction. Before the Armistice ended the work, a number of manuals had been issued for use in the schools, and others were in process of publication.[80]

The students were under military authority, with part of their time devoted to rudimentary training for army life. Living quarters and mess were often the crudest of makeshifts. For a time, St. Louis quartered the men and boys in the Y.M.C.A.[81] Oakland used the school gymnasium for a barracks and fed the men in the cafeteria.[82]

[75] Annual Report of the School Department, vol. LXXIX (Newton, Massachusetts, 1918), p. 45.

[76] Committee on Education and Special Training. A Review of Its Work During 1918, op. cit., p. 13.

[77] St. Louis, Missouri, Sixty-Fourth Annual Report of the Board of Education (1918), p. 159.

[78] Oakland, California, Report of the Superintendent of Schools (1918), p. 273.

[79] Committee on Education and Special Training. A Review of Its Work During 1918, op. cit., p. 19.

[80] Ibid., p. 19.

[81] St. Louis, Missouri, Sixty-Fourth Annual Report of the Board of Education (1918), pp. 157–158.

[82] Oakland, California, Report of the Superintendent of Schools (1918), p. 274.

In view of the hasty improvisation and temporary nature of many of the arrangements, the results were gratifying. When hostilities came to an end, 130,000 men had been trained, over 100,000 had been turned over to the army, and the remainder were ready for delivery.[83] Yet nothing illustrates more clearly the poverty of our facilities for the vocational training of men and women, and the extremely small part played by the public schools reveals how poorly they were equipped for any program of vocational education.

4. Production of Articles by School Children

Strange as it may seem, perhaps the greatest contribution made to the war effort by the vocational training organization of the public schools was the actual production of finished articles for the war machine. As has been indicated, the school kitchens were used by both children and parents for the canning of fruits and vegetables.[84] Equally important were the articles produced in the sewing rooms and the manual training shops. The major part of this work was under the direction of a quasi-public organization —the American Red Cross.

The Red Cross movement grew out of Florence Nightingale's work in the Crimean War. For many years its activities were carried on entirely by adults. Even before the European war, however, attempts were made in Sweden, France, and Spain to mobilize the children, and in 1914 the Quebec division of the Canadian Red Cross actually began to enroll boys and girls.[85]

In spite of these experiments, there is no evidence to indicate that prior to our entry into the war the American Red Cross gave any particular thought to the organization of the nation's youth. But in the spring and summer of 1917 little girls began to accompany their mothers to the Red Cross rooms to sew on garments and to knit for the soldiers. "And then," one observer remarked, "some one saw them and what they were doing, and just for a kind of curious mental exercise multiplied it by a

[83] *Committee on Education and Special Training. A Review of Its Work During 1918, op. cit.,* p. 18.

[84] See *supra,* pp. 162–163.

[85] Sarah E. Pickett, *The American National Red Cross. Its Origin, Purposes, and Service* (New York: The Century Co., 1923), p. 192.

million." The part that school children might play in the war program, if properly mobilized, defied imagination. And so, out of such beginnings, the Junior Red Cross was conceived and born in America. It was officially inaugurated on September 3, 1917.[86]

The organization was built around School Auxiliaries of the local Red Cross chapters. To become a member, a school was expected to contribute twenty-five cents for each pupil in attendance. School Committees from the local chapters offered advice and assistance, but the actual conduct of the work was purposely left in the hands of the educational officials and the teachers.

Dues were raised by the school children in numerous different ways. In Los Angeles, they collected and sold salvage; in Southern California, they harvested castor oil beans from vacant lots; in Minneapolis they made articles in the manual training shops and sewing rooms and sold them at a bazaar. The boys and girls of Lenhi County, Idaho, collected 500 pounds of wool from the trees and wire fences of the sheep ranges. Other children worked at odd jobs, raised school gardens, and produced plays.[87]

By February 28, 1919, the Juniors had contributed in membership dues over $3,700,000. By way of comparison, during this same period of twenty months, the membership dues of the adults totaled only $42,000,000. Some 11,418,385 children in the United States and 300,000 in our insular possessions were organized as members of 90,000 School Auxiliaries. This was over fifty-one per cent of the entire school population of the nation. In four states—Arizona, California, Delaware, and Nevada—every school pupil belonged to the Junior Red Cross. The cotton states made the poorest showing, the membership ranging from less than three per cent of the school population in Alabama and Mississippi to almost twenty-five per cent in Georgia.

The money raised for membership dues was not turned into the Red Cross, but was placed in special school funds from which it was drawn for the purchase of materials to be converted into finished articles.[88] All articles were carefully produced under the

[86] Henry P. Davison, *The American Red Cross in the Great War* (New York: The Macmillan Co., 1920), p. 92.

[87] *Ibid.*, pp. 95–97.

[88] *The Work of the American Red Cross During the War. A Statement of Finances and Accomplishments for the Period July 1, 1917 to February 28, 1919* (Washington: The American Red Cross, 1919), pp. 14–15.

close supervision of the national Red Cross officials from their headquarters in Washington. Written specifications, blueprints, photographs, paper patterns, and models were furnished to the teachers in charge of production. In many cases the teachers took special courses given by Red Cross nurses qualified to give sewing instruction.[89] Within a year, each School Auxiliary was given free of cost a 410 page *Teachers Manual* containing detailed instructions for carrying on the work. The school authorities were urged to read the manual carefully, paying particular attention to "the regulations concerning production."[90]

The boys and girls in the Junior Red Cross made an impressive contribution to the war effort. In the manual training shops and sewing rooms of the public schools they produced 15,722,078 articles valued at $10,152,461.96. These included surgical dressings, hospital supplies and garments, refugee garments, articles for soldiers and sailors, and furniture for nurses' homes and army camps.[91] From the sewing rooms of one city school system came the following pieces for the national organization: sweaters, trench caps, knit caps, quilts, jackets, trench coats, quilt squares, knitted scarfs, helmets, wristlets, mittens, socks, bootees, flannel skirts, flannel dresses, wash cloths, pillows, towels, rugs, baby dresses, aprons, toys for refugee children, gun wipes, and scrapbooks.[92] Out of the manual training shops came packing boxes, splints, knitting needles, games, puzzles, applicators, bread-boards, drawing boards, canes, chairs, and tables.[93] These and similar articles

[89] Dean, *Our Schools in War Time—and After*, pp. 196, 200.

[90] *Junior Red Cross Activities. Teachers Manual* (Washington, The American Red Cross, Department of Development, Junior Membership, 1918), Foreword.

[91] *The Work of the American Red Cross During the War*, p. 25. From September 3, 1917, to February 28, 1919, the children produced the following articles:

Surgical dressings	6,057,720
Hospital supplies	2,574,564
Hospital garments	444,776
Refugee garments	1,130,188
Articles for soldiers and sailors	3,174,999
Sewing for convalescent and nurses' houses	138,345
Sewing for camps	1,444,507
Furniture for convalescent and nurses' houses	70,084
Furniture for army	666,445
Miscellaneous furniture	20,450

[92] Chicago, Illinois, *Sixty-Fourth Annual Report of the Board of Education* (1918), p. 54.

[93] *National School Service*, vol. I (September 1, 1918), p. 10, and (November 15, 1918), p. 13.

poured in from the village and city schools throughout the nation. There are several reasons why the Junior Red Cross was so successful in producing articles for the armed forces. In the first place, many schools devoted their domestic science and manual training periods to the work.[94] In the second place, the work was well-organized in Washington and ably directed by H. N. Mac-Cracken, President of Vassar College. In the third place, it was widely publicized.[95] Finally, it was successful because it stood for ideals that were considered educationally sound by the great majority of educators.

The Red Cross did not attempt to force all or even part of its program on the schools; always it was the principal who decided, without any pressure from the Red Cross, which, if any, of its activities he chose to include in the curriculum.[96] The Director insisted that educational matters came first in order of importance, and only then should problems of production and finance be considered. "We hope," he explained, "to arrange an organization which will rest lightly upon the shoulders of the school teachers and indeed permit them simply to utilize the Red Cross as a means of putting into practice their educational ideals."[97] Such views were heartening to educators, and as a consequence they gave the fullest cooperation to the Junior Red Cross program.

It was the emphasis on service to others that won such enthusiastic support for the educational program of the Red Cross. The leaders of the organization were the first to admit that the making of articles was in itself of any but secondary importance. They labored arduously in behalf of health, thrift, and conservation campaigns. From it all, however, they hoped to realize a larger purpose. As the leaders of the Red Cross themselves expressed it: "Through its organization, under its flag, second only to the Star-Spangled Banner in the love of the American people, the

[94] *Biennial Report of the Superintendent of Public Instruction, 1917–1918* (Carson City, Nevada: State Printing Office, 1919), pp. 28–29, 53; California, *Third Biennial Report of the State Board of Education* (1918), p. 110.

[95] See, for example, the bulletin issued by the editors of *National School Service*, in vol. I (November 15, 1918). This was a supplementary bulletin entitled "The Junior Four Minute Men. Red Cross Christmas Call" (School Bulletin No. 4).

[96] H. N. MacCracken to the Division Managers of the Junior Red Cross, February 14, 1918. National Archives (Bureau of Education, 106–12).

[97] H. N. MacCracken to P. P. Claxton, October 3, 1917. National Archives (Bureau of Education, 106–13).

patriotic and altruistic impulses of school children can be developed into acts of practical patriotism."[98]

Perhaps the educational implications of the work were less valuable than the leaders at the time supposed. But the record shows that they won more enthusiastic cooperation from the school authorities than any of the other war agencies. It was for the Junior Red Cross program that the manual training shops and domestic science rooms were used with most effectiveness.

[98] American Red Cross to educational authorities, November 10, 1917. National Archives (Bureau of Education, 106–13).

CHAPTER VIII

TEACHING PERSONNEL

The education of the young is an essential industry.—*Remark attributed to Arthur S. Somers, President of the New York Board of Education, 1918.*[1]

Our country might conceivably be overwhelmed by superior military force, but our democracy will never be imperiled by outside attacks. Democracy is always weakened from within. Only its own feebleness or complacency destroys it. We in Europe see more clearly than you that democracy dies from lack of discipline, unwillingness to compromise, group pressure, corruption, usurpation of public power because the public is greedy or indifferent. It does unless it draws life from every citizen. Denouncing dictators get nowhere. The job of those who believe in the democratic process is to be positive, not negative, to build it up, expose and correct its mistakes, keep it alive.—*A Statement from Czechoslovakia published in The New York Times, September 25, 1937.*[2]

The success of any educational program, in time of war or peace, depends upon the ability and enthusiasm of the teachers in the classroom. Yet, commonplace as this observation may appear, actually the American teacher has never held a particularly enviable position.

Although by the end of the nineteenth century the free public school system had been firmly established and was growing rapidly, and although by this time teacher-training institutions had been in operation for over half a century,[3] many Americans continued to think of the teaching personnel of the public schools as "immature women and feeble men." Nor was the college instructor held in any great esteem—a fact of which Theodore Roosevelt showed himself to be keenly aware when, in the election campaign of 1912, he repeatedly referred to his rival as "Professor"

[1] *School and Society,* vol. VIII (September 28, 1918), p. 376.
[2] Educational Policies Commission, *The Purposes of Education in American Democracy* (Washington, D. C.: National Education Association, 1938), p. 109.
[3] Cubberley, *Public Education in the United States,* Chap. XI.

Wilson rather than as "Governor" Wilson.[4] That there was some justification for this disparaging attitude was revealed by a study of the social composition of the teaching population made in 1910 by Lotus D. Coffman. The typical[5] male school teacher secured his first position, after three years of training beyond the elementary grades, in a rural school at a salary of $390 a year. Here he remained for two years. To move to a better position in one of the near-by towns, an additional year of training was necessary. In case he wished to become a city school teacher, two more years of education, or six beyond the elementary school, were needed. The typical male teacher, in 1910, was twenty-nine years of age, had seven years of experience, and received a salary of $489 a year. Women were younger, averaging only twenty-four years of age, but their salaries were approximately the same. "What chance," Coffman asked in conclusion, "has the average American boy or girl of being wisely and intelligently educated by the average American teacher, male or female?"[6]

Under such circumstances, it was not surprising that the percentage of men entering the teaching profession was declining at a rapid rate.[7] The situation had become so serious by 1918 that the Commissioner of Education warned that "at the present rate of decrease, few men teachers will be left in the profession in the next twenty years."[8] The Wyoming State Superintendent of Education referred to male elementary school teachers as "almost an extinct genus."[9]

Two conclusions emerge from the preceding discussion: first, the scarcity of men teachers was not caused by war conditions

[4] Bagley and Alexander, op. cit., pp. 9–10.

[5] Coffman warns his readers to use the word "typical" only with great care. He describes his teacher in terms of medians, but makes it clear that "a median is a point about which individuals vary and that our hypothetical indivdual is as likely to be below as above it."

[6] Lotus D. Coffman, The Social Composition of the Teaching Population (New York: Teachers College, Columbia University, 1911), pp. 79–80.

[7] In 1880, 42.8 per cent of all teachers were men; in 1890, 34.5 per cent; in 1900, 29.9 per cent; in 1910, 21.1 per cent; in 1916, 19.8 per cent; and in 1918, 16.1 per cent. Of the 650,709 public school teachers in 1918, 105,194 were men, 545,515 women. Biennial Survey, 1916–1918 (Bureau of Education Bulletin, 1919, No. 90), p. 162.

[8] Ibid., p. 89.

[9] First Report of the State Board of Education of Wyoming (Laramie, Wyoming: The Laramie Republican Co., 1918), p. 18.

alone; second, the educational system with which the United States entered the European conflict was composed of teachers who, in general, were young and poorly prepared for the heavy responsibilities that the war thrust upon them. These facts have a direct bearing upon the relationship of the teaching profession to the war itself. When it is remembered that during the war teachers were called upon by the federal, state, and local governments, as well as pressure groups and patriotic societies of all types, to engage in innumerable war activities, it is surprising that the normal work of the schools was not more seriously disturbed. It was these young, poorly trained, inadequately paid instructors who were asked to teach the causes of the war, to organize conservation and thrift campaigns, to develop strong, healthy boys and girls, and through the children to stimulate the parents to greater war efforts.

1. The Shortage of Teachers

The effect of the European war was felt by the teaching profession long before the United States started to fight. As industry began to respond to the war needs of the belligerents, with both wages and prices steadily rising, teachers in mounting numbers left their classrooms to accept more lucrative positions.[10] By the spring of 1917, educators were becoming alarmed at the growing shortage. "There are twice as many calls for well-trained men and women as we are able to supply," wrote one school man. "Men are especially needed in agriculture, manual training, and athletics. Women are needed in normal training, languages, and all high school subjects. In these branches the jobs seek the teachers."[11]

The situation became worse during the summer. Physical training instructors were in especially great demand. The high percentage of men classified as physically unfit by the army, the increased emphasis on military training in the schools, the health campaigns that were being carried on, all served to emphasize the need for this type of instructor. In New York City, for example, the physical director, C. Ward Crampton, called for "over one

[10] Biennial Survey, 1916–1918, op. cit., p. 207.
[11] School and Society, vol. VI (July 7, 1917), p. 22.

hundred and fourteen physical training teachers" during the winter of 1917–1918. To speed up the supply, a normal school for physical training was established at New York University in the fall of 1917.[12] Particularly pressing was the need for men to fill supervisory offices, and to teach manual training, mechanical drawing, mathematics, agriculture, chemistry, physics, and other commercial, vocational, and scientific subjects.[13]

Although many of the teachers had been drawn off by the draft, the greater number had left for more attractive positions in other occupations.[14] As one educational journal noted: "The trend of the times is shown by an announcement from the Cortland State Normal School. It is to the effect that Professor R. E. Owens, of that faculty, has resigned his position and has accepted the cashiership of the National Bank of Cortland."[15] Nor, as has been indicated, was it only men who were affected; women, too, were drawn off in considerable numbers to enter industry and the civil service.[16] It was reported from Maine that civil service examinations were held "in almost all of the cities and towns," and that teachers who were being paid as low as twelve dollars a week could easily secure $1,100 or more a year from the government.[17]

Hardest hit were the rural schools where the teaching positions were least attractive and the salaries were miserably low. In certain states as many as ten per cent of the rural classrooms remained without teachers. Vermont reported that on August 15, 1918, there was a shortage of six high school principals, thirty high school teachers, eight teachers of special subjects, and over 150 rural teachers.[18] The Bureau of Education stated in 1918 that partial returns from 1,150 of the 2,964 counties in the country revealed a loss of 41 per cent of the men who had been teaching

[12] *Ibid.*, vol. VI (September 22, 1917), p. 350.

[13] P. P. Claxton to American educators, November 2, 1918. National Archives (Bureau of Education, 106–17); *Report of the Superintendent of Public Instruction: Being the Sixtieth Report Upon the Public Schools of New Hampshire* (Concord, New Hampshire: The Evans Printing Co., 1918), pp. 113–114, 195–196; West Virginia, *Biennial Report of the State Superintendent of Free Schools* (1918), p. 35.

[14] *School and Society*, vol. VI (October 27, 1917), p. 503.

[15] *Ibid.*, vol. VII (April 20, 1918), p. 470.

[16] Wyoming, *First Report of the State Board of Education* (1918), p. 17; Memorandum, June, 1919. National Archives (Bureau of Education, 106–17).

[17] Maine. *Report of the State Superintendent of Public Schools* (1918), p. 8.

[18] *Second Biennial Report of the State Board of Education. July 1, 1916–June 30, 1918* (Rutland, Vermont: The Tuttle Co., 1918), p. 15.

in 1917, and a national shortage of at least 27,000 rural teachers.[19]

By the fall of 1918, the public educational system of the United States faced what the Commissioner of Education called a "real crisis." In a letter urging the Adjutant General of the United States Army to persuade discharged soldiers to enter the teaching profession, the Commissioner warned: "Some fifty thousand schools or school departments are now closed for want of teachers. This shortage is especially great in those departments from which men have been drawn into the army, or attracted into other lines of Government work or into the various war industries."[20] From the same source came the alarming statement that "almost one-third of all American teachers were drawn out of their regular work by war conditions."[21] So serious was the situation that President Wilson felt it necessary to appeal to the public, and on November 12, the day after the Armistice was signed, he released a letter calling attention to the scarcity of teachers and urging all who were qualified to return to the classroom.[22]

2. The Problem of Salaries

As has been stated, although the draft drew thousands of instructors into the armed forces, the chief reason for the shortage of teachers was that industry offered both higher wages and, in many cases, better working conditions.[23] The educational journals and the reports of the state and city superintendents of education for the war years were filled with references to the scarcity of teachers, and in nearly every case the statement of fact was followed by a warning that only sharp increases in salaries could rectify the situation.

In 1880, wages represented seventy per cent of the total school expenditures; by 1918, they had fallen to only fifty-seven per cent of the total.[24] The average salary of high school teachers in 1918, according to a report of the Bureau of Education, was $1,031.

19 *Biennial Survey, 1916–1918, op. cit.,* p. 176.

20 P. P. Claxton to Major General Peter C. Harris. National Archives (Bureau of Education, 106–17).

21 Memorandum, June, 1919. National Archives (Bureau of Education, 106–17).

22 A copy of this letter may be read in *School and Society,* vol. VIII (November 23, 1918), p. 619.

23 *Ibid.,* vol. VIII (September 21, 1918), p. 347.

24 *Biennial Survey, 1916–1918, op. cit.,* p. 110.

California led the country with an average of $1,355; Maine was at the foot of the list with an average of only $652. Elementary school teachers fared much worse, with an average salary of only $606 for the nation as a whole. Once again California led the list with an average of $891, while Georgia stood at the foot with a "low" of $314. The average for both high school and elementary teachers was about $635 for the country at large.[25]

These figures represent the wages paid teachers in 1918, after increases had been provided in an effort to meet the rising cost of living. For the past fifty years, in fact, teachers' salaries had been rising slowly but steadily. In 1870, the average for the United States was $189; in 1880, $195; in 1890, $252; in 1900, $325; in 1910, $485; in 1915, $543; in 1916, $563; and, as already mentioned, in 1918, $635. The increase during the two years of our participation in the war amounted to about thirty-six dollars, or approximately six per cent each year.[26] In reference to this situation, the Wyoming State Superintendent of Education remarked that "we have lost both our business sense and our sense of humor."[27] Commissioner Claxton warned that if the existent standards were to be maintained, low as they were, it would be necessary to increase salaries by at least 150 per cent within the next few years.[28] The editors of *School and Society* pointedly commented that "Teachers have lost more than any other class, unless it be the children of the Nation, who in the end will suffer the most by the demoralization of the teaching profession."[29]

The true picture cannot, of course, be shown in averages. Actually, a large proportion of the teachers in the United States did not receive any salary increases during the years 1917 and 1918. One study of teachers' wages in cities of over 10,000 population reported that in the large cities only twenty-eight per cent of the elementary teachers and thirty-four per cent of the secondary

25 *Ibid.*, p. 91. Only sixteen states and the District of Columbia made a reliable separation of expenditures for the salaries of elementary and high school teachers. This represented over 31 per cent of all high school, and about 25 per cent of elementary school teachers. The Bureau statisticians concluded that "the average is presumably correct for the country as a whole."

26 *Ibid.*, p. 90.

27 Wyoming, *First Report of the State Board of Education* (1918), p. 18.

28 Conference in the Office of the Commissioner, February 13, 1919. National Archives (Bureau of Education, 106–17).

29 *School and Society*, vol. VII (May 25, 1918), p. 624.

school teachers had received salary increments since our entrance
into the war. In no case covered by the study did the increase
amount to more than twenty per cent; the average for the country was closer to five per cent.[30] While the smaller systems responded more promptly to demands for higher pay,[31] a large
number of the rural districts found it impossible under the existing tax system to raise any additional money for educational purposes. These were the areas where schools were forced to suspend
operations.[32] It was this condition, unfortunately continued after
the war, which led to the insistence upon greater state, and even
federal, aid.

If it is misleading to think in terms of averages, it is equally
deceptive to think solely in terms of a man's income. Most important to the worker is what his money will buy, not how much
he has in his pocket. In this respect, the position of the teacher,
and of all workers, became constantly more difficult as prices
rose sharply during the war years. Figures taken from *Brad-
street's* showed that the index number of prices rose gradually
from $5.91 in 1896 to $8.62 in June, 1914; during the next four
years it soared rapidly to reach a level of $17.96 by January, 1918,
and it was still climbing. In other words, a salary of $600 paid
to a teacher in the winter of 1918 was, for most purposes, roughly
equivalent to $300 in 1914 and to $200 in 1896.[33] Idaho reported
that the cost of living had increased by seventeen per cent from
1916 to 1917, while the wages of teachers had risen less than six
per cent.[34] The real income of most school people actually declined during the war years.

The difficulties of the teacher are shown most clearly when he
is compared with other workers. A survey of the monthly wages
of workers in the building trades of Huntington, West Virginia,
revealed that all were much better paid than the classroom instructors. In 1917–1918, the average monthly wage of a brick-
layer was $182; of a plasterer, $168; of a plumber, $156; of an

[30] *Ibid.,* p. 623.

[31] The files of *School and Society* for the years 1917–1918 contain in every issue
numerous references to wage increases in towns scattered over the entire nation.

[32] West Virginia, *Biennial Report of the State Superintendent of Free Schools*
(1918), p. 14.

[33] *School and Society,* vol. VII (May 25, 1918), p. 624.

[34] Idaho, *Third Biennial Report of the State Board of Education* (1918), p. 28.

electrician, $145; of a lather, $130; of a carpenter and painter, $124; of a hodcarrier, $104; and of a grade school teacher, $70.[35] Equally invidious contrasts were to be found in all sections of the country. One prominent educator of Wyoming claimed that coal miners were better recompensed than the superintendents of the best city schools, and that sheepherders received more per month than rural school teachers.[36] To the same point was the comment of a county superintendent in Florida. "Certainly," he remarked, "the State cannot expect teachers to continue in the profession at salaries which will average at least $300 per year less than is paid the average street sweeper."[37]

However one approached the problem, the fact remained that in 1918 many instructors were not paid wages sufficient for self-sustenance and had to supplement their income from other sources. As evidence of the situation, the superintendent of the public schools of West Virginia submitted the personal expense account of a primary teacher in a city school. "She was teaching quite a distance from home, which made her traveling expenses heavy," the superintendent explained. "The account covers the first four and one half months of school for the year 1917. Her salary for four and one half months at $55 a month was $247.50." Her expenses totaled $277.50. The deficit of $30 was supplied by the girl's mother.[38] To the same effect was the testimony of Representative Rankin. "Teachers in the District of Columbia can no longer afford to teach," she warned. "They are leaving the public schools by the score and entering government service in order that they may have a chance to earn a living wage. The situation is so serious as to threaten the closing of many of the lower grades in the local schools, and the possibility of consolidating the higher ones looms large." Representative Rankin went on to repeat a statement made by the directors of the Y.W.C.A. to the effect that it was impossible for young women to live in the nation's capital

35 West Virginia, *Biennial Report of the State Superintendent of Free Schools* (1918), p. 17.

36 Wyoming, *First Report of the State Board of Education* (1918), p. 17.

37 *Biennial Report of the Superintendent of Public Instruction of the State of Florida for the Two Years Ending June 30, 1918* (Tallahassee, Florida: T. J. Appleyard Printer, 1918), p. 749.

38 West Virginia, *Biennial Report of the State Superintendent of Free Schools* (1918), p. 18.

for less than $75 a month. This meant, in other words, that many of the parents of teachers in Washington were in reality subsidizing their daughters' salaries to the extent of $200 or more each year. So, the Representative concluded, we are "fostering a vicious system of basing the standard of salaries upon the personal domestic circumstances of the worker instead of upon the value of the services she is able to render."[39]

In an effort to hold teachers in the classrooms, appeals were made to patriotism.[40] Typical of this sort of pressure was a resolution adopted in 1918 by the Kentucky Educational Association:

Resolved: That men and women trained to teach should consider it their patriotic duty to hold fast to their school tasks during the period of the war. With the exception of actual military service, no department of government service can be considered more patriotic than that of teaching the children who, as men and women, will have to bear the heavy burdens and responsibilities that will follow the great war. The patriotic duty of remaining true to our professional tasks should lead us to make the necessary financial sacrifices. The teacher's financial sacrifices are no greater than those of the soldier. No less than the soldier is the teacher a necessary factor in civilization's fight for democracy.[41]

The resolution failed to point out that soldiers are well fed, well clothed, and well housed.

In other instances, boards of education ruled that instructors who signed contracts to teach during the school year must respect their contracts.[42] Since such a ruling was legally unnecessary, it revealed a certain attitude on the part of those who controlled the schools. Writing of "The Ethics of Resignation," one educator referred contemptuously to those instructors who sought to break their contracts in order to move to better paid positions. "The attitude of a teacher who thus takes 'French' (or may we not in future say 'German'?) leave is that he has to consider nothing but his own personal and pecuniary interests," this administrator bitterly remarked.[43]

[39] *School and Society*, vol. VII (January 26, 1918), p. 112.

[40] See, for example, the Commissioner of Education's letter to all teachers, November 2, 1918. National Archives (Bureau of Education, 106–17).

[41] *School and Society*, vol. VII (May 18, 1918), p. 586.

[42] *Ibid.*, vol. VIII (November 2, 1918), p. 526.

[43] John C. Futrall, *School and Society*, vol. VII (March 30, 1918), pp. 379–380.

Frequently bonuses were offered in lieu of actual wage increases. In some cases these were rejected by the teachers who wanted no temporary relief, but who demanded a more permanent solution of a problem that had been bad long before we entered the war. Now and then teachers went on strike. This happened at Royersford, Pennsylvania, and it was only after the money was raised by a citizens' committee that the teachers returned to their classrooms.[44]

Although on the whole the efforts of the teaching profession to secure adequate salary readjustments were disappointing, the struggle did help to strengthen the state and national organizations. Concerted effort on the part of the Philadelphia teachers spread to the entire state and led to direct pressure upon Pennsylvania's legislative body.[45] The West Virginia *School Journal* stated bluntly that the remedy for low wages was "the organization of a Teachers' Union, to fix minimum wages and to say to the public, 'Pay us our price or we won't work for you.' "[46] During 1918, the National Education Association conducted a vigorous campaign to secure additional members, promising that "every recruit will share with the teachers of the country the advantages of quick, decisive action. Now is the time to enlist!"[47]

3. Efforts to Maintain Standards

As we have seen, one direct result of inadequate salaries was a wholesale exodus from the classroom and the closing of thousands of schools. The situation also led to the lowering of requirements for entrance into the teaching profession.

Even before the war the normal schools and the departments of education in the colleges and universities could supply only about one in every four of the new teachers required each year. In June, 1917, the Bureau of Education estimated that approximately 130,000 new teachers were needed annually to fill vacancies in the private and public elementary and secondary schools of the United States. More than 85,000 of this number were required for the rural schools. To meet this demand, our normal schools

44 *Ibid.*, vol. VIII (December 14, 1918), p. 712.
45 *Ibid.*, vol. VIII (November 23, 1918), p. 621.
46 *Ibid.*, vol. VI (November 17, 1917), p. 592.
47 *Ibid.*, vol. VII (April 13, 1918), p. 434.

and education departments in the colleges and universities could furnish only 35,000 each year, and most of these graduates secured positions in the larger towns and cities. This left about 100,000 teachers who annually entered the classrooms with their only professional preparation a matter of several special courses taken in the public secondary schools or in county normal schools of elementary grade.[48] Irrespective of the war situation, it is apparent that the American teacher of 1917 was poorly prepared and that, as the result of a turnover of about one in every six teachers per year, the classrooms were staffed for the most part by inexperienced instructors.

During the school years 1917–1918 and 1918–1919, with the classrooms being drained of teachers and the enrollments of normal schools falling off badly, the problem of replacing trained teachers became acute. Some counties indicated that as high as eighty-five per cent of the new teachers were totally inexperienced.[49] In Vermont, normal school enrollments dropped from 400 girls in 1916 to less than 250 in the fall of 1918.[50] The New York City Board of Examiners reported that the number of pupils enrolled in the training schools of the city had fallen from 2,500 in 1916 to 1,071 in March, 1918.[51] Speaking to members of the National Security League in the fall of 1918, George D. Strayer, then President of the National Education Association, estimated that "one fifth of the boys and girls of the United States are being taught by untrained teachers," and that enrollment in the teacher-training schools was off from fifteen to sixty per cent.[52]

Various efforts were made to secure teachers and to further the training of those in service. The State Department of Education of West Virginia organized a "Reading Circle." From a list of books prepared annually by the state authorities, each teacher was urged to read at least two volumes. If in April she secured a mark of eighty-five in an examination on the designated books, she received a coupon which entitled her to one dollar extra per month

[48] H. W. Foght, "Rural-Teacher Preparation in County Training Schools and High Schools" (Bureau of Education Bulletin, 1917, No. 31), p. 4.

[49] Biennial Survey, 1916–1918 (Bureau of Education Bulletin, 1919, No. 88), p. 176.

[50] Vermont, Second Biennial Report of the State Board of Education (1918), p. 18.

[51] School and Society, vol. VII (April 6, 1918), p. 411.

[52] "The Emergency in Education," School and Society, vol. VIII (October 5, 1918), p. 416.

for the school term. Some of the normal schools in the state went a step further and offered credit through correspondence courses based on the reading circle work.[53] This program was adapted from "The National Rural Teachers' Reading Circle," organized in 1915 by the Bureau of Education and an advisory committee of the state superintendents of education in an attempt to meet the needs of the rural schools.[54]

The Bureau of Education also advocated a "teachers' house" in every community. "In order to retain them [the teachers] after they are secured there ought to be a school manse . . . a part of the necessary equipment of every school. Proper support and housing in order to secure the right type of teacher in itself constitutes a worthy program . . ." To aid the schools in the organization of such an enterprise, the Bureau prepared a special bulletin entitled *A Community Center. What It Is and How to Organize It.*[55] By the summer of 1918, Texas had built 337 teachers' cottages, and the State Superintendent of Education claimed that over 500 would be in existence by October. "The fact that so many districts have built teachers' homes," he concluded, "insures better teachers, longer tenure of office and necessarily, of course, better schools."[56] Colorado reported sixty-two in 1918;[57] Washington stated that 219 were in operation and that the "number is steadily increasing";[58] from Wyoming came the report that they were "a great help in securing and keeping teachers."[59] Although the movement was most effective in the rural areas of the West, here and there throughout the eastern and southern states, as, for example, in Franklin, New Jersey, cottages were provided by the boards of education.[60]

More effective were the requests for married women to return

---

[53] West Virginia, *Biennial Report of the State Superintendent* (1918), pp. 64–65.
[54] *Biennial Survey, 1916–1918, op. cit.,* pp. 179–180.
[55] Bureau of Education Bulletin, 1918, No. 11.
[56] *School and Society,* vol. VIII (September 7, 1918), p. 289.
[57] Colorado, *Twenty-Second Biennial Report of the State Superintendent of Public Instruction* (1918), p. 8.
[58] Washington, *Biennial Report of the Superintendent of Public Instruction* (1918), p. 90.
[59] Wyoming, *First Report of the State Board of Education* (1918), p. 48.
[60] *School and Society,* vol. VII (April 27, 1918), p. 495. See also *Annual Report for the Scholastic Year Ending September 30, 1918* (Montgomery, Alabama: Brown Printing Co., 1918), p. 29.

to the classroom. This meant, in many instances, the repeal of laws prohibiting the employment of married women. Philadelphia, Detroit, and St. Louis, to mention only three cities, had revoked their prohibitory rulings before Christmas, 1917.[61] The following spring the United States Commissioner of Education made a special appeal to both married women and to the local boards of education:

> There are in the country scores of thousands of persons, mostly women, of good scholarship and professional training, who have had successful experience as teachers but who have retired from active service. Many of these might render valuable service again in the school. As a means of relief in the present crisis, I recommend that they be called again into active service and that laws, ordinances and regulations of school boards prohibiting married women from teaching in the public schools be suspended or repealed.[62]

Numerous school districts followed this advice; nevertheless, the response was not great enough to satisfy the educational authorities, and appeals continued to be made. Many school boards were reluctant to take what to them was such a drastic step; the City of New York, for example, did not waive its ruling against married women until the fall of 1918.[63] The feeling of the women themselves was expressed in a letter to the federal educational authorities, and later, for reasons of publicity, released to the press:

> I wish to call your attention to a situation which prevails throughout the Middle West and urge your influence to remedy this injustice. As you know, most of the large cities will not employ married women as teachers in the high schools. As you also know, the War Department has placed in Class I all men whose wives are educated to earn a living. Many of these women were teachers in the larger high schools. These positions are now closed to us and we must teach in a small town— several subjects in which we are indifferently prepared—at a small wage—all because we have husbands who are giving themselves in answer to their country's call. Is this exactly fair? Kansas City, Mo., Kansas City, Kans., Topeka, Kans., and many other cities have courteously returned all applications, saying they employ no married women.[64]

[61] *School and Society*, vol. VI (December 15, 1917), p. 710.
[62] *Ibid.*, vol. VIII (August 24, 1918), pp. 226–27.
[63] *Ibid.*, vol. VIII (October 26, 1918), p. 496.
[64] *Ibid.*, vol. VIII (August 24, 1918), pp. 227.

Representative of many who opposed the employment of married women was the author of an article entitled "Pedagogy Versus Matrimony." The writer argued that married women "will in most cases either render a divided service to the schools or else evade, in ways not yet sufficiently pilloried by public opinion, the social responsibilities of the married state." His solution to the teaching problem was to pay adequate salaries to "virile, strong men, to whom we may have to pay twice or three times the salary we are to pay the celibate women."[65] Although the writer, who did not sign his name to the article, was quite correct in stating that the payment of adequate salaries was the only real solution to the problem, it helped little merely to state the fact. Most of the people must have understood this anyway, but it was the one thing that local boards of education were either unwilling or unable to do.

Under such circumstances, it was impossible to maintain the quality of the teaching personnel. The state director of vocational education in California offered to take *all* of the seniors from the division of agriculture in the Kansas State Agricultural College as teachers at $1,000 to $2,000 per year. The Dean of the college stated that hundreds of offers of a similar nature had poured in from all parts of the country.[66] From New Hampshire came the report that the entire graduating class of the state normal schools had been hired at once.[67] Even in 1917 the seniors of the Madawaska Training School of Maine were graduated two weeks before the close of the term, so pressing was the need for teachers.[68] The New Jersey Board of Education ruled that seniors in normal schools might teach during the last half of their senior year.[69] Peter A. Mortensen, Superintendent of the Chicago schools, recommended that the age limit for teaching be lowered from nineteen to eighteen years.[70] These were typical measures taken to keep the classrooms open.

Other efforts were made to replenish the supply of teachers.

65 *Ibid.*, vol. VIII (August 17, 1918), pp. 200–202.
66 *Ibid.*, vol. VII (April 27, 1918), p. 499.
67 New Hampshire, *Report of the Superintendent of Public Instruction* (1918), p. 115.
68 Maine, *Report of the State Superintendent of Public Schools* (1917). p. 50.
69 *School and Society*, vol. VIII (November 2, 1918), p. 526.
70 *Ibid.*, vol. VIII (October 12, 1918), p. 436.

An abortive attempt was projected by the American Council on Education and the French High Commission to recruit French girls, the daughters of officers killed in action, for service in American schools.[71] President Wilson suggested in a public letter that "ministers and others who were once teachers might serve a neighboring high school on half time until war demands are relaxed."[72] The Commissioner of Education urged druggists to volunteer for part-time help in the chemistry departments of the local schools, and suggested that mechanics could be of assistance in the manual training activities.[73] Although these proposals helped to emphasize the drastic need, they did little to relieve the situation.

A number of the state departments of education found it necessary to grant war emergency certificates to persons not qualified to receive regular teaching licenses.[74] The Alabama Department of Education confessed that it had been "somewhat more lenient than usual in its grading of the applicants' papers."[75] The county superintendents of Florida used such terms as "young . . . unqualified . . . inexperienced . . . untrained . . . inefficient" to describe the newly employed teachers.[76] After a survey of conditions in the fall of 1918, the Bureau of Education stated that 120,000 "new and wholly untrained teachers had been drawn into the public schools of the country, mostly boys and girls barely ahead of the classes they were expected to teach."[77] This was about twenty per cent of all the public school teachers in the country. Ample evidence is available in the reports of the state and city educational authorities to corroborate the testimony of the New Hampshire Superintendent of Education who wrote that the "quality" of teachers was "distinctly lowered," adding that

[71] Memorandum (no date). National Archives (Bureau of Education, 106–17); *Report of the United States Commissioner of Education* (1918), pp. 39–41.

[72] *School and Society*, vol. VIII (November 23, 1918), p. 619.

[73] Memorandum, November 9, 1918. National Archives (Bureau of Education, 107–23).

[74] See, for example, the reports of the State Superintendents of Maine (1917), pp. 12–13; New Hampshire (1918), p. 127; Rhode Island (1917), p. 57; Virginia (1918), p. 35; Alabama (1918), pp. 70–71; Nevada (1918), p. 16; Wyoming (1918), p. 27; Washington (1918), p. 51. This is merely a suggestive list.

[75] Alabama, *Annual Report* (1918), p. 72.

[76] Florida, *Biennial Report of the Superintendent of Public Instruction* (1918), pp. 630, 663, 693, 733.

[77] Joseph R. Hanna, Chief of the School Board Service Division, to P. P. Claxton, June, 1919. National Archives (Bureau of Education, 106–17).

this "appears to be true not only in teaching ability, but in morale."[78]

4. Teachers and the Draft

While the majority of the teachers who left the classroom during the war years entered more remunerative occupations in commerce, industry, or the civil service, thousands of men were drafted into the armed forces. Shortly after we entered the conflict, proposals were made by certain educational organizations to exempt from the draft instructors engaged in vocational training.[79] In many states, teachers of agricultural subjects were placed on the deferred list with the understanding that they were "engaged in a necessary occupation." Where this policy was not followed, many of the schools carrying on such work were forced to discontinue their agricultural curricula. In New Hampshire, for instance, ten schools abandoned agricultural activities, leaving only sixteen to conduct such training.[80]

By 1918, the educational situation had become so acute that demands for the exemption of all essential teachers were heard with increasing frequency. The president of the New York Board of Education, Arthur S. Somers, who believed, with many others, that education was an essential industry, held a consultation with the Federal Board of Exemption and with Corporation Counsel McIntyre. As a result, Somers suggested deferment for some 5,800 teachers in the city system. In order that this policy might be carried out most effectively, he recommended that the school authorities forward affidavits to the local draft boards whenever they wished to claim as essential the services of a certain teacher. To clarify the problem further, Somers urged that the school personnel be grouped in six categories: (1) teachers and principals of schools, (2) inspectors and examiners of schools, (3) superintendents of schools, (4) district inspectors and supervisors, (5) attendance officers, (6) janitors and janitor-engineers. Somers made

---

[78] New Hampshire, *Report of the Superintendent of Public Instruction* (1918). p. 127.

[79] See, for example, the resolutions adopted by a conference of school officials and teachers of Pennsylvania at State College in the spring of 1917. *School and Society*, vol. VI (July 27, 1917), p. 104.

[80] New Hampshire, *Report of the Superintendent of Public Instruction* (1918). pp. 195–196.

it clear that he was not expressing merely his personal feeling when he made this request. He had taken action, he pointed out, in response to the promptings of a number of boards of education in other cities, and he expected these cities to use a similar form of blanket affidavit.[81]

The proposal that teachers be deferred was given serious consideration by the War Department's Committee on Education and Special Training. The War Department itself was concerned over the scarcity of teachers in educational institutions with units of the Students Army Training Corps, and in secondary schools whose graduates were needed to recruit these units. Army officials feared that if the shortage grew worse, as it was rapidly doing in the fall of 1918, it would be difficult to maintain the student training corps as a reservoir of officer material. Moreover, the recent registration of all men between the ages of eighteen and forty-five threatened to drain the schools of their key teachers and administrative officials. So it was that the interests of the army paralleled the interests of educators, and the Committee on Education and Special Training insisted that the "shortages must be supplied without delay." The damage had already been done, and the army could do nothing about replenishing the exhausted supply of teachers, although it could prevent further inroads. To this end, the War Department recommended that essential teachers be deferred, with the understanding that all claims for exemption were to be made by the educational institutions in which the instructors were employed.[82]

Greater clarity was given to the War Department's announcement of this new policy in a statement subsequently issued by the Commissioner of Education to all school authorities:

The extension of the selective draft ages, by recent act of Congress, renders many school officers and teachers liable to call for military service. It is not the intention of the government, however, to call to the colors men whose services are necessary to the carrying on of the country's educational enterprise. The Provost Marshal General is

[81] *School and Society*, vol. VIII (September 28, 1918), p. 376.

[82] Grenville Clark, Secretary of the Committee on Education and Special Training, to P. P. Claxton, September 13, 1918. National Archives (Bureau of Education, 106–17). See also "Minutes of the Joint Meeting of the Committee and Advisory Board," September 18, 1918. Committee on Education and Special Training. MSS., World War Division, War Department Records.

instructing local and district boards to give deferred classification to men who are essential to the operation of educational institutions. Industrial advisers have been appointed to assist district boards in determining the validity of claims for deferred classification, or exemption in order that fundamental undertakings, including education, may not be unduly disrupted. It is, of course, understood that persons not essential to the continuance of these undertakings will not be given deferred classification on the ground of occupation.

I advise you to scrutinize with special care the teaching personnel of the school or schools under your charge with a view of determining which men teachers, superintendents, or supervisors are indispensable. In this connection you should consider the possibility of reorganizing your staff and also the possibility of replacing men of military age by others not within the limits of the selective draft, or by women. The attention of such teachers as you decide are actually essential to the carrying forward of the schools should be called to the substance of the inclosed documents in order that they may claim deferred classification when they fill out their questionnaires. In addition, the head of each school should make certain that the industrial adviser of the district board is fully informed with respect to the cases of all those teachers when their cases come before the board for decision.[83]

It is impossible to say whether or not this policy would have helped to solve the problem of the scarcity of teachers, for the war came to an end hardly a month after the War Department had announced its decision.

5. A National Employment Service for Teachers

The War Department's interest in the problem of teacher shortages led to an unusual experiment by the Bureau of Education. When, in September, 1918, the Committee on Education and Special Training wrote to Claxton warning him that the "shortages must be supplied without delay," it also recommended that the federal educational authorities prepare a register of teachers of colleges and secondary schools. The Committee suggested that these teachers be classified as to the subjects they were equipped to teach, training, professional experience, age, personality, and availability for transfer to meet war emergencies.[84]

This idea was not new. Back in 1914, the Association of Colleges

[83] School and Society, vol. VIII (October 26, 1918), pp. 492–493.

[84] G. Clark to P. P. Claxton, September 13, 1918. National Archives (Bureau of Education, 106–17).

and Preparatory Schools of the Middle States and Maryland had urged the Bureau of Education to keep a register of college teachers. Claxton himself had long toyed with a similar idea, which he called a "catalogue of brains." Nor was the suggestion that the Bureau assume the responsibilities of a national placement office entirely new to the thinking of the Commissioner. The short-lived attempt to bring French girls to American schools had been a step in this direction.[85]

The proposal that Claxton did submit to the Secretary of the Interior, however, called for a sweeping innovation in the Bureau of Education. The Commissioner asked for the creation of a School Board Service Division to register teachers and to assist state boards and other placement agencies, such as normal schools, to fill the vacancies in the nation's educational institutions.[86] After slicing in half Claxton's request for $50,000, Secretary of Interior Lane presented the plan to Woodrow Wilson.[87] The President gave his approval, and the project was started with a grant of $25,000 from the special defense fund.[88]

The Commissioner began with a nation-wide campaign to draw from retirement all those who had any experience in the classroom. While this was going on, an attempt was made to register the names, addresses, and specializations of those who had taught since 1912.[89] A second file was prepared with the number of vacancies in each county listed, and with a statement as to the "places temporarily filled, but not by qualified teachers."[90]

On paper, the project seemed promising. A number of states had established their own placement agencies during the winter of 1918–1919, but the United States Bureau of Education could cross state lines, and it was reasonable to expect that it would become "a national clearing house." Actually, by May 1, 1919, only about 17,000 teachers had been registered, and the Division had re-

[85] See *Supra,* p. 211.
[86] P. P. Claxton to F. K. Lane, September 20, 1918. National Archives (Bureau of Education, 106–17).
[87] F. K. Lane to W. G. McAdoo, October 2, 1918, *op. cit.*
[88] James F. Abel, "School Board Service Division," Unpublished MSS., June, 1920, *op. cit.*
[89] P. P. Claxton to the teachers of the country, November 2, 1918, *op. cit.*
[90] P. P. Claxton to County Superintendents of Education, November 4, 1918, *op. cit.*

sponded to 2,853 calls for teachers with approximately 15,000 nominations.[91] Nor was an attempt to draw ex-soldiers into the classrooms particularly profitable. Although about 300 young psychologists did sign up with the Bureau upon their release from the army, and although Claxton did suggest to the superintendents of the larger city systems the desirability of creating departments of psychology and research, there is no evidence that his efforts were rewarded with any appreciable success.[92] When the service was discontinued on June 30, 1919, over Claxton's protests, there were in the files the names of 14,000 active registrants who wished to secure positions, and 7,000 passive registrants who were not at the moment seeking jobs.[93] The organization was re-established for a brief period from December 1, 1919, to July 1, 1920, but it was again discontinued for lack of appropriations.[94]

From the beginning of its placement activities the Bureau had been severely handicapped. In the first place, as so frequently occurred in Washington during the war years, there was conflict between two federal agencies. A Teachers Professional Service Division had been operating in the Department of Labor since October 1, 1916, and it was planned at that time to establish ultimately a Teachers Division in each of the offices of the United States Employment Service. The Department of Labor was in the process of organizing this service when the Bureau of Education started its project in the fall of 1918.[95]

A second conflict arose between the free service organization of the Bureau of Education and the private placement agencies. These commercial bureaus normally placed about eighteen per cent of the teachers, collecting for their work approximately $3,000,000 annually.[96] Those engaged in so profitable an enterprise could not be expected to view with equanimity the encroach-

[91] Joseph R. Hanna, Chief of the School Board Service Division, to P. P. Claxton, June, 1919. National Archives (Bureau of Education, 106–17).

[92] James F. Abel, School Board Service Division, Unpublished MSS., June, 1920, op. cit.

[93] Report of George E. Walk, Assistant and Acting Director of the School Board Service Division, to P. P. Claxton, June 30, 1919, op. cit.

[94] Memorandum, P. P. Claxton, July 2, 1920, op. cit.

[95] P. P. Claxton to Representative W. W. Lufkin, February 12, 1919. National Archives (Bureau of Education, 106–17); "Minutes of a Conference in the office of the Commissioner of Education," February 13, 1919, op. cit.

[96] J. R. Hanna to P. P. Claxton, June, 1919, op. cit.

ment of a rival which proposed to offer identical services at no cost to the teachers.[97]

In the third place, the School Board Service Division was understaffed. At its maximum strength it operated under a director, an assistant director, one officer who had charge of filing and cataloguing names, a second officer who had the responsibility of selecting nominees for positions, five clerks, and nine stenographers. This was a hopelessly inadequate staff for the work that needed to be done.[98]

Finally, Claxton's superior, the Secretary of the Interior, did not appear to have been enthusiastic about the project. He cut in half the Commissioner's original request for $50,000, and early in 1919 he was suggesting that the whole division be closed "within a short time."[99] Claxton protested with some vigor, pointing out that experience had "shown the need for some permanent agency of this kind," and warning that if the Bureau of Education did not carry on the work, the Department of Labor would do so at more cost to the taxpayers. His protests were in vain. Despite additional warnings from other educators that failure to continue the service would be, as one expressed it, "a national calamity," the teacher placement experiment was abandoned.[100] The evidence indicates that it had made only a minor contribution to the problem of teacher shortages.

6. Limitations on Freedom

During the war years the activities of teachers were sharply restricted by both legislative enactments and the pressure of public opinion. Added to the problems of low salaries and the overwhelming burden of special tasks were the difficulties created by the war hysteria.[101] Nor did the restrictions come to an end with the Armistice. On the contrary, it was in the postwar years

[97] Interview with J. F. Abel, Chief Clerk of the Bureau of Education, Washington, April 15, 1941.

[98] James F. Abel, "School Board Service Division," Unpublished MSS., June, 1920. National Archives (Bureau of Education, 106–17).

[99] F. K. Lane to P. P. Claxton, February 5, 1919, op. cit.

[100] Louis W. Rapeer, Director of the National School for Research, to P. P. Claxton, July 10, 1919, op. cit. See also H. M. McManaway, Superintendent of the Virginia School for the Deaf and Blind, to P. P. Claxton, July 26, 1919, op. cit.

[101] See supra, p. 76 et passim. Many teachers were burdened with Americanization work in evening school classes.

that the real harvest of restrictive legislation was gathered. Indeed, it is ironical that the improved salary schedules, which came in the 1920's, should be accompanied by increased legislative controls over the teacher and the curriculum.

The story has been too well told to need repetition in this study.[102] In general, the laws passed in fear of disloyalty and radicalism called for (1) the requirement of affirmations of loyalty by the teaching personnel, (2) the exclusion of alien teachers from the schools, (3) the "Americanization" of foreigners, (4) the teaching of patriotism through prescribed courses in the government and history of the United States, (5) a closer scrutiny of textbooks, and (6) flag legislation and the designation of observance days.[103]

It is difficult to escape the conclusion that for the vast majority of teachers these laws and the attendant pressure of public opinion had little if any meaning. Untrained and poorly educated as most of them were, they accepted without question the prevailing opinion of the community in which they lived and taught. In the words of one student of the problem, they were "utterly uninformed and unaware of anything outside of their textbooks and the minutiae of small-town life."[104] Without ideas of their own, thousands of American teachers were incapable of even understanding what freedom meant.

At the other extreme were the intellectuals in the profession, men and women with training and ideas. As Curti has pointed out, even before we entered the war these "intellectuals had for the most part chosen their places and used such influence as they possessed to launch their fellow-citizens on the great crusade to make the world safe for democracy. In the White House a scholar

102 Bessie L. Pierce has covered different aspects of the problem in several admirable studies: *Civic Attitudes in American School Textbooks*, *Public Opinion and the Teaching of History in the United States*, and *Citizens' Organizations and the Civic Training of Youth*. Of great value is Jesse K. Flanders' *Legislative Control of the Elementary Curriculum*. Howard K. Beale has discussed in great detail the restrictions on teachers' freedom: *Are American Teachers Free?* and *A History of Freedom of Teaching in American Schools* (New York: Charles Scribner's Sons, 1941). The effect of war upon scholarship has been treated in a stimulating and able study by Merle Curti, "The American Scholar in Three Wars," *Journal of the History of Ideas*, vol. III (June, 1942), pp. 241–264.

103 Pierce, *Public Opinion and the Teaching of History in the United States*, p. 72.

104 Beale, *Are American Teachers Free?*, p. xi. These conclusions would appear to be fully corroborated by the data submitted in the preceding pages of the present study.

led the crusade. The voices of those who dissented, who urged adherence to the scholarly canons of judicious and reasonable analysis, were unheard amidst the blare of trumpets."[105] It was to this group that the most vocal, if not, indeed, the majority of public school administrators belonged.[106]

There was, however, a third type of teacher. In this company belonged the independent thinker. No one can read the wartime files of an educational journal such as *School and Society* without feeling the atmosphere of suspicion that surrounded the free-thinking American in 1917–1918. Thousands of men and women lived under what the Public Education Association of New York called "a kind of intellectual reign of terror."[107] It was these men who protested against the loyalty oaths and the dropping of German from the curriculum, who fought against the dismissals of their persecuted fellows, who defended the right of the loyal alien to remain in the classroom, and who refused to prostitute their scholarship in the name of patriotism.

The position of the American teacher in the last war was not to be envied. Much was expected of him, yet little was given in return: He was called upon for innumerable duties; he was paid the lowest of wages. He was expected to teach children to think clearly and to love their country; he himself was viewed with suspicion and, in many cases, was forced to instruct through the medium of propaganda materials that were an insult to his intelligence. It is not surprising that one third of our public school teachers left their classrooms, many never to return. It is particularly disturbing to realize that all this occurred at a time in which sanity had failed and man's only recourse was to the mad instrument of force. It is disturbing because then, if ever, we needed the keenest of minds and the coolest of tempers to educate a new generation that would be capable of building a better postwar world. Instead, we left 20,000,000 children, almost one fifth of our population, in the hands of individuals who, to a large extent, were incapable of adequately living up to their grave responsibilities. This problem weighed heavily upon the

[105] "The American Scholar in Three Wars," *loc. cit.*, p. 247.
[106] Beale, *Are American Teachers Free?*, p. 40; N.E.A., *Proceedings*, 1917 and 1918; *supra*, chaps. i and ii.
[107] Beale, *op. cit.*, p. 37.

minds of a number of educators during the war years, but their pleas for rectification were largely in vain. Perhaps a more intelligent appreciation of the importance of sound education and able leadership in the classroom might have helped to avert some of our present difficulties.

PART THREE

IN CONCLUSION

CHAPTER IX

LESSONS FROM THE FIRST WORLD WAR

SEVERAL major lessons emerge from our educational experiences during 1917–1918. In the first place, we needed greater agreement as to the function of education in a democracy. All too frequently the school buildings served merely as convenient headquarters and the children as messengers for publicity campaigns. To those individuals who used the schools for this purpose— and the list included federal officials, civic associations, and even "educators"—our educational system was hardly more than a ready-made communications organization. Those who thought in these terms used the appeal of childhood to touch the hearts and purses of the adults. Our reasons for fighting, our war aims, and our government bonds were sold through the children. Since problems of diplomacy and higher finance were not intelligible to ten-year-old boys and girls, sales resistance was overcome, not by logical argument, but by impassioned pleas. Many educators fought against this distorted conception of the place of education in the war effort. For the most part, however, they were content to follow political and civic leaders, rather than to attempt to direct public opinion. In so doing, they failed to utilize a rare opportunity to become the real leaders of American education, a position which they conceivably might have assumed.

It is difficult in the United States to secure any agreement as to educational policy. We do not have, as many countries do, a centralized system of education. Nor is it accurate to say that we have forty-eight different state systems, for in many respects the control of education is left largely in the hands of the 125,000 local school districts. Whereas in Nazi Germany educational policy is initiated and enforced by the national authorities, in our democratic-federal organization we must depend upon an enlightened public. This throws the responsibility for leadership squarely upon the shoulders of professional educators.

There were many in the First World War who accepted this responsibility with intelligence, courage, and devotion—among them Charles H. Judd, George D. Strayer, William H. Kilpatrick, and James E. Russell. But their influence was limited. Herbert Hoover and George Creel, working through powerful federal agencies, sold food conservation and patriotism by means of well-organized, extensive publicity campaigns. An organization similar to the Wartime Commission of the Office of Education, or to the Educational Policies Commission, by working in cooperation with a strengthened Bureau of Education, might have performed the same service for education. It was to our disadvantage in 1917–1918 that educators had neither agreement as to ends nor the machinery with which to appeal to the American people.

In the second place, we needed an agency in Washington with authority to coordinate the federal educational activities. Failure to agree upon the place of education in the war effort led to confusion, duplication of services, and conflict arising from overlapping jurisdiction. A seemingly endless number of federal bureaus, state educational authorities, and local pressure groups sought to use the schools for their own ends. Concerned with the problem of food were the Bureau of Education, the United States Employment Service in the Department of Labor, the Food Administration, and the Department of Agriculture itself. Two programs for training skilled workers were operating simultaneously, one under the control of the War Department's Committee on Education and Special Training, the other under the direction of the Federal Board for Vocational Education. Health and welfare activities were carried on by the Children's Bureau in the Department of Labor, the United States Public Health Service in the Treasury Department, and the Bureau of Education in the Department of the Interior, as well as by such quasi-public agencies as the American Red Cross and the Child Health Organization. Even the War Department exhibited some interest in this problem through its espousal of the "Wyoming System" of military drill and physical education. To add to the confusion, state and local groups were also active in all of this work.

It took us until nearly the end of the war to learn that in military affairs a unified command is essential. It took us months to set up a War Industries Board. But education, with its enormous investment in buildings, equipment, and personnel, and with its responsibility for the training of 20,000,000 children, derived little, if any, benefit from these experiences. The only attempt made to coordinate federal educational enterprises was the publication of Creel's semi-monthly periodical for teachers, *National School Service,* which served merely as a clearing house for printed propaganda—and this feeble attempt to reach a solution was inaugurated only two and one half months before the signing of the Armistice.

An agency to do for education what the War Industries Board did for industrial production, or what the Committee on Public Information attempted to do for all news releases from Washington, would have proved invaluable. Such an organization would not, under existing constitutional arrangements, have had the power to force the schools to take certain actions. Nor is this to suggest that such a shift of control from state to federal hands was either necessary or desirable. What we needed was an agency to coordinate the educational activities of the numerous federal departments and bureaus, thus putting an end to competing programs and the duplication of effort. Not only would such an arrangement have helped to adjust the demands of the war machine to a sound educational program under federal control, but it might, through the influence of a good example, have given more direction to our entire system of education.

In the First World War, each federal bureau decided what it wanted of the schools; then, carried away by enthusiasm, boldly made its demands upon the educators without consideration of consequences. The situation in regard to teachers offers a good illustration of the effects of this procedure. Before we had been at war many months, we were faced with a critical shortage of trained instructors. Finally, in the fall of 1918, the War Department decided to exempt from the draft those administrators and teachers essential to the war effort. By this time, of course, the damage had been done. Had the conflict continued into 1919, serious consequences might have ensued as a result of this short-sighted policy. Certainly, before the schools were stripped of their trained personnel, careful consideration should have been given to future as well as to immediate needs. This same lack of an over-all plan was apparent in our attack upon the problems of health and welfare, food, and labor supply. Only an organization in a position to see and act upon the total situation should have been permitted to pass final judgment upon such matters.

The logical agency for this service was the Bureau of Education. A number of educators, backed by the N.E.A., did propose that the Bureau be given responsibility for coordinating all federal educational activities. They had in mind a permanent arrangement for peace as well as for wartime, and their proposals called for the elevation of the Bureau to the status of a regular department with cabinet rank. But public apathy, combined with the American traditions of "general planlessness, a love of freedom, of individual enterprise, and of open goals," militated against the establishment of such an organization.[1]

In the third place, we needed in 1918—and it is perhaps important to stress this now—a reaffirmation of that faith in reason upon which the democratic way of life was founded. We fought, so many people believed, to "make the world safe for democracy," but we stimulated enthusiasm for our cause by organized campaigns to arouse the emotions of the people. Many of the lessons in patriotism used in our public schools served only to arouse hatred and antagonism. To the extent that these lessons were effective, we failed to educate for democratic living. Our sacrifice of blood and treasure in the name of democracy was a mockery if it ended only in a sharpening of the divisions within society. Judd, in his lessons on citizenship, believed that the job of educators was "to create a sense of personal responsibility, which can result only when the pupil is shown how his life is interdependent with the lives of other members of society."[2] Here were two conceptions of civic education, both sponsored by the federal authorities. The one, placing its reliance upon the emotions, sought to secure national unity by the method of indoctrination; the other, placing its faith in reason, sought to secure national unity by educating each of the pupils to assume his share of civic responsibility.

[1] The quotation is from Curti, *Social Ideas of American Educators*, p. 582.
[2] See *supra*, pp. 66–67.

Our failure in 1917–1918 was not, of course, that we encouraged Americans to love their country, but that we employed methods which were incompatible with democratic processes. To believe in democracy is to believe in the rationality and inherent dignity of man. It is to believe that the welfare of every individual is of equal importance. That is why we have a Bill of Rights. That, too, is why we could in all honesty embark in 1917 upon a "crusade for democracy." But it was illogical to shed blood upon the battlefield in the love of freedom, while at home we taught children and adults to hate man, unless he happened to be a Frenchman, an Englishman, or one of our other associates. This contributed to the serious complications which arose after the Armistice when we attempted to establish an international order based upon the right of self-determination for men of all nations. It was then that our wartime emphasis on a narrow, emotional type of nationalism returned to plague us.

In the fourth place, it is important for us to recall—confronted as we are with another period of wartime stress and postwar reconstruction—that war dislocates many of the patterns of our thought and action. In such a situation, those in a position of leadership have an unusual opportunity to give momentum to the new directions which the urgencies of war impose upon the schools no less than upon the other institutions in society.[3] Our experience during the First World War, as indicated by this study, suggests that our national leaders failed to capitalize upon many of the opportunities presented by the war because they were too much absorbed in the exigencies of the moment, too little concerned about the long-term future. Let us, by way of illustration, consider certain of those movements which were most accelerated during the war years.[4]

We have seen how federal relations to public education were quickened during the First World War. As a result of this quickened interest, numerous federal agencies began to take a new or more active part in the direction of public education. The Food

[3] For a pointed discussion of the social significance of institutional development, see Theodore Meyer Greene's "Introduction" to The Meaning of the Humanities (Princeton: Princeton University Press, 1940), pp. xxiii–xxvi.

[4] Although it is clear that the First World War was accompanied by marked changes in our educational program, it is not clear to what extent these changes can be attributed solely to the war.

Administration, the Committee on Public Information, and the Council for National Defense were all created during the war years; all were discontinued after the Armistice. Many other committees and divisions were established in the different departments and bureaus, and they, too, terminated their activities after the war. This was true, for example, of the School Board Service Division and the United States School Garden Army in the Bureau of Education, of the United States Boys' Working Reserve in the Department of Labor, of the War Savings Division in the Treasury Department, and of the Committee on Education and Special Training in the War Department. It was perhaps inevitable, with the rapid expansion of federal activities largely under the direction of the executive, that new agencies should be multiplied by the score. A certain amount of confusion was to be expected. But it was unfortunate that these new activities became the footballs of competing agencies. When this happened, as it did frequently, administrative techniques and controls became more important than long-term objectives. As a consequence, the return of peace saw the wholesale abandonment of federal programs, many of which had solid educational values, the development of which would have contributed to the re-establishment of our normal way of life.

Such was the history, for example, of those movements which were concerned with the production of food. The United States Boys' Working Reserve was not continued after the Armistice; the School Garden Army secured no further appropriations after 1919; and the activities of the Food Administration were terminated with the return of peace. Although the extension agents of the Department of Agriculture kept up their prewar work among the boys and girls of the rural areas, the public lost much of its wartime enthusiasm. With the collapse of these programs, public education sustained an enormous loss. The Youth Movements of Germany and Russia, so vital to the life of these nations, were built upon the foundations of a program of useful labor and the development, through this program, of a sense of civic responsibility. Leaders in the federal government and educators might have done as much for our own youth and for our nation. Instead, because the emphasis during the war was upon the production of food, with the development of healthy, intelligent, democratic citizens as at best secondary objectives, the public lost all interest in these activities when the food problem itself ceased to exist.

In much the same way, the American people for the most part lost interest in the problem of conservation. It is true that the thrift program, developed with such energy by the Treasury Department in 1917–1919, was not immediately abandoned. For a year or two after the war, the federal government maintained a leading part in the movement. Eventually, however, it relinquished its leadership to insurance companies, building and loan associations, and savings banks. Backed by these private agencies, thrift work played a prominent part in the public schools during the 1920's, only to lose much of its meaning in the face of a widespread campaign for installment buying during the last half of the decade. What our leaders might have done was to take advantage of the stimulus which the war gave to the thrift movement, using this opportunity to construct a really meaningful conservation program. The federal authorities stressed the purchase of savings stamps and the conservation of foodstuffs. This was important. But it was even more important that the thrift program develop in our citizens an appreciation of the nation's resources, both human and material. The very future of our country depended to a large extent upon how well we utilized these resources, whether in the name of war or peace. That the federal authorities and educators failed in 1917–1918 to teach this lesson effectively was demonstrated in the lush decade of the 'twenties with its Teapot Dome scandals, rampant extravagance, and widely accepted philosophy of eat, drink, and be merry.

The wartime impetus given to vocational education might also have been used to greater advantage had the federal government and school men viewed the situation through a larger perspective. In an effort to meet the need for skilled men, programs of training for industry and the armed forces were started immediately after the outbreak of war. Emphasizing, as they did, training in highly specialized skills, these programs were not at all what the vocational education enthusiasts wanted, but they did serve to arouse popular interest in vocational education. There can be no doubt that the war was to some extent responsible for the greater prominence given in the postwar years to industrial arts, home economics, agriculture, and commercial subjects. For the most part, however, our leaders did not understand that a man who has the duty of shouldering a gun in time of war also has the right to work in time of peace. Nor did these same leaders understand that to secure jobs for all men they would have to provide a system of vocational education far beyond anything yet envisaged, and that such a program could be provided only with vastly increased federal support. This lesson our leaders have been slow to learn, yet it was implicit in much that was done in the war years of 1917–1918.

There is, however, a brighter side to the picture. The wartime experiment in which the federal authorities took upon their shoulders the responsibility of preparing lessons in patriotism for use in the public schools came to an abrupt end with the Armistice. So, too, did much of the enthusiasm for military training in the public schools. Experience had shown that there were more efficient ways to secure civilian morale and trained armies.

Moreover, the war did exert a strong and lasting influence upon the problem of health and welfare. Prewar efforts to arouse public interest in this problem were rewarded in 1917–1918. The experiences of Europe and the revelations of our own medical examinations in connection with the draft were disturbing to the American people. Well-organized campaigns capitalized upon this concern, and tangible results were in evidence as early as 1918. Since the war, measures to protect the health and welfare of both children and adults have been adopted at an accelerating pace. Indeed, our present program of physical education, health, and welfare has many of its roots in the First World War.

The whole conflict from 1914 to 1918 helped to focus attention upon our foreign-born population. After the United States entered the war in 1917, this interest was accentuated.[5] Our hysterical reaction against "hyphenated-Americans," aroused by fear of sabotage, was accompanied by concern over the high rate of illiteracy revealed by the draft examinations. Americans realized,

[5] How the First World War stimulated our interest in the foreign-born population of the United States is revealed by Edward Hartmann in an unfinished study of the Americanization movement. This study, a doctoral dissertation at Columbia University, was interrupted when Mr. Hartmann entered military service.

many for the first time, that a large proportion of our population neither understood what democracy meant nor were in a position to learn from the printed page. As a result, Americanization activities were quickened. These were conducted before the First World War largely by private organizations, but in 1917–1918 state and federal authorities began to pay increased attention to the problem. Usually the lessons were given to adults in evening classes, but the public educational system contributed both buildings and teachers to the program. Emphasis was placed upon reading, writing, and elementary courses in civics and government.[6]

Undoubtedly of much greater value in the development of sound civic attitudes and necessary social skills was the growing program of education in the social studies. Between 1890 and the outbreak of the First World War, several national commissions of professional educators had examined the question of civic education and had recommended the inclusion of much additional social studies material in the public school curriculum. Even before we entered the conflict, new courses in civics, current events, problems of American democracy, economics, sociology, and modern American and European history were appearing with increasing frequency. There is no doubt that the war stimulated this trend toward the social studies. The federal authorities and private civic associations flooded the schools with lessons in patriotism. Newspapers, periodicals, and students' publications were filled with maps, vivid descriptions of war adventures, and analyses of the causes of the conflict. After 1918, although most of the federal activities were abandoned, private organizations continued to publish in increasing numbers papers and magazines intended to supply public school pupils with material on current social problems.

Closely related to this development was the emergence of a clearer appreciation of the public school as an instrument of social control. This prompted legislators to assume greater responsibility for civic education. Legislative provisions for the inclusion of new materials and observances in the public school curriculum, particularly in the social studies, increased notably during and

---

[6] Since the Americanization movement was concerned primarily with the education of adults, it has received only passing reference in this study.

after the war. These acts were, to a considerable degree, the result of vigorous action by such organizations as the National Security League, the National Association of Manufacturers, and the Daughters of the American Revolution. They reflected a growing awareness of the social importance of public education; whether or not it is possible to secure patriotism and social conformity by legal action remains a debatable question.[7]

In many ways the war helped to bring school and society closer together. Many teachers assumed that children were more interested in the present than in the past, more concerned about the struggle overseas than with the Punic Wars, and the study of current events was popularized to an extent undreamed of before 1917. In the sewing rooms and manual training shops the pupils made articles for the armed forces. After school, on Saturdays, and during vacation periods they helped the farmers. Boys and girls worked in their gardens, canned fruit and vegetables in the school kitchens, sold thrift stamps and bonds to their neighbors, and collected scrap materials as their contribution to victory. Physical education and health habits took on a new significance for growing boys who looked forward to an early entry into military service. Everywhere the emphasis in education was upon the immediately practical. The old struggle between the classics and the sciences was finally replaced by a new struggle between academic and vocational subjects.

There were many educators who hailed this closer union between the classroom and life as an unqualified advance for education. Others were quick to deny that the war had really vitalized education. The latter individuals were not at all impressed with the educational value of much of the wartime activity in which the children were engaged, pointing out that in many respects it was superficial and worse than useless. Of necessity, the war program was a thing of expediency, looking to the immediate needs of the nation. Although admitting that Prussianism must be de-

[7] For a discussion of the "legislative regulation of the social studies." see *The Ninth Yearbook of School Law* (Washington, D. C.: American Council on Education, 1941), pp. 140 *et seq*. For analyses of the attempts of organized pressure groups to control the social studies curriculum, see Beale, *Are American Teachers Free?* and *A History of Freedom of Teaching in American Schools;* Pierce, *Public Opinion and the Teaching of History,* and *Citizens' Organizations and the Civic Training of Youth;* Flanders, *Legislative Control of the Elementary Curriculum.*

stroyed, that the war effort must come first, many educators wanted, in addition, a type of education that would insure a more democratic society for the future, and that would guarantee to each boy and girl the fullest opportunity for the expression of his own abilities and personality.

It is impossible for many of us to look back upon our educational activities in the First World War with any degree of satisfaction. Much that we did in our schools was of permanent value to the nation. But in many ways we misused the schools for purposes that were unworthy of the name of education, committing errors of judgment that, had the war continued any length of time, might have undermined our democratic way of life. Too many of us forgot that it was the adult world which was at war—even in this age of total wars—and that to millions of younger children the blood, destruction, and death were utterly incomprehensible. It is true that we, in part, were fighting for a new and better society, yet to an unfortunate extent we neglected to prepare our children for the future of which we dreamed. It was not the least of our failures that for two years we educated for the world we hated, rather than for the world we wished the next generation to inherit.

We fight once more. The lesson should be clear. Not upon the battlefields are final victories won, but in the values a people accepts and with the machinery which is created to translate these values into life. Education, in the larger meaning of the word, is the instrument by which these values are secured. Our concern must be that the mistakes of a generation past are not repeated in the schools of today.

BIBLIOGRAPHICAL NOTES

THE footnotes of the text contain full bibliographical data. No attempts will be made to reproduce all of these specific references, or to include the many materials which, although consulted, were not cited in the study. The following notes indicate merely the general nature of the materials used in the preparation of this volume.

Manuscripts

Records in the National Archives furnished the bases for many of the sections in this volume. Part One of the study, "The Drive for Wartime Unity," was constructed largely upon the records of the Committee on Public Information. Those who use these records will find invaluable the *Classification Scheme: Records of The Committee on Public Information, 1917–1919* (Prepared by the Division of Classification, Roscoe R. Hill, Chief, and Frank Hardee Allen, Classifier, 1938). The records of the U. S. Bureau of Education, also on file in The National Archives, although incomplete, shed considerable light upon nearly all aspects of the study. This collection contains a number of unpublished manuscripts and miscellaneous documents, as well as the official correspondence of the Bureau of Education.

In addition to the documents in the National Archives, two unpublished manuscripts were particularly useful. Margaret Merriam Gearhart, *Military Instruction in Civil Institutions of Learning, 1862–1914* (unpublished master's thesis, University of Iowa, 1928) is a carefully documented study. Maxcy R. Dickson, *The War Comes to All: The Story of the United States Food Administration as a Propaganda Agency* (unpublished doctoral dissertation, George Washington University, 1942) is the product of an exhaustive examination of the Food Administration's records on file in the National Archives.

Materials dealing with the educational activities of the War Department are deposited in the World War Division, War Department Records. Unfortunately, most of these materials have been either lost or mislaid, with little of significance remaining for the historian.

The files of the Committee on Militarism in Education proved especially fruitful in the preparation of the chapter on "Schoolboys in Uniform." In 1940 the work of this organization was terminated and its records were deposited in the Swarthmore College Library. In addition to the official correspondence of the Committee, these files include numerous pamphlets, government documents, and published volumes dealing with various aspects of military training in the schools and colleges.

Correspondence and documents in the possession of Professor J. Montgomery Gambrill, formerly of Teachers College, Columbia University, now of The Johns Hopkins University, provided pertinent data on the problem of how lesson outlines were prepared by federal agencies for use in the elementary schools.

Publications of the Committee on Public Information

An important part of the Creel Committee's work was the preparation and publication of pamphlets and bulletins, many of which found their way into the schools. There are three major series of documents: The Red, White, and Blue Series, a collection of ten bulletins; the War Information Series, a collection of twenty-one bulletins; and the Loyalty Leaflets, consisting of seven pocket-size pamphlets. In addition to other information, these bulletins contain the official statement of our war aims and policies. Bulletin No. 16 of the War Information Series, *The Study of the Great War. A Topical Outline with Extensive Quotations and Reading References* (prepared by Samuel B. Harding, Professor of History, Indiana University) was distributed for use in the secondary schools of the nation.

The official story of the Creel Committee's activities is recorded in several documents. *The Complete Record of the Chairman of the Committee on Public Information, 1917–1918–1919* (Washington, Government Printing Office, 1920) contains extensive data on the operations of the Committee. Additional information, as well as political reactions to the Creel Committee, is included in the *Sundry Civil Bill, 1919*. "Committee on Public Information." *Hearing Before Subcommittee of House. Committee on Appropriations*. Part III, 61 Cong., 2 sess. (Washington: Government Printing Office, 1918). The *Official Bulletin,* a daily publication of the Creel Committee, provides a running account of the wartime activities of all the federal agencies. The semi-monthly magazine, *National School Service,* gives a picture of the educational activities carried on by the federal government in the public schools. The first issue did not appear, however, until September 1, 1918.

Other Government Publications

The *Annual Reports of the War Department* for the years from 1884 to 1900 and from 1914 to 1919 furnished some data on the educational policies and activities of the military authorities. Two documents were especially useful: *Report of the Activities of the War Department in the Field of Industrial Relations During the War* (Washington: Government Printing Office, 1919) and the *Committee on Education and Special Training. A Review of Its Work During 1918, Part 1* (By the Advisory Board, War Department, Washington: Government Printing Office, 1919.

A short, general account of the Children's Bureau is contained in *The Children's Bureau: Yesterday, Today and Tomorrow* (Children's Bureau,

Washington: Government Printing Office, 1937). The *Annual Report* of its Chief, of which the volumes from 1913 to 1922 were consulted, provides a detailed summary of the work of the Bureau. Particularly useful were the wartime publications, nearly all of which were pertinent to the present study. The *Annual Reports of the Secretary of Labor* for the years from 1916 to 1919 give a picture of child labor and its effect upon the public schools.

The wartime activities of the Bureau of Education may be traced through the *Annual Reports* of the Commissioner of Education. Statistical data are available in the *Biennial Survey,* which, in addition, contains numerous articles dealing with the various problems of education in wartime. The Bureau also published a number of miscellaneous bulletins, pamphlets, and leaflets, several of which proved useful in the present study. One bulletin published by the Bureau contained suggestions for the teaching of patriotism in the elementary schools: Charles A. Coulomb, Armand J. Gerson, and Albert E. McKinley, *Outline of an Emergency Course of Instruction on the War* (Teachers' Leaflet No. 4, 1918). A series of lessons in citizenship was edited by Charles H. Judd and Leon C. Marshall, *Lessons in Community and National Life* (prepared by the Bureau of Education in cooperation with the United States Food Administration, Washington: Government Printing Office, 1918). An outline of federal policy toward education was issued by the Bureau of Education under the title, *Government Policies Involving the Schools in Wartime* (Teachers' Leaflet No. 3, 1918). The problem of vocational education in other warring nations was discussed by Anna Tolman Smith, *Demand for Vocational Education in the Countries at War* (Bulletin, 1917, No. 36). The value of military training for schoolboys and the experience which other countries had had in dealing with this problem was discussed by W. S. Jesien, *Military Training of Youths of School Age in Foreign Countries* (Bulletin, 1917, No. 25). Recent trends in physical education were analyzed by T. A. Storey and W. S. Small, *Recent State Legislation for Physical Education* (Bulletin, 1918, No. 40). This analysis was brought up to date in 1922 by T. A. Storey, W. S. Small, and E. G. Salisbury in a bulletin carrying the same title (Bulletin, 1922, No. 1). How school children were organized to cultivate gardens was discussed by J. H. Francis, *The United States School Garden Army* (Bulletin, 1919, No. 26).

For the wartime activities of the newly established Federal Board for Vocational Education, the *Annual Report* of the Commissioner for Vocational Education is particularly valuable. An outline of the growth of vocational education in the United States is contained in a volume by Perry W. Reeves, *Digest of Industrial Education in the United States* (Washington: Federal Board for Vocational Education, 1932). The Board also prepared and published a number of manuals for use in the emergency training programs which were organized to supply men for such occupations as shipbuilding, radio operation, automobile repairing, welding, and machine shop work (Federal Board for Vocational Education, Bulletins No. 2, 3, 4, 7, 8, 9, 10, 11, 12, 16. Washington: Government Printing Office, 1918).

Educational Reports

In an effort to determine the extent and the nature of federal influence on the public schools during the war years, an examination was made of the annual or biennial reports of both state and city superintendents of education. Reports from more than thirty states, selected at random from different sections of the country, were examined for the years from 1914 to 1920. Reports from the cities of Chicago, New York, Oakland (California), Springfield (Massachusetts), and St. Louis (Missouri) were also used. These reports contain little more than a summary of the wartime activities carried on by the schools. School leaders were evidently reluctant to make any critical statements concerning the educational value of the wartime programs fostered by the federal authorities. The *Proceedings* of the National Education Association are somewhat more illuminating. Although, in general, those educators who attended the N.E.A. conventions appear to have left their critical faculties at home, there were a number of school men who did not hesitate to examine the wartime educational program in a realistic manner.

Periodical Literature

Numerous periodicals were consulted. For the most part, specific topics were checked through the *Readers' Guide to Periodical Literature,* although the complete files of several publications were examined for the years from 1914 to 1920. By far the most useful magazine was *School and Society,* which gives a reasonably complete picture of educational developments as they occur from week to week. *The History Teacher's Magazine* also gives a fairly complete record of major developments in the field of the social sciences. For a discussion of the effect of the war upon scholarship, see Merle Curti, "The American Scholar in Three Wars," *Journal of the History of Ideas,* vol. III (June, 1942). The nature and extent of military training in the public schools is revealed in *Everybody's Magazine* for the years 1916 to 1919. The editors sponsored the High School Volunteers of the United States, and the record of this organization may be traced in the monthly issues of this journal. The semi-official *Army and Navy Journal* and the *Infantry Journal* contain little data on the particular problem of military training in the public schools, although they do help to furnish a picture of the problems which the military leaders considered most pressing during the war years. *The Survey* also contains a number of articles dealing with the problem of military training of schoolboys. For a good summary of the nature and extent of military training for schoolboys, see Ping Ling, "Military Training in the Public Schools," *The Pedagogical Seminary,* vol. XXV (September, 1918). For a discussion of the health problems confronted by the schools during wartime, the files of the *American Physical Education Review,* the *American Journal of Public Health* and the *American Journal of Sociology* were particularly useful. An interesting study of the nature of patriotism may be found in

Merle Curti, "Wanted: A History of American Patriotism," *Proceedings of the Middle States Association of History and Social Science Teachers*, vol. XXXVI (1938).

Secondary Materials

There is very little secondary material dealing with the problem of federal relations to public education during the First World War. The best single volume is the study by Arthur D. Dean, *Our Schools in War Time and After* (New York: Ginn and Company, 1918), but it was written during the heat of conflict in 1918 when numerous records were unavailable and is necessarily incomplete. Some relevant material will also be found in the study by Charles Franklin Thwing, *The American Colleges and Universities in the Great War, 1914–1919* (New York: The Macmillan Company, 1920), although, obviously, this study is directed at education on the college level.

Although not directly concerned with the problems considered in the present volume, certain studies are of tangential interest and may be consulted with profit by anybody concerned with public education during wartime. Ellwood P. Cubberley, *Public Education in the United States* (Boston: Houghton Mifflin Company, 1934) furnishes background for the problem, together with some relevant material on certain specific topics. The study by Harold J. Tobin and Percy W. Bidwell, *Mobilizing Civilian America* (New York: Council on Foreign Relations, 1940) fills in a picture of the reorganization that took place in the federal government during 1917–1918. Also useful, although treating a more limited aspect of the same problem, is Bernard M. Baruch, *American Industry in the War. A Report of the War Industries Board* (New York: Prentice-Hall, Inc., 1941). A volume by Merle Curti, *Social Ideas of American Educators* (New York: Charles Scribner's Sons, 1935) contains some material dealing with the effects of the war upon education. Jesse Knowlton Flanders, *Legislative Control of the Elementary Curriculum* (New York: Bureau of Publications, Teachers College, Columbia University, 1925) analyzes the changing nature of educational legislation during a period which includes the First World War.

Certain volumes can be singled out as especially useful for an understanding of particular aspects of the problem of public education during 1917–1918. The most valuable single study of our general propaganda campaign during the First World War is a volume by James R. Mock and Cedric Larson, *Words That Won the War: The Story of the Committee on Public Information* (Princeton: Princeton University Press, 1939). For a discussion of the general nature of patriotism it is useful to consult Carleton J. H. Hayes, *Essays on Nationalism* (New York: The Macmillan Company, 1926) and Earle L. Hunter, *A Sociological Analysis of Certain Types of Nationalism. A Study of Certain Patriotic Attitudes, Particularly As These Appear in Peace Time Controversies in the United States* (New York: Columbia University Press, 1932). The problem of war hysteria, pressure groups, and teachers is discussed in a number of volumes: Bessie L. Pierce, *Public Opinion and the*

Teaching of History in the United States (New York: Alfred A. Knopf, 1926) and *Citizens' Organizations and the Civic Training of Youth* (New York: Charles Scribner's Sons, 1933); Norman Hapgood, editor, *Professional Patriots* (New York: Albert and Charles Boni, 1927); Howard K. Beale, *Are American Teachers Free? An Analysis of Restraints Upon the Freedom of Teaching in American Schools* (New York: Charles Scribner's Sons, 1936) and *A History of Freedom of Teaching in American Schools* (New York: Charles Scribner's Sons, 1941). A widely held attitude toward the value of military training for schoolboys is expressed in a volume by Colonel L. R. Gignilliat, *Arms and the Boy* (Indianapolis, Indiana: The Bobbs-Merrill Company, 1916). There are several useful volumes dealing with the nature of our wartime efforts to produce and to conserve food: Will Irwin, *Herbert Hoover: A Reminiscent Biography* (New York: The Century Company, 1928) discusses Hoover's activities as administrator of the United States Food Administration. William C. Mullendore, *History of the United States Food Administration, 1917–1919* (California: Stanford University Press, 1941) traces the history of the Food Administration. Although, like Irwin's biography of Hoover, Mullendore's study does not contain much data on the educational activities of the Food Administration in the public schools, it does furnish useful background for those interested in this specific problem. A glowing report of the achievements of the war garden movement is contained in a volume by Charles Lathrop Pack, *The War Garden Victorious. Its War Time Need and Its Economic Value in Peace* (Philadelphia: J. B. Lippincott Company, 1919). The thrift movement is discussed by Carobel Murphey, *Thrift Through Education* (New York: A. S. Barnes and Company, 1929). Especially valuable for a history of the development of vocational education in the United States is a volume by Isaac L. Kandel, *Federal Aid for Vocational Education. A Report to the Carnegie Foundation for the Advancement of Teaching* (Bulletin No. 10, Boston, Massachusetts: The Merrymount Press, 1917). The activities of the Red Cross are traced by Henry P. Davison, *The American Red Cross in the Great War* (New York: The Macmillan Company, 1920) and by Sara Elizabeth Pickett, *The American National Red Cross. Its Origin, Purpose, and Service* (New York: The Century Company, 1923). No student who wishes to understand the position of the teacher during the First World War can neglect the volume by Lotus D. Coffman, *The Social Composition of the Teaching Population* (New York: Bureau of Publications, Teachers College, Columbia University, 1911). Although published several years before we entered the war, this study reveals the type of teacher upon whom was thrust the problems of wartime education. Certain portions of the studies by Beale and Pierce, previously cited, also contain valuable information about the problems of teachers in the First World War.

The reader who is interested in a particular topic will find numerous additional references to further reading, both primary and secondary, in the footnotes which document the problem under discussion.

AMERICAN EDUCATION:
ITS MEN, IDEAS, AND INSTITUTIONS
An Arno Press/New York Times Collection

Series I

Adams, Francis. **The Free School System of the United States.** 1875.

Alcott, William A. **Confessions of a School Master.** 1839.

American Unitarian Association. **From Servitude to Service.** 1905.

Bagley, William C. **Determinism in Education.** 1925.

Barnard, Henry, editor. **Memoirs of Teachers, Educators, and Promoters and Benefactors of Education, Literature, and Science.** 1861.

Bell, Sadie. **The Church, the State, and Education in Virginia.** 1930.

Belting, Paul Everett. **The Development of the Free Public High School in Illinois to 1860.** 1919.

Berkson, Isaac B. **Theories of Americanization: A Critical Study.** 1920.

Blauch, Lloyd E. **Federal Cooperation in Agricultural Extension Work, Vocational Education, and Vocational Rehabilitation.** 1935.

Bloomfield, Meyer. **Vocational Guidance of Youth.** 1911.

Brewer, Clifton Hartwell. **A History of Religious Education in the Episcopal Church to 1835.** 1924.

Brown, Elmer Ellsworth. **The Making of Our Middle Schools.** 1902.

Brumbaugh, M. G. **Life and Works of Christopher Dock.** 1908.

Burns, Reverend J. A. **The Catholic School System in the United States.** 1908.

Burns, Reverend J. A. **The Growth and Development of the Catholic School System in the United States.** 1912.

Burton, Warren. **The District School as It Was.** 1850.

Butler, Nicholas Murray, editor. **Education in the United States.** 1900.

Butler, Vera M. **Education as Revealed By New England Newspapers prior to 1850.** 1935.

Campbell, Thomas Monroe. **The Movable School Goes to the Negro Farmer.** 1936.

Carter, James G. **Essays upon Popular Education.** 1826.

Carter, James G. **Letters to the Hon. William Prescott, LL.D., on the Free Schools of New England.** 1924.

Channing, William Ellery. **Self-Culture.** 1842.

Coe, George A. **A Social Theory of Religious Education.** 1917.

Committee on Secondary School Studies. **Report of the Committee on Secondary School Studies, Appointed at the Meeting of the National Education Association.** 1893.

Counts, George S. **Dare the School Build a New Social Order?** 1932.

Counts, George S. **The Selective Character of American Secondary Education.** 1922.

Counts, George S. **The Social Composition of Boards of Education.** 1927.

Culver, Raymond B. **Horace Mann and Religion in the Massachusetts Public Schools.** 1929.

Curoe, Philip R. V. **Educational Attitudes and Policies of Organized Labor in the United States.** 1926.

Dabney, Charles William. **Universal Education in the South.** 1936.

Dearborn, Ned Harland. **The Oswego Movement in American Education.** 1925.

De Lima, Agnes. **Our Enemy the Child.** 1926.

Dewey, John. **The Educational Situation.** 1902.

Dexter, Franklin B., editor. **Documentary History of Yale University.** 1916.

Eliot, Charles William. **Educational Reform: Essays and Addresses.** 1898.

Ensign, Forest Chester. **Compulsory School Attendance and Child Labor.** 1921.

Fitzpatrick, Edward Augustus. **The Educational Views and Influence of De Witt Clinton.** 1911.

Fleming, Sanford. **Children & Puritanism.** 1933.

Flexner, Abraham. **The American College: A Criticism.** 1908.

Foerster, Norman. **The Future of the Liberal College.** 1938.

Gilman, Daniel Coit. **University Problems in the United States.** 1898.

Hall, Samuel R. **Lectures on School-Keeping.** 1829.

Hall, Stanley G. **Adolescence: Its Psychology and Its Relations to Physiology, Anthropology, Sociology, Sex, Crime, Religion, and Education.** 1905. 2 vols.

Hansen, Allen Oscar. **Early Educational Leadership in the Ohio Valley.** 1923.

Harris, William T. **Psychologic Foundations of Education.** 1899.

Harris, William T. **Report of the Committee of Fifteen on the Elementary School.** 1895.

Harveson, Mae Elizabeth. **Catharine Esther Beecher: Pioneer Educator.** 1932.

Jackson, George Leroy. **The Development of School Support in Colonial Massachusetts.** 1909.

Kandel, I. L., editor. **Twenty-five Years of American Education.** 1924.

Kemp, William Webb. **The Support of Schools in Colonial New York by the Society for the Propagation of the Gospel in Foreign Parts.** 1913.

Kilpatrick, William Heard. **The Dutch Schools of New Netherland and Colonial New York.** 1912.

Kilpatrick, William Heard. **The Educational Frontier.** 1933.

Knight, Edgar Wallace. **The Influence of Reconstruction on Education in the South.** 1913.

Le Duc, Thomas. **Piety and Intellect at Amherst College, 1865-1912.** 1946.

Maclean, John. **History of the College of New Jersey from Its Origin in 1746 to the Commencement of 1854.** 1877.

Maddox, William Arthur. **The Free School Idea in Virginia before the Civil War.** 1918.

Mann, Horace. **Lectures on Education.** 1855.

McCadden, Joseph J. **Education in Pennsylvania, 1801-1835, and Its Debt to Roberts Vaux.** 1855.

McCallum, James Dow. **Eleazar Wheelock.** 1939.

McCuskey, Dorothy. **Bronson Alcott, Teacher.** 1940.

Meiklejohn, Alexander. **The Liberal College.** 1920.

Miller, Edward Alanson. **The History of Educational Legislation in Ohio from 1803 to 1850.** 1918.

Miller, George Frederick. **The Academy System of the State of New York.** 1922.

Monroe, Will S. **History of the Pestalozzian Movement in the United States.** 1907.

Mosely Education Commission. **Reports of the Mosely Education Commission to the United States of America October-December, 1903.** 1904.

Mowry, William A. **Recollections of a New England Educator.** 1908.

Mulhern, James. **A History of Secondary Education in Pennsylvania.** 1933.

National Herbart Society. **National Herbart Society Yearbooks 1-5, 1895-1899.** 1895-1899.

Nearing, Scott. **The New Education: A Review of Progressive Educational Movements of the Day.** 1915.

Neef, Joseph. **Sketches of a Plan and Method of Education.** 1808.

Nock, Albert Jay. **The Theory of Education in the United States.** 1932.

Norton, A. O., editor. **The First State Normal School in America: The Journals of Cyrus Pierce and Mary Swift.** 1926.

Oviatt, Edwin. **The Beginnings of Yale, 1701-1726.** 1916.

Packard, Frederic Adolphus. **The Daily Public School in the United States.** 1866.

Page, David P. **Theory and Practice of Teaching.** 1848.

Parker, Francis W. **Talks on Pedagogics: An Outline of the Theory of Concentration.** 1894.

Peabody, Elizabeth Palmer. **Record of a School.** 1835.

Porter, Noah. **The American Colleges and the American Public.** 1870.

Reigart, John Franklin. **The Lancasterian System of Instruction in the Schools of New York City.** 1916.

Reilly, Daniel F. **The School Controversy (1891-1893).** 1943.

Rice, Dr. J. M. **The Public-School System of the United States.** 1893.

Rice, Dr. J. M. **Scientific Management in Education.** 1912.

Ross, Early D. **Democracy's College: The Land-Grant Movement in the Formative Stage.** 1942.

Rugg, Harold, et al. **Curriculum-Making: Past and Present.** 1926.

Rugg, Harold, et al. **The Foundations of Curriculum-Making.** 1926.

Rugg, Harold and Shumaker, Ann. **The Child-Centered School.** 1928.

Seybolt, Robert Francis. **Apprenticeship and Apprenticeship Education in Colonial New England and New York.** 1917.

Seybolt, Robert Francis. **The Private Schools of Colonial Boston.** 1935.

Seybolt, Robert Francis. **The Public Schools of Colonial Boston.** 1935.

Sheldon, Henry D. **Student Life and Customs.** 1901.

Sherrill, Lewis Joseph. **Presbyterian Parochial Schools, 1846-1870.** 1932 .

Siljestrom, P. A. **Educational Institutions of the United States.** 1853.

Small, Walter Herbert. **Early New England Schools.** 1914.

Soltes, Mordecai. **The Yiddish Press: An Americanizing Agency.** 1925.

Stewart, George, Jr. **A History of Religious Education in Connecticut to the Middle of the Nineteenth Century.** 1924.

Storr, Richard J. **The Beginnings of Graduate Education in America.** 1953.

Stout, John Elbert. **The Development of High-School Curricula in the North Central States from 1860 to 1918.** 1921.

Suzzallo, Henry. **The Rise of Local School Supervision in Massachusetts.** 1906.

Swett, John. **Public Education in California.** 1911.

Tappan, Henry P. **University Education.** 1851.

Taylor, Howard Cromwell. **The Educational Significance of the Early Federal Land Ordinances.** 1921.

Taylor, J. Orville. **The District School.** 1834.

Tewksbury, Donald G. **The Founding of American Colleges and Universities before the Civil War.** 1932.

Thorndike, Edward L. **Educational Psychology.** 1913-1914.

True, Alfred Charles. **A History of Agricultural Education in the United States, 1785-1925.** 1929.

True, Alfred Charles. **A History of Agricultural Extension Work in the United States, 1785-1923.** 1928.

Updegraff, Harlan. **The Origin of the Moving School in Massachusetts.** 1908.

Wayland, Francis. **Thoughts on the Present Collegiate System in the United States.** 1842.

Weber, Samuel Edwin. **The Charity School Movement in Colonial Pennsylvania.** 1905.

Wells, Guy Fred. **Parish Education in Colonial Virginia.** 1923.

Wickersham, J. P. **The History of Education in Pennsylvania.** 1885.

Woodward, Calvin M. **The Manual Training School.** 1887.

Woody, Thomas. **Early Quaker Education in Pennsylvania.** 1920.

Woody, Thomas. **Quaker Education in the Colony and State of New Jersey.** 1923.

Wroth, Lawrence C. **An American Bookshelf, 1755.** 1934.

Series II

Adams, Evelyn C. **American Indian Education.** 1946.

Bailey, Joseph Cannon. **Seaman A. Knapp: Schoolmaster of American Agriculture.** 1945.

Beecher, Catharine and Harriet Beecher Stowe. **The American Woman's Home.** 1869.

Benezet, Louis T. **General Education in the Progressive College.** 1943.

Boas, Louise Schutz. **Woman's Education Begins.** 1935.

Bobbitt, Franklin. **The Curriculum.** 1918.

Bode, Boyd H. **Progressive Education at the Crossroads.** 1938.

Bourne, William Oland. **History of the Public School Society of the City of New York.** 1870.

Bronson, Walter C. **The History of Brown University, 1764-1914.** 1914.

Burstall, Sara A. **The Education of Girls in the United States.** 1894.

Butts, R. Freeman. **The College Charts Its Course.** 1939.

Caldwell, Otis W. and Stuart A. Courtis. **Then & Now in Education, 1845-1923.** 1923.

Calverton, V. F. & Samuel D. Schmalhausen, editors. **The New Generation: The Intimate Problems of Modern Parents and Children.** 1930.

Charters, W. W. **Curriculum Construction.** 1923.

Childs, John L. **Education and Morals.** 1950.

Childs, John L. **Education and the Philosophy of Experimentalism.** 1931.

Clapp, Elsie Ripley. **Community Schools in Action.** 1939.

Counts, George S. **The American Road to Culture: A Social Interpretation of Education in the United States.** 1930.

Counts, George S. **School and Society in Chicago.** 1928.

Finegan, Thomas E. **Free Schools.** 1921.

Fletcher, Robert Samuel. **A History of Oberlin College.** 1943.

Grattan, C. Hartley. **In Quest of Knowledge: A Historical Perspective on Adult Education.** 1955.

Hartman, Gertrude & Ann Shumaker, editors. **Creative Expression.** 1932.

Kandel, I. L. **The Cult of Uncertainty.** 1943.

Kandel, I. L. **Examinations and Their Substitutes in the United States.** 1936.

Kilpatrick, William Heard. **Education for a Changing Civilization.** 1926.

Kilpatrick, William Heard. **Foundations of Method.** 1925.

Kilpatrick, William Heard. **The Montessori System Examined.** 1914.

Lang, Ossian H., editor. **Educational Creeds of the Nineteenth Century.** 1898.

Learned, William S. **The Quality of the Educational Process in the United States and in Europe.** 1927.

Meiklejohn, Alexander. **The Experimental College.** 1932.

Middlekauff, Robert. **Ancients and Axioms: Secondary Education in Eighteenth-Century New England.** 1963.

Norwood, William Frederick. **Medical Education in the United States Before the Civil War.** 1944.

Parsons, Elsie W. Clews. **Educational Legislation and Administration of the Colonial Governments.** 1899.

Perry, Charles M. **Henry Philip Tappan: Philosopher and University President.** 1933.

Pierce, Bessie Louise. **Civic Attitudes in American School Textbooks.** 1930.

Rice, Edwin Wilbur. **The Sunday-School Movement (1780-1917) and the American Sunday-School Union (1817-1917).** 1917.

Robinson, James Harvey. **The Humanizing of Knowledge.** 1924.

Ryan, W. Carson. **Studies in Early Graduate Education.** 1939.

Seybolt, Robert Francis. **The Evening School in Colonial America.** 1925.

Seybolt, Robert Francis. **Source Studies in American Colonial Education.** 1925.

Todd, Lewis Paul. **Wartime Relations of the Federal Government and the Public Schools, 1917-1918.** 1945.

Vandewalker, Nina C. **The Kindergarten in American Education.** 1908.

Ward, Florence Elizabeth. **The Montessori Method and the American School.** 1913.

West, Andrew Fleming. **Short Papers on American Liberal Education.** 1907.

Wright, Marion M. Thompson. **The Education of Negroes in New Jersey.** 1941.

Supplement

The Social Frontier (Frontiers of Democracy). Vols. 1-10, 1934-1943.